British History in Perspective
General Editor: Jeremy Black

PUBLISHED TITLES

C. J. B...

Jeremy Black ... Eighteenth-Century ...

D. G. Boyce *The Irish Question and British Politics, 1868–1996 (2nd edn)*
Keith M. Brown *Kingdom or Province? Scotland and the Regal Union, 1603–1715*
A. D. Carr *Medieval Wales*
Eveline Cruikshanks *The Glorious Revolution*
Anne Curry *The Hundred Years War*
John W. Derry *British Politics in the Age of Fox, Pitt and Liverpool*
Susan Doran *England and Europe in the Sixteenth Century*
Seán Duffy *Ireland in the Middle Ages*
William Gibson *Church, State and Society, 1760–1850*
David Gladstone *The Twentieth-Century Welfare State*
Brian Golding *Conquest and Colonisation: the Normans in Britain, 1066–1100*
Sean Greenwood *Britain and the Cold War, 1945–91*
S. J. Gunn *Early Tudor Government, 1485–1558*
J. Gwynfor Jones *Early Modern Wales, c. 1525–1640*
Richard Harding *The Evolution of the Sailing Navy, 1509–1815*
David Harkness *Ireland in the Twentieth Century: Divided Island*
Ann Hughes *The Causes of the English Civil War (2nd edn)*
I. G. C. Hutchison *Scottish Politics in the Twentieth Century*
Ronald Hutton *The British Republic, 1649–1660 (2nd edn)*
Kevin Jefferys *The Labour Party since 1945*
T. A. Jenkins *Disraeli and Victorian Conservatism*
T. A. Jenkins *Sir Robert Peel*
H. S. Jones *Victorian Political Thought*
D. E. Kennedy *The English Revolution, 1642–1649*
D. M. Loades *The Mid-Tudor Crisis, 1545–1565*
John F. McCaffrey *Scotland in the Nineteenth Century*
Diarmaid MacCulloch *The Later Reformation in England, 1547–1603*
W. David McIntyre *British Decolonization, 1946–1997: When, Why and How Did the British Empire Fall?*
A. P. Martinich *Thomas Hobbes*
Roger Middleton *The British Economy since 1945*
W. M. Ormrod *Political Life in Medieval England, 1300–1450*
Richie Ovendale *Anglo-American Relations in the Twentieth Century*
Ian Packer *Lloyd George*
Keith Perry *British Politics and the American Revolution*
Murray G. H. Pittock *Jacobitism*
A. J. Pollard *The Wars of the Roses*
David Powell *British Politics and the Labour Question, 1868–1990*
David Powell *The Edwardian Crisis*
Richard Rex *Henry VIII and the ...*

British History in Perspective
Series Standing Order
ISBN 0–333–71356–7 hardcover
ISBN 0–333–69331–0 paperback
(outside North America only)

You can receive future titles in this series as they are published by placing a
standing order. Please contact your bookseller or, in case of difficulty, write to us
at the address below with your name and address, the title of the series and the
ISBN quoted above.

Customer Services Department, Macmillan Distribution Ltd
Houndmills, Basingstoke, Hampshire RG21 6XS, England

Scottish Politics in the Twentieth Century

I. G. C. Hutchison

palgrave

First published 2001 by
PALGRAVE
Houndmills, Basingstoke, Hampshire RG21 6XS and
175 Fifth Avenue, New York, N.Y. 10010
Companies and representatives throughout the world

PALGRAVE is the new global academic imprint of
St. Martin's Press LLC Scholarly and Reference Division and
Palgrave Publishers Ltd (formerly Macmillan Press Ltd.)

ISBN 0–333–58874–6 hardback
ISBN 0–333–58875–4 paperback

This book is printed on paper suitable for recycling and
made from fully managed and sustained forest sources.

A catalogue record for this book is available
from the British Library.

Library of Congress Cataloging-in-Publication Data

Hutchison, I. G. C.
    Scottish politics in the twentieth century/I. G. C. Hutchison.
        p.   cm.—(British history in perspective)
    Includes bibliographical references (p.   ) and index.
    ISBN 0–333–58874–6
    1. Scotland—Politics and government—20th century.   I. Title: Scottish
politics in the 20th century.   II. Title.   III. Series.

DA821. H88 2000
320.9411′09′04—dc21   00–030892

10 9 8 7 6 5 4 3 2 1
10 09 08 07 06 05 04 03 02 01

Printed in China

P; P. J.; M. K.; H. A.

CONTENTS

TABLES

PREFACE

It is remarkable that, despite the major historic developments in Scottish politics in recent years, only a limited amount of academic research into the political history of the country in the twentieth century has been published. There have of course been numerous studies by political scientists since the later 1960s, but almost all of these have been focused on the contemporary situation, with rarely more than a cursory historical survey included. Among historians, attention has tended to concentrate on a few select episodes. The most active field of investigation has been left-wing Clydeside politics during and immediately after the First World War. The second area covered has been the history of the Scottish self-government question. A scattering of material does sketch in certain other phases, overwhelmingly dealing with the Labour Party, frequently in the form of biographies. Only M. Fry's stimulating *Patronage and Principle*, which appeared in 1987, attempts an overall coverage of the period since 1900 – and then encompasses the century in rather a restricted length.

This book attempts to redress this deficiency by offering a sustained account of Scottish politics from the turn of the century until 1979, followed by a briefer discussion of the last twenty years. All the main parties are considered throughout the entire period, with the amount of space allocated between them reflecting some rough approximation to the weight and influence of each during the period under discussion, rather than using their current strength as the criterion. So, the Conservatives and Liberals are generally discussed rather more fully, and Labour and the Scottish Nationalists perhaps less so, than a present-day standpoint might adopt.

The changing social and institutional frameworks within which politics operated are outlined in a broad manner. Too often these have been perceived as static over time, or else their present complexion is back-projected in an uncritical and undifferentiated manner. But there were two crucial disjunctures – one after the First World War and the other in the later 1950s – both of which contributed to the reorientation of the pattern of politics.

Because of the dearth of secondary material for several themes and periods, this work is substantially based on primary sources, few of which have been systematically explored by researchers before. The main archives used have been those of the party organisations, at both central and constituency levels. Unpublished manuscript material left by individuals, drawn from all the major parties, has also been consulted. This last has been done in an effort to penetrate behind the mostly rather bland and highly selective volumes of memoirs produced by prominent Scottish politicians.

Trends in, and facets of, the whole of the country are dealt with, instead of assuming that treating exclusively with 'Glasgow and twelve miles round' will reveal all the essential elements of Scottish politics. This is especially the case when considering non-Labour politics, although even for Labour a wider geographical canvass can amplify the accepted picture. The importance of regional distinctions within Scotland has been a persistent feature of twentieth-century politics, and was probably most starkly illuminated by the varying degrees of support given to devolution by different parts of the country in the 1979 referendum. The highly localised circulations of the four largest cities' broadsheets confirm this: to this day there is no really national newspaper in Scotland.

This survey seeks to avoid a sort of Whig interpretation of twentieth-century Scottish politics, such as that currently held among some sections of opinion, namely that the advent in 1999 of a Scottish parliament was the culmination of a long, central and inevitable process. As the sources used here reveal, it is striking how rarely the question of Scottish Home Rule featured as the matter of prime moment in Scottish politics for much of the first seventy years of this century. Furthermore, when the topic was raised, its contemporary impact was often rather less significant than posterity has imagined, so that failure to deliver a measure of devolution rarely provoked electoral hubris.

Another assumption which may be overstated is that Scottish politics have long been distinct from the rest of Britain. On the whole, it seems more accurate to see such trends as fluctuating: at some times conforming quite closely to, and at other times deviating markedly from, the general British norm. It is therefore true that differing nuances and emphases could often be detected – for instance, the greater priority attached to the land question before 1914, and the significance of housing policies for most of the period since 1914. But of course, regional political variations within the rest of mainland Britain also obtained to greater and lesser degrees over the century.

The continuing involvement of Scottish politicians at the heart of the British system indicates a considerable element of convergence. Six prime ministers this century have either been Scots or represented Scottish constituencies, against thirteen English. Further, both the Labour and Liberal Parties have been led by several Scots who never made it to 10 Downing Street. Labour had Keir Hardie, Arthur Henderson and John Smith. For the Liberals, with Sir Archibald Sinclair, Jo Grimond, David Steel and Charles Kennedy as leaders, Scots have been in command for over half of all the years since 1935. The relative ease with which individuals from England and Scotland could find seats in the other country also testifies to this congruence. The comparison in this respect with Ireland, which was hermetically sealed from the remainder of Britain in the nineteenth and early twentieth centuries – and indeed this persisted after the establishment of the Northern Ireland state – is highly revealing.

Even in the period since the early 1970s, when the Scottish Nationalists rose dramatically, there has not been a continuous pattern of bifurcation between Scotland and England. Thus, for nearly a decade after 1979 the Nationalists looked to be in eclipse, with the Liberal/SDP centre parties more dominant, rather as in England and Wales. So the suddenness and intensity of the upsurge of backing for the SNP in this decade may be viewed as a new and epochal trend, as much as the evolving trajectory of past trends. In this sense at least, Scotland may be truly on the threshold of a new politics. Then again, it may yet prove to be merely another high blip in the erratic pulse rate of nationalist electoral support.

I wish to thank my colleagues Professor D. W. Bebbington, Dr J. L. M. Jenkinson, Professor G. C. Peden and Dr J. J. Smyth for advice and informed discussion on diverse aspects of this book. Dr P. Lynch read the manuscript and commented critically but helpfully on the text. None of these individuals is in any way responsible for any errors of fact or perversities of interpretation which remain.

I gratefully acknowledge permission given by the following to quote from copyright material owned by them: Sir John Gilmour, Bt (Gilmour of Montrave MSS); Penguin Books (incorporating Hamish Hamilton) kindly allowed me to quote a passage from R. H. S. Crossman, *Diaries of a Cabinet Minister*, vol. 1.

If there are any holders of copyright material whose consent has inadvertently not been obtained, I can only offer profuse apologies and undertake to rectify all such omissions in subsequent editions.

I. G. C. H.

ABBREVIATIONS

Ann. Rep.	*Annual Report*
ASTMS	Association of Scientific, Technical and Managerial Staff
BSP	British Socialist Party
BUF	British Union of Fascists
CLP	Constituency Labour Party
COSLA	Convention of Scottish Local Authorities
CPGB	Communist Party of Great Britain
CWC	Clyde Workers' Committee
EHR	*English Historical Review*
EUL	Edinburgh University Library
GMWU	General and Municipal Workers' Union
GWEC	Glasgow Workers' Electoral Committee
ILP	Independent Labour Party
LP	Labour Party
LRC	Labour Representation Committee
LUA	Liberal Unionist Association
MSP	Member of the Scottish Parliament
NAS	National Archives of Scotland (formerly Scottish Record Office)
NEC	National Executive Committee (Labour Party)
NLS	National Library of Scotland
NMLH	National Museum of Labour History
NPS	National Party of Scotland
NUWSS	National Union of Women's Suffrage Societies
SAC	Scottish Advisory Council (Labour Party)
SCWS	Scottish Cooperative Wholesale Society
SDF	Social Democratic Federation
SDP	Social Democratic Party

SHR	*Scottish Historical Review*
SHRA	Scottish Home Rule Association
SLA	Scottish Liberal Association
SLF	Scottish Liberal Federation
SLP	(1) Scottish Liberal Party
	(2) Scottish Labour Party
SMF	Scottish Miners' Federation
SNP	Scottish National Party
SSHA	Scottish Special Housing Association
SSP	Scottish Socialist Party
STUC	Scottish Trades Union Congress
SUA	Scottish Unionist Association
SWPRC	Scottish Workers' Parliamentary Representation Committee
TGWU	Transport and General Workers' Union
UA	Unionist Association
UDC	Union for Democratic Control
UFC	United Free Church
WCG	Women's Co-operative Guild
WSPU	Women's Social and Political Union

1

THE LIBERAL ASCENDANCY, 1900–14

I

The most apparent difference between Scottish and English politics in the Edwardian era was the greater strength of the Liberal Party in Scotland. The electoral pattern is revealing. Whereas in England the Conservatives won six of the seven general elections between 1886 and 1914, in Scotland they achieved this just once, in 1900; while the sole Liberal triumph in England was in 1906. At the last pre-war election, the Liberals held 58 of the 70 Scottish seats.[1]

Scotland was thus a safe haven for English Liberals in the pre-war period. Some, like Asquith, wisely chose to launch their parliamentary careers in Scotland. Others fled north after rejection in England: the most famous instance being Winston Churchill, who moved to Dundee in 1908 after his Manchester constituency spurned him. So serious had the influx of Englishmen become by 1911 – they made up nearly a quarter of Liberal MPs – that a protest was mounted by party activists at the proposed nomination of Gladstone's grandson for Kilmarnock.[2] In a mirror image of the Liberal position, eminent Scottish Conservatives tended to seek English seats. From the outset of his parliamentary career, Arthur Balfour opted for an English constituency. Bonar Law, Balfour's successor as leader, ousted from his Glasgow seat in 1906, promptly picked up Dulwich and, subsequently, Bootle. His return to Glasgow in 1918 denoted the profound changes in Scottish politics ushered in by the war.

1

The prevailing support for Liberals was also indicated in the slow progress marked by Labour. Although the origins of a separate Labour party lay in Scotland, and Scots were prominent in the early phase of the party's development, Labour nevertheless found Scotland electorally difficult before the war. While the two front-rank Labour politicians of this period, Keir Hardie and Ramsay MacDonald, were Scottish, they never held Scottish seats. It is highly significant that in England the Liberals felt compelled in 1903 to reach a pact with the fledgling Labour Party in order to avoid electoral clashes. But in Scotland, the Liberals were so much more confident that no similar deal was struck. The Gladstone–MacDonald pact was instrumental in securing a sizeable Labour presence in Westminster in 1906. In Scotland, however, with no agreement in place, Labour struggled to win seats against universal Liberal opposition. Nor did matters improve in subsequent polls. Labour's share of the Scottish vote fell between the two 1910 elections, from 5.1 per cent to 3.6 per cent. In England, the decline was less steep – from 6.9 per cent to 6.4 per cent – while in Wales it rose from 14.9 per cent to 17.8 per cent. The party's National Executive Committee was so worried by the poor results in Scotland that it sent a high-powered committee north the following year to identify the problems.

The reasons for these cross-national disparities lie in the greater strength of the Liberal tradition in Scotland, the weaknesses of the Tories and the particular problems confronting Labour. But in the longer term the prevalence of the Liberals might seem less assured.

II

At the very start of this period, the strength of the Liberals primarily derived from their identification with the central preoccupations of nineteenth-century politics in Scotland, which could be described briefly as religion, free trade, franchise reform and the land question. The impact of these issues was intensified because they were intertwined. To a growing degree, however, these were wasting assets, as the issues and social processes which underpinned them seemed less relevant in the new century. The challenge for Liberals was how to husband this legacy, yet simultaneously to develop a social reform agenda which would ensure the adherence of the working-class electors who now had the alternative of Labour on offer. The grafting of certain of these older features on to the new collectivist agenda adopted by the Liberal government after about 1908 contributed signally to the greater success of the party in Scotland.

Religious dissent was for three main reasons a potent factor in creating support for the party in later nineteenth-century Scotland. First, there was a high degree of doctrinal uniformity, as the overwhelming number (between 80 per cent and 90 per cent) were Presbyterian. Secondly, the numerical balance between state church and secession Presbyterians was very close. In some areas – the western Highlands, certain larger Lowland cities – the Church of Scotland was probably in the minority.[3] This fuelled the case for disestablishment in the eyes of many. Lastly, the major grievance of many dissenting Presbyterians – the Disruption of 1843 – was still within memory. The upshot was the growth in the last quarter of the nineteenth century of a robust Scottish disestablishment campaign which resulted in five motions being moved in the Commons between 1886 and 1895, attracting an impressive degree of support from Scottish MPs.[4] The cause was thus much more advanced in Scotland than in England, so committing many to the Liberal Party whose equivalents in England had tended to drift over to Conservatism.

Yet disestablishment was dwindling as a political rallying cry after about 1900, as even one of its staunchest supporters, the Free Church leader Robert Rainy, was prepared to admit. In that year the two main dissenting Presbyterian churches (the Free and the United Presbyterian churches) amalgamated. Soon thereafter it became apparent that the newly formed United Free Church (UFC) would merge with the Church of Scotland, and although fusion was not achieved until 1929, the process had been set in motion well before 1914. In this context, disestablishment was becoming irrelevant, and so the Scottish disestablishment lobby lost members rapidly after 1900.

Even though religious questions seemed to be in eclipse, the continuing impact of evangelicalism remained stronger than in England. The anti-drink crusade, which had, after all, begun in Scotland, continued to carry social and political weight, especially among dissenting Presbyterians, up to the outbreak of war. Indeed, its impact on the first generation of Scottish ILP socialists was enormous. The passage in 1913 of a Scottish local veto temperance measure revealed the extent of these influences. There was little likelihood of a similar measure in England (in this respect, as with disestablishment, Scotland was much closer to Wales than to England).[5]

A second pillar of traditional Liberal values which had a higher appeal than in England was free trade. By the 1900s there were many English Conservatives ready to embrace protectionism. In Scotland there were considerably fewer, so that the tariff reform crisis, precipitated in 1903, produced deep fissures in Unionism, as discussed in the next section. But the significance of free trade went beyond creating disarray in the Conservative camp. An additional benefit for Scottish Liberals was that it forged internal unity after several years of friction caused by the challenge mounted by the Liberal Imperialists.[6] One reason for the party's poor performance in the 1900 general election had been internal dissension, because the appeal of Liberal Imperialism was strong in Scotland. Irish Home Rule had been particularly unpopular in Scotland, because of the very close geographic, ethnic, religious and commercial links with Ulster. The great vigour of Liberal Unionism in Scotland testified to this.[7] So a diminution of its saliency seemed to offer prospects of winning back Liberal Unionists, who, as is discussed below, were less well integrated into the Conservatives than in England, and therefore were seen as ripe for reconversion from their apostasy of 1886.

Moreover, Scotland was perceived to have a very powerful identification with the Empire, where so many had emigrated and where so much of Scottish business and investment was located. If the Liberals could adopt a more positive position on Imperialism, this could only be beneficial: the extent of popular support in Scotland for the Boer War had surprised many Liberals, and was held by some party analysts to have played a contributory role in the 1900 electoral setback. The Liberal Imperialists attracted individuals who had largely withdrawn from political involvement from about 1886. These included prominent businessmen like the shipowner Joseph Maclay, and the chemical manufacturer Sir Charles Tennant, along with a clutch of university professors.

Just as important for boosting Liberal Imperialism in Scotland were the individuals involved. Its leader was Lord Rosebery, the dominant figure in Scottish Liberalism from the early 1880s and revered by his fellow Scots only slightly less fanatically than Gladstone. In addition, two of his most prominent lieutenants, R. B. Haldane and H. H. Asquith, sat for Scottish seats. The Liberal Imperialists collided quite violently with orthodox Liberals, whose British leader was another Scot, Sir Henry Campbell-Bannerman. Haldane masterminded Liberal Imperialist organisation in Scotland, and a bitter struggle for control of the party was waged at the turn of the century, both in the constituencies and on executive bodies of the Scottish Liberal Association.

Escape from this ever-deepening vortex of dissension was afforded by tariff reform. All Liberals, Imperialist or otherwise, were agreed on the sanctity of the free trade principle. Asquith was shrewdly designated by

Campbell-Bannerman as the leader of the rhetorical war against protectionism, thus sealing the restored unity of the Liberals. The Scottish wing of Liberal Imperialism was wound up well ahead of its English partner and a united Liberal Party turned to look outwards to attack the protectionist Tories.[8] The general election result of 1906 was accordingly a resounding verdict by the Scottish voters in defence of free trade. But the difficulty for the Liberals was that there was no guarantee that many of the disenchanted Unionists would remain in the Liberal camp once the threat of protectionism receded.

The land question had a deeper resonance and a more central location in Scottish than English politics. One of the major conclusions reached by Labour's 1911 inquiry into the Scottish political situation was that '... the Land Question in Scotland dominates everything else. Scotland has stood by the Liberals because it hates the House of Lords and the landlords ...'[9] The reasons for the greater prominence given to land in Scotland reflect three highly formative forces in the nineteenth century. First, the impact of the First Reform Act of 1832 was much greater than in England. The Scottish electorate rose by 1,500 per cent (from 4,500 to 65,000), whereas in England it increased by a mere 80 per cent.[10] The landowners were blamed for having retained virtually complete control under the grossly exclusive unreformed system. Hence the reputation of the Liberals as the bringers of the vote to the Scottish people was reinforced and linked to anti-landownership.

The Disruption of 1843 sharpened these feelings, as a core issue in the secession was the conflict between the wishes of evangelical congregations and the legal rights of lay patrons, who were mostly lairds, over the selection of ministers. After the Disruption, hostility was further stoked by the refusal of numerous landowners to make land available for the new church to erect churches and schools. In many rural areas where one individual frequently controlled all the land in the vicinity, this was oppressive, and so many landowners were identified as enemies of religious freedom, such as the duke of Buccleuch, who held vast estates all over the south-east. Some at least of the disestablishment agitation launched by the Free Church had an element of revenge upon the landed class.

The revolt of the Highland crofters against their landlords in the 1880s gave new and weightier impetus to the land question in Scotland at a time when there was no equivalent episode in England. The crofters' protest movement received much publicity, and a pronounced wave of sympathy for the crofters was provoked in Lowland cities, often spearheaded by Radicals already critical of landownership patterns. The presence of many Highlanders in Lowland cities ensured that the folk-memory of these events persisted across the whole country.[11]

The land question remained a core element in Scottish politics, thanks in good measure to the eventual passage in 1911, after several abortive attempts, of the Sinclair Land Act. This act, which was much more radical than its English counterpart, sought to extend to Lowland small-holders tenurial rights and opportunities to purchase holdings similar to those granted to Highland crofters in 1886.[12] The vehement resistance offered to the measure between 1905 and 1910 by Scottish landowners stirred deep passions on the reformers' side. The spectacle of some of the largest proprietors – often the descendants of those vilified in the nineteenth century, like Buccleuch – orchestrating a vociferous campaign of opposition to the popular mandate wielded by the Liberal government kept the land debate in the forefront. In the December 1910 election campaign the veto deployed by the House of Lords on the Scottish land measure featured nearly as prominently in Liberal propaganda as the rejection of Lloyd George's budget.[13]

The 1911 land measure represented the culmination of the nineteenth-century concept of land reform, viz. promoting free trade in land by reducing monopoly ownership and creating a small peasant proprietor class. But land formed a bridge between old and new liberalism which was particularly effective in Scotland. One major consequence of the crofters' campaign was to introduce a more radical analysis of landownership. For many Liberals, the 'single tax' policy became very attractive. This tax on landownership, especially on the incremental value of land, won wide support in Scottish left Liberal circles from the 1890s. It slotted effortlessly into the New Liberalism of the 1900s, with its emphasis on social reform and collectivist interventionism by the state in the workings of the market. The single tax simultaneously offered an analysis of, and a solution to, the major social problem in Scotland, working-class urban housing, which was emerging as a political issue being vigorously addressed by socialists and radicals.[14]

The confluence of these two streams of liberalism, with the land question occupying a core position, was achieved by Lloyd George's 1909 budget and his subsequent land campaign, which might have been tailor-made to evoke maximum enthusiasm north of the border. In the summer of 1914, the Liberals set up a Land Campaign Committee to press the case for the single tax as the solution to both the acute social problems in Scotland and the iniquities of rating as a system of financing local government.[15] This was regarded by many as more electorally palatable than Labour's socialisation remedy, as a significant element within the ILP itself confessed. At the 1912 AGM of the Glasgow Liberals a jubilant member highlighted its significance: 'In the taxation of land values they had the key to the whole position.'[16]

A kindred fusing of old and new was seen with Home Rule for Scotland. Initially developed in the mid-1880s as an attempt to render Irish self-government more acceptable in Scotland, where Liberal Unionism was strong, by the eve of war the demand for a Scottish legislature had acquired a new rationale. The older nationalistic right to self-determination was now almost subsumed by the argument that urgent and radical action was needed if the social ills afflicting Scotland – notably rural decline and urban squalor – were to be redressed. A Westminster parliament was too clogged up with imperial business to handle competently Scotland's peculiar problems. National regeneration, a key social radical concept, was thus explicitly conjoined with Home Rule in the propaganda material produced by left Liberals in the last few years of peace.[17]

These radical approaches were enthusiastically taken up by the left ginger group, the Young Scots, and increasingly from 1906 the intake of Scottish Liberal MPs became dominated by social radicals. A symbol of this was Sir Henry Campbell-Bannerman's replacement in 1908 as MP for the Stirling Burghs. Sir Henry had been the epitome of rather old-fashioned Liberalism. His successor, Arthur Ponsonby, was identified with collectivist policies, and indeed one friendly correspondent suggested to him that he could well be leader of the Labour Party. Several who had hitherto been identified with the more traditional Liberal policy concerns now embraced the modish approaches: J. W. Gulland switched from church-related issues to advocating state-funded social insurance, while the wealthy landowner R. C. Munro Ferguson emerged from sulking over the Land Act to contemplate enthusiastically the nationalisation of mining royalties and state afforestation projects. The collectivist solutions to social difficulties, extending to the adoption of a minimum wage and beyond, were all eagerly debated in the party's constituent elements. The emergence of this cadre of social radicals – spearheaded by Churchill, MP for Dundee from 1908 – rejuvenated the party and, equally important, kept it immune from the electoral challenges posed by Labour. Socialists on the eve of war were left complaining that too many Scottish Liberal MPs were at least as far to the left as Labour, so that no breakthrough was achievable. For instance, the ILP's journal, the *Forward*, observed of J. W. Pratt, the member for West Lothian from 1913:

our chief objection to him is that he has chosen to associate himself with the Liberal party . . . In one respect Mr Pratt is a dangerous man. His platform ability, his knowledge of the socialist case, and his strong humanitarian (if not socialist) sympathies could be used with damaging effect against Labour candidates on behalf of the Liberal aspirants for Parliament.[18]

A similar indication of Liberal confidence in Scotland on the eve of war could be drawn from the widespread support given by the party to women's suffrage. While Asquith and Churchill, two of the main targets of the suffrage campaigners, did sit for Scottish constituencies, the question was in two respects relatively well contained by Scottish Liberals. First, the party in general had few problems in contemplating female enfranchisement. The demand had a long history of support in Scottish Liberal circles: the male and female members of the great Victorian Radical family, the MacLarens, had been identified with the cause from at least the 1860s. Most of the leading women in the campaign in the immediate pre-war era were Liberals: Mrs Greig, the president of the Scottish Women's Liberal Federation, was active in the formation in 1902 of the Glasgow suffragist society. The Women's Liberal Federation was one of the staunchest supporters of the whole movement, and its growing involvement in the cause can be seen in the shifting balance of articles carried in the federation's magazine. In 1909 it published 17 pieces on free trade and temperance, and only two on female suffrage. But by 1912, there were only seven articles on free trade and temperance, whereas there were twelve on votes for women.

There were also numerous male Scottish Liberal suffragists. Forty-three Scottish Liberal MPs in the December 1910 parliament supported female enfranchisement: this proportion, three-quarters, comfortably exceeded the English figure. Several Liberal municipal authorities, such as Aberdeen and Dundee (Churchill's seat) petitioned parliament on behalf of the cause. Electorally the Scottish Liberals felt that neither the intervention of pro-suffrage candidates nor – especially after 1910 – the backing given by militant suffrage campaigners to Labour posed any serious threat. Only one by-election loss (Midlothian) could remotely be ascribed to the votes for women question, and even here there were more compelling causes – a bungled Liberal candidature, an Irish Unionist campaign.[19] There was an implicit confidence that, with so many Liberal women in key posts in the suffrage movement, it was unlikely that there would be serious damage inflicted on the party. Additionally, as discussed below, Labour in Scotland had a difficult relationship with women suffrage campaigners, in contrast to the position in England.[20]

Liberal confidence was reinforced by the nature of the campaign in Scotland, which was overwhelmingly constitutionalist in approach. In 1914 there were 66 branches of the suffragist National Union, with Liberals very active in most branches. The suffragettes, by contrast, could muster only four branches of the Women's Social and Political Union, and 13 of the Women's Freedom League (a less extremist splinter from the WSPU). In contrast to England, acts of violence were less frequent, less extreme, and they began later, for it was not until 1912 that the Scottish suffragettes opted to use violence. Despite this relative moderation, the WSPU lost one of its Scottish organisers, Helen Fraser, who switched in 1908 to the suffragist National Union, in protest at the rising tone of violence emanating from the English suffragettes.[21]

Just as the ideological stance of pre-war Scottish Liberals suggests no terminal atrophy, so the organisational condition of the party does not indicate that irreversible decay had set in before the outbreak of war. At the start of the twentieth century, to be sure, there were signs of inadequate constituency administration. A survey carried out by Scottish party headquarters in 1902 revealed that only just over half of the constituencies had satisfactory machinery, while fully one-fifth was virtually unorganised. Several seats, including Campbell-Bannerman's own constituency, still remained dependent on the personal influence of the MP, rather than having a permanent and fully representative association. The electoral setbacks of 1895 and 1900, together with the protracted disputes within the party between the Liberal Imperialists and the mainstream, no doubt contributed to the sense of organisational decay. But the changed political climate from 1903 coincided with the task of revamping Scottish organisation being entrusted to Lord Tweedmouth, who by 1906 had completely overhauled the party machinery. But his achievements were not a one-off; a continuing raft of improvements were sustained right up until the end of peace. Seats were revitalised by enthusiastic younger MPs: Ponsonby at Stirling from 1908 and MacCallum Scott in Bridgeton from December 1910 galvanised their moribund local parties and built them up to fighting standard by 1914.[22]

The results were manifold. Constituencies were everywhere put on a broad representative footing, with the central organisation – the Scottish Liberal Association (SLA) – promoting a steady improvement in the quality of organisation in the localities. The use of properly trained agents was encouraged wherever possible; in 1910 an association was set up to professionalise the paid organisers. Much of their attention was directed to registration work. For many years the Unionists had held a major advantage in this, and the loss of several seats by the Liberals in the 1895 and 1900 elections could be ascribed to massive registration drives conducted by the Tories.

Activists' support for the Liberal Party remained high and confident. Local association membership continued to be buoyant, rising in Dundee by 15 per cent from 1,100 in 1907 to 1,279 a year later. Subscriptions also held up: the amount given to the Glasgow party in 1913 was the highest ever, while the number of subscribers to party headquarters rose by 10 per cent between 1907 and 1911. So there was no sign of disgruntled Liberals turning away from the party, even after the radical social reform legislation enacted between 1908 and 1911. For instance, the Aberdeen association was deemed to be in its best ever organisational shape by 1914, after a dip in the late 1900s. Propaganda work was also sharpened and maintained at maximum activity up to the start of war: touring vans brought lecturers to isolated rural communities in summer campaigns – in 1913, for example, the theme was Irish Home Rule. At the same time a vigorous street-meeting programme was held in towns, and in Glasgow, factory gate meetings were introduced in a bid to counter the socialist message.

The women's wing grew promisingly over this period, with branches flourishing despite – or perhaps because of – the government's paralysis over votes for women. In 1914, it boasted a membership of 25,000 in 174 branches, well ahead of the 1904 tally of 11,000 in 70 branches. Moreover, the branches were pretty alive, holding frequent meetings. The main strength of the women's organisation was not in rural, declining areas, but in the central urban-industrial belt. In addition to purely social activities, women Liberals did much solid political work. Many meetings of a propagandist nature were held by women, but they also undertook leafleting and canvassing. In the west of Scotland their work at elections was singled out for praise. It is a sign of the strength of the women Liberals that they launched a magazine for their members in the west of Scotland. This journal conveyed a full picture of an active, well-supported and politically engaged movement throughout the pre-war decade.

The Young Scots offered an equally eloquent proof of pre-war Liberal vitality. Founded in October 1900, in the depths of the Boer War, in order to help promote the anti-war argument, the movement later expanded to become both a Liberal recruiting vehicle and a sort of radical think-tank for new policies, while simultaneously maintaining its formidable propagandist work. The Young Scots proved an invaluable testing ground where a new generation of aspiring MPs could serve their political apprenticeship: J. W. Gulland and J. M. Hogge, both subsequently Liberal Chief Whips, were the most outstanding instances. New ideas were also ventilated in the Young Scots circles. In particular, the social reform policies of the New Liberalism were adapted to Scottish circumstances by the Young Scots: as noted, they were deeply involved in developing the land and home rule questions in new social radical directions. The total Young Scots membership of perhaps 10,000 in 1914 was probably double that of the Scottish ILP. The Young Scots branches, about 60, were spread over a wide geographical area, with a considerable number in Lowland urban-industrial areas.[23] Their achievements in mobilising Liberal support at elections were recognised, and more than one Tory commented ruefully on the numbers of Young Scots and energy shown by them in comparison to the Unionist young men.

There were no signs, then, of the Liberals being either an ageing party, or one abandoning working-class districts to retreat to rural outposts. Rather it was Labour that was struggling to make the breakthrough before 1914. It is also noticeable that the Young Scots were politically catholic (or promiscuous): their number included Fabians and ILP sympathisers such as D. M. Stevenson and R. E. Muirhead, so underlining the fuzziness of party dividing lines on the left before 1914. This point is often made with reference to the ILP and to the openness of the columns of that party's journal, the *Forward*, to heterodox opinions. There was, in other words, a Progressive Alliance in Scotland, as in England. It is perhaps relevant to note how many pre-war Liberals wound up in the inter-war period as Labour supporters, without necessarily having experienced a 'Road to Damascus' conversion to socialism. Such figures as James Barr, Arthur Ponsonby, MacCallum Scott, J. L. Kinloch and E. R. Mitchell exemplified this pattern.

III

Clearly, as we have seen, the external context within which the Unionists had to operate was more hostile in Scotland than in England. But there were also related forces which further impaired their progress before the war. These included the narrow social bases of the party's support, the uneasy alliance within the party between Tories and Liberal Unionists and the deep fissures opened up by tariff reform. As a result of these features, pre-war Unionism in Scotland was both less extreme and less innovative than in England.[24]

Tariff reform deeply divided Scottish Unionists. Landowners and industrialists alike were overwhelmingly hostile to protectionism. For the former, Scottish agriculture (in which grain was less important and dairy and meat production more significant than in England) was booming and had no need of protection: hence Tory laird MPs like Sir Michael Shaw-Stewart and Sir John Stirling-Maxwell opposed the issue. For the latter, since the Scottish economy was primarily based on the heavy industries and textile sectors, both dependent on international markets and expanding world trade for their prosperity, there was little attraction in ending free trade. So jute barons from Dundee, shipbuilders on the Clyde and coal and steelmasters throughout the central belt found common cause in resisting tariff reform. The only Clyde shipbuilder in parliament, J. M. Denny, along with J. G. A. Baird, representing the most powerful iron and coal concern in Scotland, could not endorse tariff reform. The newspaper which acted as the voice of the west of Scotland business interest, the *Glasgow Herald*, violently attacked Chamberlain's protectionist scheme in the run-up to the 1906 general election.

The question fomented an internal struggle for mastery of the party analogous to that caused within the Liberal Party by the Liberal Imperialists. The Scottish Secretary, Lord Balfour of Burleigh, left the cabinet over the issue. Some Liberal Unionist MPs such as Alexander Cross defected back to the Liberals in protest, while several Unionist free traders simply chose to retire in 1906 rather than fight on an issue they disagreed with. Free Fooders complained that the Chamberlainites were conspiring to ensure that only tariff reformers won candidature nominations in the 1906 and 1910 elections. The free traders responded to this perceived assault in two ways. One approach was to work at a national level in liaison with the English Free Food organisation to combat protectionist propaganda and manoeuvrings. The key man in Scotland to take this approach was C. B. Renshaw, MP for West Renfrewshire. The other strategy was to wield influence at the local constituency level with a view to sabotaging the tariff reform agitation. The retiring MP for Roxburghshire, Arthur Elliot, declined to endorse his replacement Unionist candidate in 1906 because of his protectionist leanings. Elliot was at the heart of a movement which threatened that the Free Fooders might secede *en bloc*, hoping in this way to induce the Unionist Party to retreat from commitment to tariff reform.

The disunity rampant among the higher echelons of Scottish Unionism had a damaging impact on grassroots activists. Some, such as the Vice-president of the Paisley association, switched sides to the Liberals on grounds of principled opposition to tariffs. Others felt disheartened by the internal feuding and withdrew from party work. It was a commonplace observation in post-mortems on the 1906 election that there was a dearth of the usual volume of helpers, and some large branches, for instance Dunfermline, were stated to be virtually extinct by early 1906. The significance of this divide in Unionism was that it did not follow the long-standing tension between Liberal Unionists and Conservatives, but both camps included supporters from the two components of the Unionist Party.

The party never fully broadened its social base: too often it was seen as merely the party of lairds and their lawyers. A Scottish landowner who had sat for an English seat before contesting Berwickshire in January 1910 drew the party leader's attention to the exclusive and introverted character of Scottish Toryism: 'In many Scottish Committees there is a "County-family" feeling of exclusiveness still somehow maintained, quite unsuited to these democratic days.'[25] This reflected the distinctive social structure, class relations and mentalities of rural lowland Scotland.

There was not in Scotland an automatic rural deference vote which landlords could deploy to boost their electoral position. Between 1906 and 1914 only a handful of county seats could be said to display evidence of deferential tendencies. Even the mighty duke of Buccleuch, owning vast tracts of south-eastern Scotland, could not guarantee delivery of seats there. Tenant-farmers operated under a business relationship with landowners, with little scope for paternalism. Moreover, tension between laird and farmer over game laws and other agricultural questions had been acute in the 1860s and 70s and was still present a generation later in many areas.[26] There was no mass docile landless labourer class dependent on the squire for work or support: instead there were radical and self-consciously independent ploughboys who regularly moved from farm to farm, often on an annual basis. Many Tories perceived the major obstacle in the counties to be these agricultural skilled workers, who remained resolutely impervious to the blandishments of Unionism. Seasonal tasks like harvesting were carried out by migrant workers from Ireland or the Highlands, so there was no class of landless labourers residing in estate villages on the English pattern.[27] Hence the whole structure of the rural community as found in England, with its shared values reinforced by deference to the estate owner, was not easily available in Scotland. As a result, the Liberals were as strong in Scottish seats with a heavy agricultural presence as in urban-industrial ones.

The Unionists' problems worsened as many territorial magnates were beginning to disappear in the twenty years before the war. Traditional landowners were running into acute financial difficulties, and either sold up to raise cash or were forced out by bankruptcy. By 1914, in the south-west, lords Galloway and Queensberry were in severely reduced circumstances, while in the north-east the duke of Fife had liquidated his vast holdings in Banffshire. Their replacements were not always landowners on the same scale, as estates were often subdivided for ease of sale.[28] The new owners lacked the local prestige based on history and antecedents enjoyed by the outgoing class. Even the core of Unionist support was now being gradually eroded.

The Conservatives found it well-nigh impossible to compensate for their rural weaknesses by making a breakthrough into the urban middle class in the later nineteenth century. It was this element which provided the basis for the resurgence of the English Tories under Disraeli and Salisbury. By contrast, only Falkirk (occasionally) and Glasgow (once) of the major Scottish burgh constituencies returned a Tory between 1832 and 1886. Hence the secession in 1886 of the Liberal Unionists was highly beneficial to the Tories. The anti-Home Rule Liberals were particularly well supported in the urban west of Scotland, where a mix of religious, commercial and intellectual factors operated forcefully, so that in Glasgow all seven seats fell to Unionism in 1900, neatly reversing the complete whitewash suffered by the city's Tories in 1885.[29] Two consequences followed. Scottish Liberal Unionists fought and won more seats than in England: in 1900, 13.4 per cent of both candidates and MPs in England were LUs, in Scotland the respective figures were 40.0 per cent and 47.2 per cent. They also provided the majority of Unionist MPs with a non-landed and more business or professional background than the Conservatives. So, in 1900, 11 of the 17 Liberal Unionist MPs (65 per cent) were businessmen or professionals, but only 8 of 19 Conservatives (42 per cent) fell into this category.

In England, amicable co-operation between Conservatives and Liberal Unionists was the rule from the start, so that by the mid-1890s fusion had been largely accomplished. But in Scotland there was constant friction and contention. The amalgamation of the two parties did not occur until 1912, largely at the behest of the English leadership, and the merger process was acrimonious on both sides. Part of the recurring trouble was that the Liberal Unionists in Scotland included numerous radicals, who were never reconciled to joining formally with the Tories. Indeed, in the tariff reform controversy, Liberal Unionist free traders explicitly argued that the best means of preventing heavy desertions to the Liberal Party was to retain a separate Liberal Unionist identity.[30]

However, Liberal Unionist organisational weakness triggered merger talks after the poor results in the 1910 elections. The decision to call the unified party the Scottish Unionist Association, with the word 'Conservative' omitted, indicated the degree of influence still wielded by the Liberal Unionists, and the sensitivity of Tories to their partners' feelings. Of course in Scotland the term 'Unionist' conveyed a double appeal: it clearly wooed the Orange-inclined working-class element, as well as retaining the Liberal Unionist identity.

The Scottish Conservatives also sought to open up links with more working-class urban elements. The focus for the attempted nexus was provided by the Orange Order. From the 1880s, the Glasgow Conservative Association had one seat on its Executive reserved for a representative of the city's Orange lodges. The movement had grown rapidly in the later nineteenth century: by 1900 the most careful calculation suggests it had 25,000 members. The institution had grown in response to the arrival of Irish Roman Catholic immigrants, and tended to be most active across Lowland industrial Scotland. It was particularly numerous in the western and central coalfields and in manufacturing towns, such as Greenock and Glasgow. The order clearly latched on to the Presbyterian anti-Catholic tradition in Scotland, but it was reinforced by the presence of many Ulster Protestant immigrants, who had settled in the west of Scotland, moving more easily in the host community than their Catholic compatriots, and who brought with them the sectarian spirit well established by mid century in northern Ireland.[31] The disciplined and coherent organisational structure of the order seemingly offered a ready made machine for delivering support at elections.

Yet the Orangemen were of no more than marginal use to the Tories. For one thing, being overwhelmingly working-class, many of them did not have the parliamentary franchise. While Orange-backed candidates polled well in elective bodies with lower franchise qualifications, such as school boards, these votes were less significant for parliamentary contests. Secondly, it proved counter-productive: the order, unlike its Ulster parent, was not socially broad-based; instead it was drawn overwhelmingly from the working class, with the merest smattering of middle-class involvement. Only in a small number of seats – possibly Greenock, parts of Lanarkshire and occasionally Glasgow Bridgeton and Camlachie – were there some political dividends, but these were balanced by the loss of middle-class voters, alarmed by the public violence and sectarian disorders associated with Orangeism in many parts of Scotland. Yet it was to the middle class that the essential message of Unionism was directed.

By about 1906 it had become clear that a new approach by the Unionists to capture working-class voters was required. Under the aegis of the Scottish Whip from 1912, the party devoted a good deal of attention to trying to reach this class. A major effort was to strive to check the success of the Liberal press, most of all the Dundee-based *People's Journal*, which was blamed for the depth of radical feeling, especially in the rural parts of the east of Scotland. In the west, the *Daily Record* was perceived as the main Liberal advocate. Local pro-Tory newspapers were accordingly funded, such as the *Mearns Leader*, begun in 1913. Also in 1913, the *People's Politics* (with its conscious acknowledgement of the Dundee radical organ in its title) was launched, mainly targeted not so much at agricultural workers as at industrial workers, particularly in the west. It quickly proved highly successful, as an initial print run of 10,000 was expanded within six months of its inception to 55,000.

Working-men speakers were also recruited to address audiences in a language and an accent which would strike a response. W. P. Templeton, a Falkirk wood-turner, was recruited for this purpose. To reinforce the appeal to the working class, the Workers' League was formed, with the objective of providing a general anti-socialist message. The creation in the Glasgow region of a Democratic Unionist Association further underlined the interest of the Tories in this social group, and the desire to reach them with less recourse than in the past to Orange, anti-Home Rule appeals. Another body, the Scottish Labour Federation, was formed in 1913, soon claiming 3,000 adherents. The federation's speciality was street political meetings in industrial areas, countering socialist propaganda by likewise using open-air speakers.[32] Nevertheless, it is difficult to see that this frenetic activity yielded immediate political dividends: in by-elections before 1914 in working-class seats, the Unionist vote did not normally grow significantly; it was rather the split of the anti-Tory vote between Labour and Liberal which aided Unionists.[33]

One casualty of the internal divisions of the 1900s was organisation.[34] In the later nineteenth century, the Tories had been especially effective in registration work, for which a paid organiser in the constituency was essential. Nevertheless, an internal inquest after the 1906 débâcle pinpointed serious administrative defects. In particular there was a tendency to leave too much of the organisational workload to the organiser, with little assistance from ordinary members. Where the organiser was a part-time post (usually a local solicitor), this was highly unsatisfactory. A sustained drive to remedy this defect meant that by 1913 most constituencies had a full-time professional agent in lieu of the part-time worker, and general constituency organisation was more representative and competent.

The role of women was also considered. By 1909 there were over 1,900 enrolled in the women's section of the West Aberdeenshire association, and this was pretty well a hopeless seat. The Primrose League was much less important in Scotland than in England in recruiting women to the Tory cause. There were fewer habitations north of the border, and the movement never entered the political consciousness of the Scottish Tories as it did in England. On the other hand, one advantage of having women directly involved in the party was that explicitly political work could be developed quite systematically. Day schools and study circles to instruct women in the issues of the moment were well established by the outbreak of war. Women were also widely engaged in distributing party literature and undertaking registration work, although, unlike the Liberal women, they did little canvassing or public speaking. The party also sought to cater for the young. The Junior Imperialist League, launched in the immediate pre-war years, established a number of branches in Glasgow and elsewhere. Political education was mixed with social activities. League members did hold street meetings and so forth, but their endeavours were not on the same level as the Liberal Young Scots.

The lines of command within the united party were carefully delimited in the administrative reorganisation of 1911–12. The practice of leaving the development of party organisation to one individual, the Party Agent, was stopped. This position was seen as being imposed on Scotland by the London-based managers of the party, and the person often lacked the political clout within Scotland to have changes put into practice. From 1912 the leadership of the Scottish party, particularly in administrative matters, was entrusted to the newly created office of Scottish Whip. As an MP, the Scottish Whip would provide a natural link between the requirements of activists in Scotland and the activities in parliament of the MPs. In addition, it gave Scotland rather more self-government than heretofore, presumably in the hope that direct contact with the Scottish scene would mean a more sensitive approach.

The drive for efficiency and the struggle to reach a new audience was of course financially draining. The Scottish national organisation, the

National Union, was assisted by the Political Committee of the Scottish Conservative Club, which channelled funds to seats which were deemed organisationally backward. With this substantial support the Unionist machinery seemed in good heart in 1914. But there were those who still felt uneasy. The party, it seemed to some, was over-dependent on the professional class of agents and organising secretaries, with little real vitality being shown by the rank and file membership. The candidate for East Fife denounced the calibre of grass-roots activists as 'timid and impossible people ... *chicken-hearted*'.[35] Financially, too, the local associations were prone to rely on funding from a tiny handful of individuals, usually landowners or businessmen, rather than having a wide range of small donors. On the eve of the war, a number of marginal constituencies, such as Midlothian, Roxburghshire and Peebles & Selkirkshire, were deemed by internal party assessors to be in a highly unsatisfactory condition. Certainly in a number of key respects, such as mobilising women, youth and general membership, the Unionists could not be said to be ahead of the Liberals. It was to be well over fifty years before the Unionists' primacy in organisation was challenged again.

There was a curious colourlessness to Scottish Conservatism just before 1914. On the one hand, there was less involvement in the diehard opposition mounted by reactionary peers to the Liberal political and welfare reform programme. Some 41.2 per cent of all peers, but only 17.6 per cent of the diehards, owned land in Scotland.[36] Even the resistance in Ulster between 1911 and 1914 to the third Home Rule Bill aroused a more muted reaction in Scotland than many on both sides of the Irish Channel anticipated, given the furious Scottish reaction to the previous two bills. Irish Home Rule was rarely cited as a prominent factor in by-election results between 1910 and 1914. When Sir Edward Carson led an Ulster Unionist deputation on a tour of Britain in 1912 to stir up opposition to the bill, an estimated 100,000 turned out at Liverpool to give support, but in Glasgow, a mere 8,000 attended.[37]

On the other side, however, there were few Scottish Unionists who appeared interested in the attempts made by progressive Unionists to move the party's policies in a more advanced direction. On female suffrage, the party had no clear view. The Liberal Unionist Women's Association was disposed to support the campaign, and Lady Frances Balfour, the sister of Arthur, was one of the strongest Conservative women exponents of franchise reform in Britain. But there were also extremely vociferous anti-suffragists. The marchioness of Tullibardine (the future duchess of Atholl, and the first Scottish woman MP) was drawn into politics by her opposition to the matter. Another prominent anti-suffragist was Mrs Parker Smith, whose husband James was a leading tariff reformer and key Unionist strategist in Scotland in the decade before 1914.[38]

Much of the impetus to rethink Toryism in England came from a desire to promote the agenda of social reform. This of course was the obverse side of the economic case for tariff reform. A problem for the Unionists north of the border in trying to push for social reform was that the party lacked a tradition of Scottish Tory democracy. The origins of this radical Toryism in England in the 1830s had been less pertinent in Scotland, because the New Poor Law of 1834 did not apply in Scotland, and the equivalent measure, introduced in 1845, represented less of a break with previous practice. The relative unimportance of deference in Scottish social relations, as noted earlier, again minimised the potential for a social reform tradition. By the 1900s, Scottish industrialists committed to Unionism seem to have seen workers' welfare as a matter for the individual firm to adopt. Several offered company housing, paid pensions to retired employees and provided social amenities in the locality. But, presumably, they preferred this to be intimately bound to the firm's specific strategies, rather than as part of a responsibility placed on all of society. In some parts of Scottish industry, workplace relations deteriorated sharply from the 1890s, and it may well be that employers resisted efforts to, as they might see it, shore up the workers with social security measures.[39]

Hence the efforts of the party's candidate in Paisley in the early years of the century to promote the concept that Unionism would champion the interests of the working classes of the town resulted in his repudiation by the controlling interests in the local party. The textile manufacturers and engineering works owners were not prepared to tolerate radical Toryism in the constituency. The candidate was effortlessly deselected and a more amenable replacement found.[40] There were almost no Scottish MPs involved in the party's Social Reform Committee, which flourished in the final pre-war phase. Composed of about 25 MPs and a dozen or so figures outside parliament, this group strove to develop a progressive Unionist social policy framework. Only one Scottish MP, H. J. Mackinder, was a member, and he was an Englishman. Arthur Steel-Maitland, a Scottish landowner, was also involved, but his political career was based entirely in England. It is typical of the incoherence of the party that it could establish no clear position on the land question to combat the Liberals' runaway agitation, so that in the pre-war by-elections

Unionist candidates had to improvise policy with no clear direction from the centre.

IV

The performance of Labour in Scotland is at first sight perplexing, given its double head-start there. From Keir Hardie's candidacy in the Mid-Lanark by-election of 1888 the Scottish Labour Party was formed. This was the model for the Independent Labour Party, founded five years later in 1893, with which the Scottish Labour Party itself merged. Secondly, the formation of the Labour Representation Committee in England in 1900 was preceded by a few months by its Scottish equivalent, the Scottish Workers' Parliamentary Election (later Representation) Committee (SWPRC). Yet, as already noted, in electoral terms, Labour in Scotland lagged behind right up until the outbreak of the First World War. The barriers to Labour's advance took four forms: organisational defects; ideological conflict between constituent sections; divisions within the working class; the franchise system.

The formation in 1900 of the SWPRC at a conference attended by 266 delegates from a range of institutions seemed to give the Scots not only an earlier but also a broader base of working-class involvement. The co-operative movement and the miners' union both attended the launch proceedings, whereas in England, these two bodies did not participate. It is, however, not necessarily the case that Scotland was politically further to the left. To a degree the situation reflected institutional and administrative differences as much as ideological ones. Scotland, with 3.7 per cent of the total population unionised in 1892, lagged substantially behind England's 4.9 per cent, and moreover Scottish unions were often very highly localised with a small membership.[41] Because of these weaknesses, trade unions could not do electoral deals with the Liberals. Moreover, being industrially feeble, unions tended to seek amelioration of their members' conditions through political processes rather than workplace action. Also, the Scottish labour movement had faced stiffer legal challenges, so the desire to create a political party was stronger. There was also the wish to obtain better access to government departments and to be granted separate representation on public bodies dealing with the interests of organised labour in Scotland. And Whitehall tended not to differentiate between Scottish and English labour organisations in these matters.[42]

Until 1908 the SWPRC handled Labour politics north of the border, and did so with singular lack of efficiency or distinction. Part of the problem lay in the fact that many British-wide unions looked primarily to the LRC, believing it inefficient to share finances and other resources with the SWPRC. The SWPRC secretariat was noticeably less well-organised than the LRC (ironically run by a Scot, Ramsay MacDonald). The upshot was that constituencies received little information about available prospective candidates, propaganda was haphazard and central assistance towards struggling local parties was inadequate. The end of the Scottish party's existence came after its pursuit of a distinctive electoral strategy collided with its London-based sister, the Labour Party. The latter strove at by-elections in 1908 in Montrose and Dundee to reach a *modus vivendi* with the Liberals. The SWPRC, impervious to this, initially contemplated intervening more aggressively. The British trade unions decided to withdraw all support from the SWPRC, which was rendered impotent. Thereupon the SWPRC was swallowed up by the Labour Party, but there was an uneasy transition period. It was only in the two or three years before the war that improvements began to be recorded: the party had no city-wide organisation in Glasgow until 1912. More significantly, attempts to establish a Scottish Council to oversee party affairs languished, as the component sections first squabbled among themselves, and then with the London executive on central matters like its composition, its funding and its scope for evolving policy. Thus the movement in Scotland lagged several years behind in devising competent structures.[43]

Friction between the socialist wing of the party, the ILP, and the trade union wing persisted unabated throughout the pre-war years. The ILP in Scotland outperformed the rest of Britain: in 1910 it had about 5,000 members (one sixth of the British total) in some 130 branches. The true membership was probably half as much again, mainly because many could not afford to pay the subscription fees. Yet these are still very low figures compared to the other parties: the Glasgow ILP had about 1,300 members in 1913; the Glasgow Unionists had nearly 7,500 in 1911, while Dundee Liberals in 1908 numbered 1,279. Moreover, ILP support was characterised by volatility. Branches were formed, flourished and folded in remarkably short periods. The movement was mainly successful in recruiting among the lower middle class – particularly clerical workers – and the skilled working class: around two-thirds of the office-bearers of Glasgow branches between 1895 and 1911 came from these two groups. The bulk of the unskilled seems to have remained impervious to the ILP message: only two of the 80 Glasgow branch secretaries traced were labourers.[44]

Before 1914 the ILP never became a mass or even a moderately popular party, thus rendering mobilisation of the Labour vote extremely problematical. Looking back from the post-war age, one veteran member expressed astonishment at the rapid progress made since 1918, recording that in 1913–14 the movement in Glasgow seemed on the verge of collapse. At the Govan by-election in 1911, the ILP declined to nominate one of its number for candidature, believing that only a trade unionist had any hope. Yet Govan was regarded by many as a major ILP base and in 1918 it was the only Clydeside seat to go to Labour, and then with an ILP member as candidate.[45]

The ILP's essential strength was as an educational and evangelising movement. Its highly influential propaganda sheet, the *Forward*, begun in 1906, had reached a circulation of 10,000 by the start of the war. The party was famous for its public campaigning, with street-corner meetings, addresses in cinemas on Sunday nights and summer sessions at holiday resorts. It did not pay any great heed to working up electoral machinery, voter registration or even systematic canvassing. Its membership saw themselves as embarking on a long-term campaign – or, as James Maxton liked to envisage it, sowing the seeds which would come to fruition in some distant harvest-time. The prevailing assumption was that few immediate dividends would be won.[46]

The ILP's message was straightforward and fairly easy to absorb, having no heavyweight ideological lumber to transmit. Marxism was for most not a particularly influential force in the movement. The ILP represented an ethical vision of socialism which had certain things in common with Liberal radicalism. In particular, land reform, temperance, free trade and the right to national self-determination were all shared values. The ILP's interest in Scottish Home Rule was again close to Liberalism.[47] For some ILPers the values of Presbyterian, small-town or rural Scotland were the norms to be attained. *Our Noble Families*, the first book written by Tom Johnston, the editor of the *Forward*, was an attack on the land-owning nobility of Scotland, a classic Liberal target.[48]

Nevertheless, most ILPers shared a concern about poverty and the plight of poor people: it was Maxton's experience as a teacher in the East End of Glasgow which converted him to socialism. A sense of class consciousness was also a uniting characteristic of the elements in the ILP. However, their socialism was, as the social bases of the membership reveal, essentially targeted at the skilled worker, and there was frequently some uncertainty about the poorer sections of the working class. The ILP was reluctant to support full adult suffrage, which would have brought into the electorate not just the female socio-economic equals of the existing voters, but also a mass of semi- and unskilled working-class individuals. Perhaps its main ideological success was in broadening the message of socialism from a close focus on industrial production to a wider framework of municipal reform, housing improvement, etc. The emphasis on municipalising the trams and using the profits to under-write housing costs, so making rents affordable for the poor, was a significant marker for the future. At the time, however, this line of approach had to contend with the Liberals' preference for land tax, and much of the electoral evidence indicates that the socialist case had not made much headway.

Moreover, the ILP was a fairly broad church, embracing left Liberals as well as Marxists. The pages of the *Forward* reflected a catholicity in which writers of different opinions could state their case freely. The party enjoyed reasonably good relations with the SDF/BSP in the pre-war years, often reaching agreement to work together on campaigns, for instance against unemployment. Nevertheless, there were important repositioning exercises being conducted among the socialist groupings in the period. On the one hand, the ILP established its ascendancy over the SDF as the main socialist organisation, and it also secured its special relationship with unions in the emergent Labour Party. In addition, the ILP defined its differences from the Socialist Labour Party's industrial route to socialism.

The more Marxist-orientated SDF had in some places an initial advantage over the ILP. In Aberdeen, for example, the Federation was historically stronger than the ILP, but the split in the former of 1903, which resulted in the formation of the Socialist Labour Party, crucially debilitated the SDF. Furthermore, the SDF's mounting hostility towards the Labour Party allowed the ILP to marginalise its rival. The Aberdeen Workers' Electoral Committee, formed by the Trades Council in 1900, had contained both the SDF and the ILP, but when its successor, the Aberdeen Burgh Labour Party, was established in 1909, the SDF declined to participate, so abandoning the field to the ILP.[49]

In the four years before the First World War, there was a great deal of industrial unrest. Strikes abounded in many of the major industries in Scotland: most notably, the Singer's sewing machine workers industrial action in 1911, a three-month miners' strike in 1912, and the Leith dockers' three-month strike in 1913. These brush-fires of anarcho-syndicalism can be regarded as the harbingers of the acute unrest on Clydeside in the war, as some have recently argued.[50] Yet there is little evidence of widespread solidarity for these episodes: the Paisley mills, for example, resolutely ignored the disputes in neighbouring towns, while the Aberdeen Trades Council declined to identify with the strike movement in central Scotland.[51] The outcome of the symbolic Singer's strike was defeat for the unions and workers, and this effectively discredited the strategy of achieving socialism by the route of factory action. This was a serious setback for the Socialist Labour Party, which had been at the core of these strikes, and the result was to confirm the superiority of the ILP. The ILP had vigorously denounced the concept of anti-parliamentary socialism along the lines espoused by the syndicalists. The *Forward* never wavered in its repudiation of the Socialist Labour Party's line, and this left the ILP in a stronger position over its rivals by August 1914.[52]

Trade unions in Scotland were not particularly socialist in outlook, although some prominent union leaders, most notably Robert Smillie of the Lanarkshire miners, were. But others were still not far removed from Liberalism: the Midlothian miners' leader, running as the Labour Party candidate in a by-election in the constituency in 1912, pronounced himself a loyal follower of Gladstone. The Labour MP for Dundee from 1906, Alexander Wilkie, was secretary of the shipwrights' union and he remained chairman of a Liberal club in Newcastle. These Lib–Lab union leaders adopted a highly critical stance towards the ILPers, who reciprocated with added venom. So George Barnes, MP for Glasgow Blackfriars & Hutchesontown, and the erstwhile secretary of the engineers' union, forbade the most eloquent apologist for ILP socialism in Scotland, J. Bruce Glasier, to help in his election campaign. The ILP denounced several union candidates for their anti-socialist and reactionary views: for instance in Dundee and Midlothian. These rifts dogged the Labour Party right up to the war. Attempts to frame a constitution for the Scottish Council of the Labour Party were temporarily derailed when union elements, led by the miners, objected to the allocation of what they deemed over-generous representation on the executive committee to the ILP and kindred socialist societies.[53]

There was, however, a degree of electoral advance notched up by Labour, more so in local government than parliamentary terms. The Glasgow Workers' Electoral Committee ('the Stalwarts') was set up in 1895, combining the local trades council, the co-operative movement, the ILP and the Irish Nationalists. Its objective was to run candidates for the city council. The programme adopted was not overtly socialist, but it did address working-class concerns, and included the municipalisation of the liquor trade, a minimum wage and taxation of land values. Similar bodies followed in Edinburgh in 1899 (the Edinburgh Workers' Municipal Committee) and Aberdeen in 1900 (the Aberdeen Workers' Electoral Committee). The Stalwarts did establish a presence in Glasgow city chambers. In 1897, there were 11 GWEC representatives elected, but by 1908, the year in which it is sometimes claimed the case for socialism received a major boost in the west of Scotland as a result of the severe economic recession, only one 'Stalwart' remained. By 1914, however, recovery seemed apparent: there were 17 Labour Glasgow councillors, well above the highest total reached in the time of the Stalwarts. Yet this was not a wholly satisfactory position: the new council had been increased from 75 to 111 because of the extension of Glasgow's boundaries in 1912, so that proportionately there was no greater presence than about twenty years earlier. Moreover, the party was concentrated in a handful of wards – 11 in all – yet even so, it did not monopolise the representation of these districts.[54] Indeed, Dundee, with 10 Labour councillors out of 34, had a better record. Elsewhere, there were few clear inroads on the eve of war: Paisley had the same number of Labour councillors in 1913 as in 1900, and in Aberdeen, between 1909 and 1913 only one Labour councillor sat.

The working class was not yet united behind Labour. Many still adhered to Liberalism, as we have seen. The impact of the Irish Roman Catholic community on the development of Labour before 1914 is sometimes portrayed as negative. Relatively larger than in England, this was a well-drilled political force. The Catholic Union, founded in 1880, successfully mobilised votes in school board contests to protect the church's educational interests. The main Irish nationalist party had by 1914 12,500 Scottish members (one fourth of the British total) in about 100 branches. Theological hostility, together with political expediency, are the reasons sometimes advanced to explain Labour's failure to enlist the support of this solidly working-class grouping. Nevertheless, this is rather over-simplistic for a variety of reasons.

First, the political clout at parliamentary elections of the Irish Catholics was severely limited. A careful study suggests that over half of adult males in this ethno-religious category were disenfranchised in the later nineteenth century. In the January 1910 election, it was estimated that at most two Scottish seats might have gone to Labour if the Irish vote had been solidly behind the party.[55] Therefore, Labour's poor electoral showing was not caused by the absence of the Irish vote. Secondly, the church did not systematically seek to suppress all manifestations of socialism among its members. John Wheatley, the founder of the Catholic Socialist Society, was not persecuted by the hierarchy, notwithstanding the vapourings of the odd over-zealous priest. Wheatley's group was so minute – its maximum size was 100, with 50 members the more usual number – that it posed no menace. Moreover, Wheatley's version of socialism, an attempt to reconcile Catholic ideas with socialism by stressing society's responsibilities to the underprivileged, was far removed from the Marxist godless materialism denounced by the church authorities.[56]

Thirdly, the electoral politics of Irish nationalism were not universally anti-Labour. Mostly their vote went Liberal, given the imminence of a Liberal government legislating for Home Rule, but tactical subtlety meant that the vote could be given to Labour as a warning to backsliding Liberals: George Barnes held Glasgow Blackfriars & Hutchesontown from 1906 in good part on this basis. Where the cause of Irish nationhood was not relevant, there were few inhibitions about supporting Labour, as the episode with the Stalwarts in Glasgow showed. This grouping foundered in the early 1900s through no fault of the Irish. There were influential individuals within the Irish Catholic community highly sympathetic to the aspirations of Labour, including Charles Diamond, the owner-editor of the community's newspaper, and John Ferguson, the leading Irish Nationalist, who helped Keir Hardie launch his Scottish Labour Party in 1888. Moreover, Labour itself was not blameless: many ILPers, coming from a strong Presbyterian background, were ambivalent about relations with Irish Roman Catholics. Tom Johnston is a good instance of this.

Labour had difficulty winning women over to their side. English-based women's suffrage activists visiting Scotland commented on the vestigial presence of women in Scottish left-wing movements such as the ILP. Margaret Irwin, an early secretary of the STUC and the organiser of women into trade unions, is an obvious exception, but the prevailing tone of the socialist and labour organisations was male-oriented. The equivocation which the Scottish socialists displayed over women's suffrage, as noted above, probably alienated many.[57]

Labour also encountered difficulties because of the lower Scottish enfranchisement rate. The average percentage of adult male enfranchisement in 1911 for Britain was around 64 per cent, but in the Scottish burghs, it was 57 per cent. In Dundee, however, only 48 per cent of adult men in the city had the parliamentary vote. There were three broad reasons for this: the legal technicalities regarding the lodger franchise in Scotland; the Scottish custom of the tenant not paying rates in low-quality property, when personal payment of rents was a *sine qua non* for gaining the vote; and the high mobility of labour, because of the cyclical nature of the heavy industry sector and a large pool of casual labour, which meant that many did not reside the required period (about eighteen months) to get on the registers. These debarments bore most heavily on the working class. About 55 per cent of the delegates on Glasgow Trades Council were on the electoral registers in 1910–11 and 1911–12, but only 45 per cent were on both years' rolls. These individuals were normally the most active and 'respectable' elements of the working class, so it may not be unreasonable to infer that among the less skilled groups the enfranchisement figure was even lower.[58]

On the other hand, there is no guarantee that Labour was disadvantaged by the vote factor: as we have seen, much of the party's message was geared to the lower middle-class and upper working-class categories. It is significant that even in those local government spheres where a broader franchise than the parliamentary qualification operated, for instance, school boards and parish councils, Labour was not making any advances of note before the war. The final indicator that Labour had not effected any seismic change in political allegiances came with the outbreak of war. Scotland, and especially its working-class element, rallied enthusiastically to the patriotic call. Proportionately more Scots than English volunteered, and the problem was to keep key workers at home in production for the war effort. The socialist message of international working-class solidarity against the capitalist war was mostly disregarded.

Hence the position in the summer of 1914 can be summed up as follows. In some contrast to England, the Liberal Party was holding up well in Scotland: membership and finances were not slipping to any degree; electorally the party retained most of its seats in by-elections. The Unionists were still trying to establish the basis for a sustained assault on Liberalism and to cement the differing strands in the party into a harmonious whole. Labour faced a variety of internal problems before it could take on the Liberals with any prospect of success, and progression was not always linear. On the five occasions Labour fought North-East Lanarkshire between 1901 and 1911, their lowest poll shares occurred in the last two elections.[59] The party's performance in the 1911–14 Scottish by-elections fell below the results obtained in England. The party won no seats, and the best it could manage was to contribute to the Liberals losing a trio of constituencies (Midlothian, 1912, South

Lanarkshire, 1913, and Leith, 1914) to the Tories. But even here, other influences may have damaged the Liberals: Ulster loyalists certainly claimed Midlothian as a scalp for their electioneering work on the mainland. In Scotland, plans for the next general election (due in 1915) indicated that Labour expected to contest proportionately fewer seats than in England. But the gradual growth of Labour could also be discerned. The party was gaining a presence in council chambers: in 1915, Labour had 13 county and 69 town councillors (although Glasgow, relatively speaking, was still in 1913–14 performing less well than ten to fifteen years earlier). Organisation was at last becoming tighter: city-wide Labour parties were installed, and the Scottish Advisory Council, finally instituted in 1915, permitted a broader approach to machinery to be adopted. Importantly, too, voter registration work was being pursued systematically. In the coalfield areas of Fife, Ayrshire, Midlothian and Lanarkshire, the miners' unions had appointed political agents, who enrolled many Labour sympathisers, with William Watson leading the way in Fife.[60] Yet there were deficiencies: in 1914 the majority of trades councils as well as a good number of trade unions were not affiliated to the party. Ominously, too, many urban-industrial seats were not among Labour's target constituencies. So, in Aberdeen, which in 1918 returned one of only seven Labour MPs in Scotland, it was not intended in 1914 to contest the next election.

2

THE RISE OF UNIONISM AND OF
LABOUR, 1914–39

I

The extent of the transformation in Scottish politics can be presented starkly: in August 1914 there were 54 Liberal MPs, but ten years later only 8, while the number of Conservative MPs rose over the same period from 13 to 36 and Labour from 3 to 26. By 1924 the last two parties were rather closer to the levels of support they enjoyed in England. The comprehensive defeat of Asquith in 1918 at East Fife, a seat he had held for over thirty years, and the humiliation of a lost deposit at Glasgow St Rollox inflicted on MacKinnon Wood, Liberal Scottish Secretary between 1912 and 1916, epitomised the Liberal collapse. By 1924 the extent of the party's retreat was clear, as large tracts of the country were Liberal-free zones: in west central Scotland the party fought a mere 5 of 31 seats, winning only one (Greenock).[1] Most of the few remaining Liberal Lowland urban seats (e.g., Dundee, Greenock and Leith) were held because of a pact, formal or otherwise, with the Tories. Elsewhere, too, Liberals crumbled with little resistance. The north-east Lowland rural constituencies, formerly a hot-bed of impregnable Liberalism, mostly dropped into the laps of Conservatives, sometimes to the surprise of the victors, as in Moray & Nairn in 1923. Only the Highlands, where social and ideological changes were perhaps less rapid, remained steadfastly Liberal.

In the 1920s, Scottish Liberals tended to be less active electorally – and less successful in garnering votes than in England – but the position was

Table 2.1   The Liberal poll, England and Scotland, 1922–35

	% of Seats Fought		Share of Vote		% of MPs	
	England	Scotland	England	Scotland	England	Scotland
1922 Ind. Lib.	57.3	67.6	19.6	21.5	9.0	21.1
Nat. Lib.	20.0	46.5	7.6	17.7	6.3	16.9
1923	73.8	83.1	29.9	28.4	25.1	30.9
1924	57.1	47.9	17.6	16.6	3.9	11.3
1929	86.1	63.4	23.6	18.1	7.1	18.3
1931 Lib.	17.3	19.7	5.8	8.6	3.9	10.0
Nat. Lib.	5.7	11.3	3.4	4.9	4.7	11.3
1935 Lib.	27.0	22.5	6.3	6.7	2.2	4.2
Nat. Lib.	6.3	12.7	3.4	6.7	4.5	10.0

Source: F. W. S. Craig, *British Electoral Facts, 1832–1987* (Dartmouth, 1989), tables 1.22–27.

reversed in the 1930s. However, the Liberals in Scotland were always more efficient at translating votes into seats.

A significant element in the problems faced by the Liberals arose from redistribution changes contained in the 1918 Franchise Act. For the first time, the boundary commissioners were enjoined to create, as far as practicable, constituencies of equal population size. The upshot was a double blow for the Liberals: 11 of the 13 seats abolished had generally been Liberal before 1914, and the new seats were reallocated away from the northern and southern peripheries in favour of the central urban-industrial area. Glasgow itself gained eight seats, while the southern and northern regions fell from 16 to 10.[2] Labour was much assisted by the reallocation of seats to the industrial regions, the Tories probably less so.

Labour also performed equally unevenly: in the 1920s, Scotland was doing better than England, but the drop in support in 1931 was more accentuated than in England. Though Scotland recovered solidly by 1935, even with the ILP vote added, the party had not regained the share of the vote achieved in its best year (1929), yet in England 1935 was the best share of the poll in the inter-war era.

The inter-war years were the most successful period electorally for the Scottish Tories since 1832. From having been the largest party in only one of the 20 elections held between then and 1914, they had the most MPs in four of the seven inter-war contests. Subsequently, they have been the biggest party in only two of the fourteen elections since the Second World War. Moreover, the level of support for the Tories in Scotland drew much closer to that in England: in 1922,

Scotland was just 60 per cent of the English poll share, by 1935, it was up to 85 per cent.

II

The Unionists were helped by a pronounced shift in the political stance of four key national institutions, namely the Church of Scotland, the legal and educational systems and the press. These had a strong impact in a country which had no parliament of its own: to a degree they represented official Scotland and spoke for the nation. Before the war they had either been neutral, or there was a Liberal balance to check pro-Conservative leanings. After 1918 many of these restraining elements disappeared, leaving the Unionists holding the commanding heights.

Between the wars the press moved emphatically towards the Tories from a pre-war position of rough equipoise between Liberal and Unionist. In three of the four main cities before 1914, both parties had a supportive daily paper.[3] By the mid-1920s, these Liberal organs had all gone. In Dundee and Aberdeen, they were each taken over by the Tory rival; the titles may have been incorporated in the mastheads, but the politics were rigorously Unionist. In Glasgow, the *Daily Record*, long a powerful exponent of Liberalism, was bought out by Conservative press magnates, and its politics switched accordingly. When new papers appeared, they were pro-Tory: the Glasgow *Bulletin*, a stablemate to the *Herald* launched in 1915, addressed a lower-middle class readership in Unionist tones. The stoutly Unionist *Sunday Post*, begun in 1914, was read almost universally in Scotland.

Most Scots tended not to read the London daily press, and the only metropolitan paper to make a serious incursion into the Scottish market was the right-wing *Daily Express*. Lord Beaverbrook, himself of Scottish origin, launched a Scottish edition in 1928, a venture in which he took close personal interest. Labour's *Daily Herald* struggled in Scotland, and even the ILP weekly, the *Forward*, had passed its peak by the later 1920s.

The Liberals also lost influence through changes in the content of the *People's Journal* following a transfer of ownership after the war. It altered from its pre-war role as a standard-bearer of radicalism, especially among rural areas, into an anodyne mix of stories and sentimental Scottishness. Local newspapers also changed colour. Before 1914, it was customary for most areas to have Liberal and Tory papers in rivalry. By the outbreak of the Second World War, most places had only one paper, and these were usually either Unionist, or neutral: in 1913, 59 journals defined themselves as Liberal, 51 as Unionist, and 101 gave no affiliation. Twenty-five years later, 13 were Liberal, 51 Tory, and 133 neither – although several Unionist-leaning papers placed themselves in the last category (e.g., the *Glasgow Herald* and the *Dundee Courier*), so understating the pro-Unionist bias. It may be no coincidence that the two larger towns still with a Liberal daily paper in 1939 – Greenock and Paisley – were among the few surviving substantial urban Liberal bases.

So alarmed were the Liberals at the destruction of their press outlets that the SLF endeavoured in 1936 to strike a deal with the *Weekly Glasgow Herald*. The *Weekly Herald*, which had only tenuous connections with the eponymous daily, was in financial difficulties. The Liberals tried to induce party members to take out annual subscriptions to the paper in the hope of the *quid pro quo* of being given a full page per issue to put forward the Liberal viewpoint. The scheme foundered quickly, leaving the Liberals voiceless.[4]

In the pre-1914 decade, the political benefits to the Liberals of its traditional links with non-established Presbyterianism were, as we have seen, in decline. After 1918, changes in Presbyterianism meant the Tories were the party which gained most. The merger between the UFC and the Church of Scotland in 1929 resulted in the absorption of the more Liberal-inclined dissenters into the larger state church, so that the opinions of the latter prevailed. Even before then, the UFC had diluted much of its erstwhile radicalism: the impact of Labour and an aggressive working-class pushed many clergy and laity into the Tory camp from about 1924.[5] After the union, the expanded Church of Scotland enjoyed enhanced prestige, speaking for the vast bulk of Presbyterians in a way it had not been able to claim for over a century. The role of the Church's General Assembly as a surrogate Scottish parliament was now more credible.

The Presbyterian churches were pretty conservative throughout this period, showing little interest in, and less commitment to, issues of social reform. There was overwhelming and continuing church support for involvement in the First World War.[6] After the war the Church of Scotland was much exercised by what it perceived to be the 'Irish menace' to Scottish values, and the Kirk called for the repatriation of the Irish population from Scotland. Since the bulk of the Irish Catholics (Protestant Irish were not in the Church's sights) were Labour voters, the political undertones were clear.[7] The General Strike of 1926 was roundly and universally denounced by Presbyterian churches as an onslaught on social stability.[8] The Church of Scotland took little overt interest in the social and economic consequences of the 1930s recession. The leading minister who sought to involve the church in these questions, George MacLeod, was effectively marginalised, and instead the church, under the commanding leadership of John White, himself an active Unionist, avoided political criticism of the government.[9]

The higher reaches of the Scottish legal system also became inextricably linked to the Tories. Before 1914 the Liberals had attracted many eminent Scottish lawyers into parliament: the two Liberal Lord Chancellors of 1905–16 (Loreburn and Haldane) had been Scottish MPs. Eleven advocates sat as Liberal MPs between 1892 and 1914, and only six as Unionists. After 1918, a sea-change occurred: no advocate entered the house between the wars as a new Liberal MP, while 24 sat as Tories. So overwhelming was the Tory presence that the first Labour government used Unionists to fill the posts of Lord Advocate and Solicitor-General. Labour managed to field one of its own in 1929, but he stayed loyal to MacDonald in 1931, leaving Labour bereft of advocates until Robert Gibson won Greenock in 1936. The Tories benefited doubly: in the twenty years before 1914, nine Liberal and four Unionist MPs became sheriffs or judges, but between 1918 and 1939, there were 14 Unionists and only one Liberal promoted to the bench from the Commons. This predominance arguably forged, if only subconsciously, a close identification between the party and a key national institution. More practically, the Tories had the presence of powerful forensic talents in parliament to promote the party's cause: J. S. C. Reid was regarded by many as one of the most formidable debaters in the Commons.

In the education sector, perhaps the area which Scots saw as most influential in shaping national characteristics, the Tories were dominant. This had been true before 1914 at university level. The party had firmly controlled the return of MPs for the university seats, and after 1918 this continued. The impression was therefore created that the educational elite was heavily Tory. MPs were often eminent academics (for instance, Professor Sir John Kerr, a distinguished zoologist), or men of renown in public service (John Buchan and Sir Henry Craik). One of the most graphic indicators of the limited extent to which Labour reached beyond working-class voters is the party's performance in the Combined Scottish Universities constituency. All graduates of the Scottish universities were entitled to vote. Given that socialist schoolteachers had entered the demonology of the right at the time of the 'Red Clydeside' election of 1922, one might expect that, as secondary teaching was an

Table 2.2   The Labour poll in the university seats, 1918–35

	Camb.	Eng.	London	Oxford	Wales	Scot.
1918	11.1	18.4	31.7	6.0	19.2	12.2
1922	–	12.2	19.2	–	24.6	–
1923	–	21.9	17.6	–	–	–
1924	–	–	–	–	40.6	9.3
1929	9.2	–	–	–	24.9	10.7
1931	–	–	–	–	–	–
1935	19.2	–	30.4	17.6	38.7	–

Notes:

1   'Eng.' stands for Combined English Universities, i.e., all except Cambridge, London and Oxford.

2   The percentages relate to the first total of votes cast: additional votes acquired under the proportional voting scheme used for certain of these seats have been disregarded.

3   Labour fought four by-elections in the Scottish constituency, polling thus: 1927, 12.3 per cent; 1934, 20.8 per cent; 1935, 17.3 per cent; 1936, 12.4 per cent. All except the last were straight fights.

all-graduate career (and many primary teachers were possessors of the Ordinary MA), there would be strong support for Labour. In addition, the radicalisation of students in the 1930s might have helped Labour in that decade. In reality, Labour contested the constituency only fitfully, running in three of the seven general elections. When candidates did stand, they were pretty unsuccessful: in a by-election in 1936, the Scottish Nationalist candidate polled double Labour's vote. Comparisons with the rest of the British universities seats puts Labour's Scottish record in perspective, as Table 2.2 suggests. The clearest indication of the political leaning of schoolteachers is seen in the formation in 1926 of a Glasgow Unionist Teachers Association. By 1933, it claimed 800 members.[10]

III

While it is undoubtedly the case that the war created major problems for the Liberals, other, broader factors also contributed to the party's eclipse. The challenge of war took two broad aspects.[11] First, Scottish Liberal MPs were disproportionately Asquithian: in the Maurice Debate vote in 1918, the litmus test for defining positions *vis-à-vis* Asquith and Lloyd George, 22 Scottish MPs voted on Asquith's side and 17 against. As Asquithian Liberals were punished by the electors in 1918 for their perceived 'disloyalty' over the Maurice Debate, the impact in Scotland was thus severe.

Secondly, the internal schisms produced by the war had serious consequences for party strength and morale. Among MPs, the elements of the New Liberalism which had been so potent before 1914 were scattered politically. Some, such as Ponsonby, opposed the war from the outset. A number of radicals, including J. W. Pratt and A. MacCallum Scott, followed Lloyd George and Churchill into coalition with the Conservatives in 1916. Others, however, remained loyal to Asquith: J. M. Hogge and J. W. Gulland, two of the most vocal pre-war radicals, were leading instances of this. Moderate, centrist MPs were equally divided: Sir Henry Dalziel was strongly pro-war, while P. A. Molteno stood by Asquith.

The 1918 election augmented the Liberal disarray. Proportionately twice as many Coalition Liberals stood in Scotland (43 per cent of Coalition candidates), as in England (22 per cent). Hence the split was deeper and more pervasive in Scotland, as considerably more of the contests occurred between Liberals: in four out of 70 seats, there were two Liberals in the field, while this happened in only five of the 456 English constituencies. The hostility persisted in the 1922 general election, when in 16 (23 per cent) seats Asquithian Liberal fought National Liberal. This compares with 34 (6.7 per cent) in England.

The Liberal breach, formalised in 1920, was exceptionally bitter in Scotland and left a lingering hostility. The extent of support for the Lloyd George wing can be seen in the disaffiliation from the SLF in 1920 of nearly one-quarter of all local associations. Lloyd George also took away many of the best members of the SLF administrative staff. Organisation on both sides of the divide became inadequate, and in particular, the drop in subscribers proved catastrophic. It was extremely difficult for either faction to develop branches in seats where the other was officially in control. The willingness of Lloyd George to contemplate running a candidate against Asquith in the Paisley by-election of 1920 when no Unionist initially came forward added greatly to the rancour.[12]

The conflict at the higher levels had a deleterious impact on grassroots supporters. Some local associations were, indeed, in conflict with their MPs over the war: Arthur Ponsonby, W. M. R. Pringle and G. B. Esslemont were in varying degrees deselected or forced to quit because their criticism of the conduct of the war collided with constituency activists. Besides this direct tension, the sight of party leaders squabbling viciously led to disaffection and withdrawal from party involvement by ordinary members. The grass roots simply withered: in a stronghold like Stirling, solidly Liberal since 1832, it was reported in 1922 that the local party had 'still to be revived from the state of hibernation which has existed since the days of the war'. Associations reported a disturbing lack of younger members: in Aberdeen in 1920 the need to recruit young men was stressed, yet two years later the South constituency chairman wished to resign because of his defective hearing, suggesting no great influx of members.[13]

Yet the Liberals' precipitate decline between 1918 and 1922 seemed to be arrested thereafter. The process of reunification in 1922–3 passed over quite amicably: a new structure incorporating members of both sides got to work briskly, reuniting constituency organisations, as in Caithness & Sutherland, where the National Liberal MP, Archibald Sinclair, made the transition effortlessly. The general election of 1923 seemed to encapsulate the new mood of optimism. A united party fought on a historic rallying cry – free trade – and 22 seats were won. Still, this resurgence proved illusory. The preponderance of the seats won in 1923 were either uncontested (5), or held in straight fights with either Labour (6) or Unionist (9). In 1924, Labour intervened in eight of the nine seats where there had been a straight Liberal–Tory contest the year before, winning only one (Edinburgh East), but the Liberals lost in all. In addition, in two of the five uncontested 1923 wins the Liberals faced a challenger in 1924, and lost both.

The year 1923 also underlined the degree to which support for the Liberals was at best only partial. Asquith's decision to prop up a minority Labour administration evoked a wave of shocked hostility in Scotland; even in his own constituency leading Liberal businessmen publicly complained about the decision. By the 1924 general election the Liberals were in difficulty: money dried up, organisation shrivelled and the party found itself unable to contest many seats. In England, Liberals fought 280 seats in 1924, against 360 in 1923, a fall of about 22 per cent; in Scotland, the decline, from 59 to 34, was in the order of 43 per cent. The 1929 general election revealed that financial and personal resources were still in short supply, and the Liberals fought 45 seats in Scotland, that is 63 per cent of the total, whereas over 87 per cent of English seats were fought. The withdrawal of an important subsidy from London in the aftermath of the election confirmed the enfeebled state of Liberalism north of the border.[14]

In 1931 the party suffered severely from the permanent defection of many local activists into the Tory camp. In Clackmannan & East Stirling, the Alloa town clerk, a prominent Liberal, seconded the nomination of the Unionist candidate at the selection meeting.[15] A considerable number of MPs stayed loyal to the coalition in 1933 when the issue of free trade led to the departure of the Samuelites from the National government: only four Scots crossed with Samuel and 28 others to the opposition benches. Local party organisation in many seats simply collapsed, even in those with a recent history of Liberal representation. In South Midlothian & Peebles, where the Liberals had got between a fifth and a quarter of the vote in the 1920s, the association was stated in 1934 not to have been functioning for some time.[16]

In the 1930s, the praiseworthy object of trying to maintain good relations with those sundered (only temporarily, it was believed) after 1933 created considerable confusion and hampered clear decision-taking. National Liberal activists and constituencies still took part in SLF deliberations. At a meeting after the 1935 general election to decide whether Liberals should co-operate with National Government candidates at the next contest, National Liberal MPs Sir Godfrey Collins and J. P. Maclay took a prominent part in the debate. They lost, but by only 166 to 102.[17] This must have sent out a rather muffled message to voters.

The Liberals suffered severely from a long-running financial crisis throughout these years. The SLF's annual revenue was about one tenth that of the Tories, and covered only three-quarters of annual expenditure. The overdraft limit was constantly being breached, and salaries were often months in arrears. Drastic cuts in the 1930s – dismissing staff, reducing salaries, moving from prestigious offices – did not solve the basic condition. The main cause was the fall in paying supporters. The internal feuding of the 1920s was held to have made fund-raising difficult, while the protracted economic depression also blunted donors' willingness to contribute. By 1927 they numbered only one half of the pre-war 2,000, and deaths continually lowered the total still further. As an official remarked in 1937, the party relied on 'the generosity of a few', so the loss of any individual was serious. There was a particularly severe crisis in 1932, when two substantial backers died.[18]

The results were profound. The structure of the central machinery was highly deficient. It was chronically understaffed: at one point the party secretary was himself collecting subscriptions door-to-door when he should have been engaged in higher grade work. The party could barely afford cars for its organisers, so that constituencies were left to their own devices. No women's organiser was appointed until the late 1920s.

The SLF had only a very tenuous relationship with some constituency parties. Local autonomy was the norm, with no apparent need to liaise with the centre. Some Liberal associations were totally beyond any influence: Montrose Burghs, a Liberal seat, was said in 1932 never to consult the SLF 'about anything' and had had 'no official connection with the federation for years'. When the centre tried to impose its will, it was openly rebuffed. The East Fife, East Perthshire and Greenock parties all rejected the SLF's suggestion that they run a Liberal candidate in by-elections in the 1930s. East Perthshire actually disaffiliated, and Greenock threatened to do so. When the SLF, on the other hand, tried to induce the West Perthshire Liberals to withdraw in the by-election of 1938, to leave the duchess of Atholl with the prospect of victory, compliance came with the utmost displeasure and only after the direct intervention of the national party leader, Archibald Sinclair.[19]

Local independence was encouraged by the evident lack of communication on the part of the SLF. In 1928, a survey of constituencies' activities for that year found that local parties had held 700 public and social meetings, and had raised £7,500. This was all to the SLF's surprise, as it commented: 'This statement indicated that there was more activity than was known'.[20] Affiliation fees from the localities were occasional windfalls, rather than regular payments: at a key policy meeting in 1936, twelve constituencies were debarred from voting because of non-payment of affiliation dues. These included six in traditional Liberal areas – the seat represented by the national leader among them.[21]

The effect of these adverse factors was apparent in the atrophy of many constituency parties, which the central administration was unable to redress. Given the intra-party tensions still prevalent after the Asquith–Lloyd George reunion, the party secretary decided to discontinue visits to constituencies until the conflict was resolved. It was noted in 1926 that the disputes served to create 'misunderstandings and jealousies and bewilder the rank and file'.[22] As the Aberdeen South local secretary pointed out, if no central funds were available to help contest a seat, what incentive was there for activists to go on?[23] Maintaining membership levels was a recurrent problem. In Dundee, they hovered around the 900 mark for most of the 1930s. This was quite adequate, but rather exceptional, as Dundee was one of the few urban Liberal seats, but before 1914 the figure had been 1,279, over one third higher.

The involvement of members was also sketchy. At the annual general meetings of two wards in Dundee between 1925 and 1935 the average attendance was nine and seven.[24] Local organisations were regularly reported as defunct, e.g., Edinburgh Liberal Council in 1933, Midlothian South & Peebles Association in 1934. The west of Scotland was almost entirely abandoned in organisational terms: in 1928 it was felt 'perhaps a little dangerous' to try building up support in Glasgow.[25]

Great difficulties were encountered in finding candidates, and then in funding them properly. The party struggled in 1929 to reach the target number of contests given it by party headquarters in London, so incurring a severe reprimand from Herbert Samuel about the poor state of organisation in Scotland as compared to England.[26] In 1937, the Liberals were toiling to find suitable candidates, even though the party planned to fight a mere handful at the next general election.[27] Thus the Liberals were reduced to minimal functioning levels by the Second World War.

But the problems of the Liberals were not due solely to internal crises, significant though these were. Partly it was because structural factors operated against them. The franchise element of the Fourth Reform Act of 1918 wounded the Liberal party, as well as the redistributive element already discussed. Asquith's opposition before 1914 to female enfranchisement now rebounded on him and, by extension, his supporters. It was widely accepted that in East Fife a large number of the new women voters went against him for this reason.[28] As discussed later, the advent of an increased male electorate benefited Labour, and afforded few gains for the Liberals.

The Liberals' difficulties were also policy-based. They had little to offer the working class and social progressives after 1918. Many joined Labour, for a range of reasons. Arthur Ponsonby found that the only local elements prepared to back his anti-war stance were ILP members, and after the war he joined the Labour Party. Certain Young Scots – for example, Revd James Barr – who had been anti-war, made a similar journey. MacCallum Scott went to Labour because he perceived it to be the sole vehicle for achieving his collectivist reforming objectives. Others, like William Wedgwood Benn and A. M. Livingstone, the MPs for, respectively, Leith and the Western Isles, left for Labour in disgust after Lloyd George became leader of the party in 1926, thus underscoring the superficiality of the reunion of 1923. On the other hand, as is discussed below, the right-inclined sections of Liberals were effectively poached by the Tories.

Additionally, the wellsprings of the older nineteenth-century liberalism, which still retained considerable appeal before 1914, were either no longer powerful or not a monopoly of the party. Thus, temperance did not seem as effective a solution to acute social problems as the state interventionist remedies such as subsidised public housing which came to the forefront after 1918. In any case, Labour took up the anti-drink appeal more effectively. The old potent appeal of free trade also dwindled. It resurfaced in the 1923 election to boost the Liberal vote, as many businessmen still rejected protectionism as a cure for the ills of traditional Scottish industry. Yet by the end of the decade, acceptance of protection was widespread: the imposition in the 1930s of tariffs evoked limited protest in Scotland. The *Glasgow Herald*, vociferous in defence of free trade in 1923, acquiesced in the new policy with equanimity.

Again, the land question appeared less pertinent. Urban social conditions now had a more convincing collectivist solution on offer from Labour. In rural areas, state attempts to promote smallholdings were not very successful, with few making a living on their plots. Similarly, the break-up of great estates afforded tenant farmers the chance to buy their farms, so there was no call for sweeping land legislation by this class, who rather became acutely hostile to any legislative encroachment on their newly acquired property rights. Agricultural labourers were likewise unimpressed by Liberal land policy, being instead attracted by Labour's emphasis on improved rural working and living conditions rather than by the right to be a struggling small farmer. Nonetheless, taxation of land values, the pre-war rallying cry, was still invoked by Liberals twenty years on. It appeared in the party's 1935 general election programme, touted as a replacement for rates.

Yet, even on land issues, the party seemed too timid and marginal. The initial report of the Liberal Party's Scottish Rural Land Inquiry in 1928 was referred back in order to tone down the section on landownership because, as several members of the SLF executive stressed, there was an 'undue emphasis' on 'the principle of purchase' for smallholdings. In addition, the opportunity to say something distinctive on urban land, which might have allowed a Liberal perspective on the housing question, was missed. Pressed for time, the enquiry's members concentrated on the rural element, deciding simply to look at the English version's urban recommendations, and 'see how far any of these could be fitted in to Scottish conditions'.[29] This emphasised the rural, anti-urban perspective of the party in an age of intensifying class consciousness.

This focus on a slightly backward-looking, small-town or rural vision of Scotland is of a piece with the line taken by the Liberal candidate for Dundee in the 1929 election. The topic he chose for an address to the Rotary Club in one of Scotland's most industrial cities was 'The Importance of Virile Rural Life', and subsequently he spoke to Broughty Ferry voters on land drainage.[30] Likewise, the SLF's 'Call to Arms' in the 1935 general election placed the values of small-scale localism above efficiency and professionalism in local government. It deplored the 1929 local government reforms which had scrapped the plethora of small authorities and introduced large unitary authorities.[31] A similar impression of being rather antiquated came from Dingle Foot, the MP for Dundee from 1931. While he did protest at low unemployment benefit scales and called for housing reform, he was violently opposed to all signs of corporatism and the extension of the role of the state, whether from Labour or the Tories. Instead he insisted on the absolute need to protect the individual from a centralised bureaucracy.[32] As is shown below, progressive Unionism had moved away from this perception to a more statist approach.

Moreover, the party could show remarkable ineptitude in shaping its policies to relate to current circumstances. When the SLF drew up a policy statement in 1937, there was surprise among members of the executive at the absence of any reference to agriculture. A special committee was promptly set up, and a report was produced the following year. This omission is quite astonishing, given that the Tories were, as is discussed later, facing great unpopularity in rural areas over their treatment of Scottish farming, and since, additionally, the Liberals were essentially a party of non-industrial regions.[33]

But the deeper problem for the Liberals was that in an age of political allegiance primarily determined by highly polarised class relations, there was little room for a middle of the road, classless party. The working-class Liberal had moved comfortably to Labour in the early post-war period; some radicalised by war-time factors, others reassured of the essential pragmatic nature of Labour, as indicated below, and happy to follow the lead given by the prominent converts from radical Liberalism to Labour. The middle class, unsettled by the strident rhetoric of the militant socialists, sought security with the Tories: the reaction of the Paisley business community to Asquith's decision to prop up the minority Labour administration of 1924 is revealing, as is the movement of UFC ministers to the Tories in the 1924 election.[34] The Liberals were effectively confined to areas where class-consciousness was not a prevailing feature.

IV

The vitality and *élan* of the Scots Tories between the wars, perhaps buoyed up by their striking electoral advances, was underscored by their full participation in the British party, to a degree unparalleled before or since. Five Scottish MPs held Cabinet posts outside the Scottish Office portfolio: it was forty years after 1945 before this happened again.[35] Scots were also prominent in the intellectual development of Toryism between the wars: Noel Skelton is usually regarded as the coiner of the most pregnant concept in modern Conservatism, 'a property-owning democracy'.[36] The duchess of Atholl's *Women and Politics*, published in 1931, was a skilful propaganda effort; and Walter Elliot's *Toryism in the Twentieth Century* (1927) was the main work in a series aiming to expound the Conservative position on contemporary affairs.

One factor of considerable significance in the dominance of the Unionists was their superior organisation, which easily outstripped Liberal and Labour in comprehensiveness and efficacy. By 1927, barely a dozen constituencies did not have a full-time agent/organiser, whereas the Liberals and Labour alike had a mere handful. Financially the party was healthy: between 1923 and 1932 the central organisation enjoyed an average annual income of £13,000. This contrasts with the virtually bankrupt Liberals and the permanently cash-strapped Labour Party. In addition, the Conservative Clubs in Edinburgh and Glasgow continued their pre-war activities of raising regular large amounts to supplement the party's income. Party membership was buoyant: there were around 30,000 in Glasgow alone in 1931, a figure substantially in excess of the total for Labour in the whole of Scotland.

In its propaganda methods the party showed an alertness to social trends and to Scottish sensitivities. The party noted in 1937: 'Modern conditions call for modern methods of treatment: it is becoming increasingly difficult to secure the interest or attention of electors along former lines of procedure.'[37] In 1930, to meet this challenge, cinema vans were introduced, mixing a political message with material of wider interest. They reached an audience at once both large (3,000 in one constituency in a given year) and new:

a feature of these [cinema van] meetings is the opportunity they provide for members and prospective candidates to reach a section of the electorate not readily attracted to more ordinary meetings.[38]

In response to complaints that leaflets emanating from London did not address Scottish concerns, the Scottish Whip's Office assumed responsibility for Scottish literature, and published a number of leaflets which were seen as effective, particularly one rebutting Scottish nationalism, which appeared in 1932.[39]

The major achievements in organisation, however, arguably lay in mobilising women and the young. From the passage of the 1918 Franchise Act, women were given a high and visible place: each constituency association was required to have a woman as one of the two vice-presidents; the first woman Scottish MP was a Tory, and with 16 candidatures in the inter-war period, the party easily outperformed Labour (12) and the Liberals (6). Rank and file involvement was systematically worked up: by 1924 there were around 400 sections, with central women's organisers appointed to handle these. Political education of women members was attended to, with lectures, day and weekend schools and an annual conference laid on. Women took a full role in electioneering – canvassing and holding kitchen and garden meetings – as the party acknowledged in 1924:

> The women are indefatigable in taking their share of organisation and propaganda and in acquiring a knowledge of politics, and are showing much less diffidence than formerly in standing alongside the men in Party warfare.[40]

The Tories were also far more successful than their rivals in catching younger supporters, mainly through the vehicle of the Junior Imperial League. The league was revived after 1918 and targeted 15 to 25-year-olds. By about 1930 there were 20,000 members in 250 branches. While the movement had a range of social functions to attract recruits, it also carried out serious political work such as canvassing during elections and holding educational meetings to diffuse knowledge of party policies and principles. Not only did it form a bridge to draw people into the adult party association, the league also brought on future leaders: in 1938, two league activists were elected to Glasgow City Council.[41] The Young Unionists began about 1923, and took in eight to 15-year-olds. Most of its branches were in the west of Scotland. Meetings seem to have been primarily for entertainment purposes: a Young Unionists Choir was formed, taking part in adult party concerts. But on Empire Day, members in the Glasgow area marched to the city cenotaph – in the 1930s these numbered from 400 to 600.[42]

It is nevertheless important to bear in mind that the organisational prowess of the Tories can be overstated. The agents in Scotland were less well trained than those in England, and did more routine office work and fund-raising than real political duties. Financially the party was hit by the economic difficulties of the 1930s: in five years after 1929 SUA revenue fell by 50 per cent, and some headquarters staff were laid off. The huge membership included many social rather than political affiliations: most local parties ran bridge and whist clubs which were very popular. Glasgow Kelvingrove's afternoon sessions in a local hotel and a dance hall drew in 'many people not previously interested in our work'.[43] Certainly the party officials were perennially worried about the limited enthusiasm of members for political education courses, and schemes were started up only to falter and decay and then be relaunched some years later: this happened in 1926–8 and 1934–8. There is also evidence from Glasgow Cathcart in the early 1930s that membership figures and levels of organisational activity may have been significantly inflated.[44] Nevertheless, despite these deficiencies, the party had an incontestably superior political machine to its competitors.

Of course, organisation alone does not explain the Tory success in this period. In West Aberdeenshire, a long-standing Liberal constituency, there was only a partial Tory organisational structure in place in 1923. At the dissolution of parliament, the local party decided initially not to contest the seat, as it had established branches in barely half of the constituency's parishes.[45] Yet in the end a candidate was run in 1923, and the seat was won, remaining Tory thereafter for over forty years.

The transformation of the Unionists from the bedraggled rump of pre-war Scotland into the ascendant party between the wars owed much, not simply to its organisational competence, but also to its success in policy matters and in reacting adroitly to social processes. In the area of policy, rehabilitation began with the war period.[46] The issues shifted from those peace-time preoccupations in which the Tories appeared at a grave disadvantage. Winning the war, in terms both of fighting and of supporting the military effort unstintingly, was what the Tories were identified with. The Liberals appeared weak and then divided, while Labour was easily (if unfairly) stigmatised as anti-war. The Tories, by contrast, had a good war. Many were on military service, and reaped electoral dividends afterwards: the most obvious beneficiary being Colonel Sprot, who returned with a distinguished army record to unseat Asquith. Almost exactly one half of the Unionist MPs elected in 1918 had a military title, which only just over one tenth of Liberals had (and none of Labour).

The Unionists' work on recruiting committees and the like gave them a high profile in war work, while the contribution of heavy industry to the economic basis for victory may also have boosted the Tories. Many of

Table 2.3   Military men in the 1918 general election

	Unionist		Labour		Liberal	
	No.	%	No.	%	No.	%
Candidates	16	45.7	0	0	6	10.0
MPs	13	46.4	0	0	4	12.5

Note: 'Liberal' includes both Coalition and Independent (Asquithian) Liberal.

the owners of large engineering and shipbuilding concerns were Unionist, and several who had been involved in war-time production sat in parliament after 1918 – e.g., T. S. B. Adair, G. Murray. Liberal employers were more to be found in textiles, consumer goods and services, none of which were to the fore in the war effort. It is vital to remember that the war was immensely popular in Scotland, and that this lingered long into the peace, borne on by the building of local war memorials, the Scottish National War Memorial, and the ubiquity of ex-servicemen's associations.

The main plank in the Unionist electoral strategy for the inter-war period was, in essence, to secure the adhesion of the bulk of the former Liberal vote. Two approaches were adopted. On the one hand, the socialist bogey was exploited, on the other a relatively progressive stance on economic and social issues was elaborated.

Playing the anti-extremist card was pretty easy in Scotland. The legacy of 'Red Clydeside' from 1915 to 1922 created the setting, to be perpetuated and elaborated over twenty years. The cry of the extreme socialist menace was well worked in 1924, and it was again successful in 1931, when fears of 'WILD EXTREMES OF NATIONALISATION AND EXTRAVAGANCE', as one candidate put it, created a climate of near-panic.[47] As instanced earlier, many Liberals who remained impervious to Unionist propaganda in the previous decade now hastened to endorse the Tories at the 1931 election. Indeed, the party made remarkable gains not just in middle-class seats, but actually carried off almost all of the mining seats.[48]

Yet this avenue of advance had limitations. For one thing, Labour was not everywhere and always radical: as is discussed below, the moderates gained a clear pre-eminence from the mid-1920s. Also, the Tories could alienate middle opinion if they appeared intransigent ultras. The espousal of tariff reform in the 1923 general election upset many in the political centre, not least the normally soundly Unionist *Glasgow Herald*. Likewise, some of the party's setback in the 1929 election was ascribed by

insiders to the impression that the Tory government had behaved excess-
ively harshly towards the miners in the aftermath of the 1926 strike.[49]

The Unionists were aware that the Liberals had to be handled carefully, for they still posed, or so it seemed to many Tories, the threat of an
electoral comeback. In a number of seats, it was the Liberals who offered
the realistic alternative to Unionism, as they had only a vestigial presence in urban-industrial areas, but lingered in rural and middle-class
seats. The added problem offered by a Liberal resurgence was that this
could split the anti-socialist vote and allow Labour to squeeze in. The
1929 election encapsulated these factors. Six of the eleven Tory seats lost
to Labour fell because of a new Liberal intervention. A further five were
lost to the Liberals themselves.

The Tories felt particularly vulnerable to the Liberals in the 1930s
because the agricultural crisis threatened to jeopardise the gains the former had made in the previous decade among the farming community.
The Unionist-dominated government was roundly and repeatedly con-
demned at Tory Party conferences for failing to tackle the agricultural
depression: as late as 1938 criticisms were still being aired.[50] English
cereal growers, being mainly wheat farmers, received a subsidy which
the Scots, who were more barley and oat producers, were denied until
the very end of peacetime. When support to oats was finally conceded,
Bob Boothby, the MP for East Aberdeenshire, whispered to his newly
elected West Aberdeenshire colleague, 'Kemsley, this has made your
seat safe for life'.[51]

In these circumstances, the Tories were extremely solicitous of the
sensitivities of the Liberals. Thus, Scottish Unionist MPs voted quite
differently to English members at the decisive Carlton Club meeting in
1922: the latter voted by 179 to 71 to end the coalition with Lloyd
George's Liberals, whereas the former went overwhelmingly – by 17 to 7
– for continuation, not rupture.[52] The Unionists were also normally
quite prepared to strike deals at general elections with the Liberals, and
in this they were more accommodating than the English party. In 1918,
the proportion of Lloyd Georgites given the coupon in Scotland (43.1
per cent) far exceeded England (21.9 per cent), and 1922 National Liberal candidates in Scotland (33) were almost equal to Unionists (36) but
in England they constituted only one quarter (95) of Tory candidates
(406). In 1923, with tariff reform to the fore and Liberal reunion
achieved, Tory–Liberal pacts were harder to secure. In 1924, under the
shadow of a Labour administration, some sort of arrangement between
Tories and Liberals was reached in at least 44 constituencies. In 1929,

with Lloyd George spearheading an attempted Liberal revival, there were very few deals.[53]

In 1931, the compacts between Tory and Liberal were much tighter in Scotland than in England. In the former there was only one three-way fight in 71 constituencies, but in the latter there were 50 in 512 constituencies. Liberal and Unionist normally competed in Scotland only when Labour was absent. The extent of the concessions made by the Tories was reflected in the proportionately larger number of Liberal and National Liberal MPs returned in Scotland (23.4 per cent of all Coalition MPs), compared to England (9.2 per cent). In 1935, the settlements reached in 1931 mostly held good.

The idea of a natural co-existence between Liberal and Tory was heightened by local government election practice. Here, an anti-Labour alliance was constructed by the Conservatives, in which front parties were erected. In some places, they were called Moderates, elsewhere Progressives. But everywhere the concept was to pull in Liberals (and any other anti-socialist groupings), while leaving the muscle and might in the hands of the Tories. When the future Tory MP Herbert Moss decided to enter municipal politics, he was informed by the Glasgow Unionist secretary, Sir Lewis Shedden, that all new men (sic) had to start by fighting in the East End, and that Parkhead ward had a vacancy. Accordingly, Moss ran there – under Moderate party colours.[54] Normally, however, there were places at the top of the municipal parties for Liberals: Lord Provost Garnet Wilson in Dundee, and Bailie James Gray in Glasgow being very prominent instances.

The spill-over was of course that co-operation was easily extended to parliamentary contests, epitomised by the Tory–Liberal sharing of the two candidatures from 1922 in the sole dual-member constituency in Scotland, Dundee. Between 1906 and 1914, a similar electoral arrangement had prevailed in that city – but then it had been between Liberal and Labour. Likewise, the Tories declined to monopolise all three seats in the Scottish universities constituency, instead always carefully ensuring that one was held by a Liberal.[55]

The importance for the Scottish Tories in being alert to Liberal feelings was highlighted by the 1936 Greenock by-election. On the death of the National Liberal MP, Sir Godfrey Collins, the Unionists refused to accept either of the two replacement candidates proposed by the Liberals. Instead the Tories insisted on one of their party standing as a 'National' candidate. Liberals in the seat were very disgruntled about this imposition, and Labour won the seat on a swing of 7.5 per cent. It is significant that at the local elections held less than a month before, Labour had lost three seats to the anti-socialist grouping, who thereby took control of the council.

In order to induce Liberals to support them, the Tories posited themselves as the natural inheritors of the great nineteenth-century Scottish Liberal tradition. 'The Unionists were carrying forward the underlying values of the former [i.e., Liberals]', it was claimed in 1928.[56] This progressive stance was exemplified in three ways: first in the party's response to other political movements, secondly by its choice of personnel for office and as MPs, and thirdly by the espousal of forward-looking policies.

One consequence was that the Unionists became less interested in wooing the Orange vote, which, as we have seen, had been occasionally practised in the pre-1914 days. While the order flourished in the 1920s and 1930s, it had a very limited political role. Mostly its attraction was simply a social one, and also of course it was seen as a means of enhancing employment prospects. But, as noted below, working-class Orangemen appeared to vote Labour regularly and in large numbers. In a very few seats, the Tories did intermittently court the order's members. Some fishing for Orange votes occurred when prominent Catholics stood for Labour: Wheatley in Shettleston in the early 1920s was a prime target for this sectarian approach. But on the whole, these appeals were eschewed, presumably because, as in the pre-1914 era, they collided with the main strategy of securing moderate, middle-class support.[57]

The Tories had no truck with right-wing extremism. The intervention of popular Protestant parties in Glasgow and Edinburgh municipal elections in the 1930s was robustly criticised. The Glasgow Tories promptly denounced all efforts to inject sectarianism into British politics. The preferred solution was to reconstruct the anti-Labour municipal alliances along more effective lines, so that within a few years the two Protestant parties were in eclipse. Fascism was equally sturdily repudiated. When a Unionist MP, Colonel Thomas Moore, wrote an encomium of the British Union of Fascists ('The Blackshirts have what the Tories Need'), the party hierarchy gave him a stern warning. The Glasgow Unionists in 1937 yoked Fascists and Communists together in disapproval of 'revolutionary and anti-democratic parties'.[58]

Fascism was not particularly successful in Scotland. Oswald Mosley did take two Scottish MPs with him when he formed the New Party, but they were heavily defeated in their own seats in the 1931 election.[59] Membership of the BUF in Scotland seems to have been very slim, with a handful of activists in the main cities and a sprinkling of sympathisers elsewhere. Few prominent figures in Scottish public life associated with the movement, apart from the occasional upper-class oddity like the earl of Glasgow. The small number of Jews living in Scotland (rather than rosy assumptions about the Scots' natural aversion to anti-Semitism) may partly explain the BUF's difficulties, and the counter-propaganda mounted by the numerous ILPers and Communists, who were, as in Aberdeen and Glasgow, prepared to disrupt Fascist meetings, also contributed. Equally pertinently, Mosley's wholehearted support of Irish nationalism probably alienated many potential right-wing sympathisers.

Scottish nationalism posed an intriguing challenge to the Tories. As noted later, the Scottish Party, formed in 1932, had a right-wing proclivity, and the potential damage was underscored when the secretary and most office-bearers of the Glasgow Cathcart Unionists seceded in 1933 in order to advocate a form of Scottish self-government. The gravity was enhanced by the obvious likelihood of Liberals, long the party of Home Rule, being won over to the Scottish Party. The upshot was the production in 1932 by the Scottish Unionists of a pamphlet presenting the case against nationalism. The importance, especially in the realm of economics, of the union was emphasised. But in addition the Unionists made concessions to the mood of self-government. The Gilmour Report of 1937 was the prelude to greater administrative devolution for Scotland. The erection of St Andrew's House, opened in 1939, gave – literally and metaphorically – concrete expression to the Unionists' understanding of Scottish aspirations. The enhancement in 1926 by the Conservative government of the office of Scottish Secretary to a full Secretaryship of State was pointed to as a sign of the long-term commitment to furthering Scotland's prestige by the Tories.[60]

In terms of the human face of Unionism, the party increasingly strove to project a kindlier image than its pre-1914 appearance. There were seven Scottish Secretaries during periods in which the Unionists were in government (either on their own or as the major member of coalitions). Four were Liberals, three Unionists. All of the latter were firmly in the liberal camp of Unionism; indeed one, John Colville, had run under Lloyd George's Coalition Liberal colours in 1922.[61] Unionist MPs were equally on the left side of the party. In 1922 there were no more than a couple of diehards, and in the 1930s there were really only three on the right (F. A. MacQuisten, Colonel T. Moore and Major A. H. M. Ramsay). More typical was the progressive Unionism epitomised by Walter Elliot, Robert Boothby and the duchess of Atholl. Elliot had always advocated state activity to regulate the excesses of the market and was a powerful proponent of the role of government in dealing with social problems. Boothby was an early Keynesian, whom the Liberals did not bother running against because they regarded him as one of them. As he put it himself: 'I am a progressive MP for a progressive constituency'.[62] The duchess of Atholl perhaps carried this tendency to extremes. A strong champion of women's rights, she supported the republican side in the Spanish Civil War and also opposed appeasement. In the immediate post-war years of political flux, she and her husband were in favour of the formation of a centre party, yoking Tories and Liberals together.[63]

Scottish Toryism developed a distinctive voice on economic and social policies which showed some drift from English Conservatism, which, so recent studies have argued, was fairly resistant to statist solutions. The adoption of an interventionist approach was central to the Unionist appeal in Scotland. In part this allowed them to reassure Liberals that the Tories were not reactionaries. The party's central organisation contended that Unionism:

> has no lack of sympathy for the 'underdog'. One of its main objects throughout its life has been to raise the standard of life of the people. It has done much to improve it and it will continue to do so.[64]

It also sent an especially strong message to women, who were believed to be very concerned over social conditions. A women's organiser for the party pointed this out:

> Why should they leave the Labour Party to bring forward all the great social evils? They [women] wanted to get into the Unionist Party – progressive and kindly people who were really out for the good of the country.[65]

The most important issue developed by the Unionists to establish their social concern credentials was housing. Because of the inferior housing conditions in Scotland, this topic had greater salience than in England. The manner in which the Labour party had succeeded in mobilising support after the First World War through this question, as considered later, gave impetus to the Tories to seek to reclaim lost ground. And, of course, housing, as Labour had spotted, was of immense importance for women voters. The Unionists accepted the centrality of bad housing as contributing to a wide range of social problems. In 1935, the SUA explained that poor housing was the prime cause of 'misery, bad health and moral deterioration . . . Good housing must be the basis of all the social services and of medical and moral welfare.'[66]

The Tories constantly reiterated the need for state-subsidised house-building as the only realistic cure for the crisis. It was agreed, for instance, that there should be no opposition to Labour's 1924 Housing Act, because it was a serious attempt to solve the problem. The Tory government's slum clearance programme of the 1930s was warmly applauded by the Scottish party.[67] The party's record was stressed in propaganda literature as far superior to that of Labour: in 1927, it was pointed out, the Tories built five times the number of municipal houses put up under Labour in 1924. This commitment to public sector provision was demonstrated not just at the level of central government, but also at the layer of local administration. Most of the councils in Scotland were under Tory (or at least a Tory-dominated anti-socialist party) control for the bulk of the inter-war years, yet there was rarely any shirking of the need to build subsidised housing. For instance, virtually all of the 2,155 houses built by Clydebank burgh council between 1919 and 1939 were put up when the Progressives were in power. Walter Elliot, indeed, became so irritated as Scottish Secretary with what he believed to be foot-dragging by Labour-run municipalities that he set up the Scottish Special Housing Association in 1937, designed to build even more state-subsidised housing stock.[68]

A measure of the resolution of the party to tackle the housing question in a non-ideological manner was shown in a sharp internal squabble during the spring of 1935. Many party activists in the west of Scotland championed the rights of the private rented sector, arguing that impending government legislation would be highly detrimental to these landlords' interests, instead benefiting the state sector of the housing market. Owners of rented property formed one of the core supports of Unionism, as a Glasgow MP observed: 'we were creating enemies among our own people – which we could ill afford'. Yet the party hierarchy and government ministers were obdurate in rejecting the private sector lobby's campaign: the bill was not altered to take account of their protestations. As the party's senior figure in the western area argued, the Unionists could not project the image of 'acting simply in the interests of the property-owning classes'.[69]

Although housing was, naturally, the centrepiece of the Unionists' progressive policy programme, other questions received a similar treatment. Enhanced pension payments for widows, orphans and the elderly alike were a frequent call, 'realising that on our production and successful operation of such a scheme depends to an incalculable extent the permanent betterment of social conditions'. The 1925 pension bill was greeted as a highly beneficial reform, and in the 1930s the British social services were hailed as the most generous anywhere.[70] While a junior minister at the Scottish Office, Walter Elliot launched an experimental free school milk scheme in the bigger cities in 1927, and in 1929 this was extended to cover the whole country.

In the climate of the inter-war era, Tories in Scotland viewed unregulated capitalism as anachronistic. The organ of the west of Scotland business class, the *Glasgow Herald*, in 1935 urged an end to calls for a return to 'an individualist system which changing economic conditions had rendered unworkable'. Instead, support should be given to 'the forces of ordered progress and stability', typified by the approach adopted by Godfrey Collins and Walter Elliot.[71] This position was echoed by a party leaflet which alluded to the party's 'belief in the authority of the state over private interests for the good of the whole community'.[72] Unemployment was denounced time and again as a social evil which should be eliminated as rapidly as possible. The Tories were disinclined to persecute trade unions. In the aftermath of the 1926 general strike, the party's Western council overwhelmingly rejected – by a margin of ten to one – a motion to strip unions of most of their bargaining powers.[73]

The party operated at several levels to hold together the anti-Labour front. It promoted efficiency: the local government reform of 1929 swept away many small administrative units, and instead a more centralised, large-scale set of authorities was established to reap economies of scale. While many, mostly Liberals and Labour, deplored the elimination of small local democratic institutions, the government stressed the gains in efficiency and professionalism which would ensue. This was calculated to appeal to, among others, businessmen, who resented local taxes and were themselves amalgamating and consolidating. Derating of industrial property was a more tangible benefit for businessmen offered by the Tories, and substantially cut local tax burdens on enterprise.[74]

In accord with the argument propounded by the *Glasgow Herald* in 1935, namely that *laissez-faire* economics were redundant, Scottish Unionist leaders, both political and industrial, became ever more involved in the development of corporatist strategies by the state between the wars. Elliot was a major advocate of state involvement in economic affairs in order to smooth the unevennesses of markets. He applied his ideas directly to agriculture when he held that portfolio in the early 1930s, and pressed for these precepts to be applied to industry.[75]

It is striking how many of the top businessmen in Scotland were at the heart of the British corporatist trend. Viscount Weir, owner of the Glasgow engineering concern, was perhaps the most active proponent of corporatist solutions to economic and social issues among the British business community, as his membership of the Mond-Turner committee testifies. His leadership of the main employers' association in the inter-war years gave him immense weight in government circles. Sir Andrew Duncan, Sir James Lithgow, and Sir Andrew Bilsland were all seminal figures in shaping this approach, which ran counter to crude market forces economics. One of the largest coalmasters in Scotland, Sir Adam Nimmo, expounded this standpoint in 1934 when he urged the need for planning in every industry, as it was preferable to relying on 'the free play of unbridled forces'. All of them were, beside their business roles, strong supporters of the Unionist party.[76] Prominent among MPs strongly committed in the 1930s to planning were Boothby and Sir Robert Horne, who sat for Glasgow Hillhead. It is perhaps significant that the most pro-corporatist minister in Stanley Baldwin's 1924–9 administration was the Scot Sir Arthur Steel-Maitland.

The extent to which the Unionists had transformed themselves was perhaps most aptly attested to in 1926 by a leading ILP MP, Rosslyn Mitchell. He lauded John Gilmour, the Scottish Secretary: 'Your actions so little resemble the Toryism of my youth', with the result that 'I believe the rigidity of party lines is slackening'.[77] The remarkably buoyant performance of the Scottish Tories after the Second World War may owe something to the manner in which the party had avoided the obloquy visited upon their English counterparts for neglecting the acute social, and economic problems of the 1930s.

V

Much of the stereotype of Scotland as left-wing derives from the 'Red Clydeside' tradition. This is mainly based on three episodes in and around Glasgow during and immediately after the First World War. The first key phase embraces the crisis in the munitions factories in the winter of 1915–16. An umbrella organisation of militant shop stewards, the Clyde Workers' Committee (CWC), liaised to protest against the war-time industrial policy of dilution (the replacement of skilled by unskilled labour) through industry-wide strikes. The Prime Minister, Lloyd

George, addressed a rowdy meeting of workers on Christmas Day 1915, followed by the suppression of the *Forward* journal and the prosecution of its editor and printer for sedition. The leaders of the CWC were jailed or expelled from Glasgow. The second episode, virtually contemporaneous with the industrial protest, was a rent strike – staged in protest at the hiking of house rents – which resulted in prosecutions of working-class women for non-payment in 1915. The government stepped in and froze rents at their August 1914 levels for the duration of the war. Thirdly, in January 1919, a general strike in the west of Scotland culminated in disorder in George Square, Glasgow, with troops placed on standby in the city by the nervous authorities.

These hectic episodes, it has been argued, demonstrated the spread of socialist ideas among the working class. Membership of the ILP rose very sharply as the war drew to a close: by 1919, it reached 9,000, whereas in 1917 it had been a mere 3,000. These forces all combined to result in Labour winning a remarkable 10 of the 15 Glasgow seats in the 1922 general election. The scale of support for Labour in Glasgow was far in excess of any other major British city: in Birmingham and Liverpool, the party won not one of, respectively, 12 and 11 seats. Furthermore, several of the Clydeside MPs (for example, James Maxton, John Wheatley and David Kirkwood) were sharply to the left of most of the Parliamentary Labour Party. Additionally, the ILP sponsored a far higher share of Scottish than English MPs in the 1920s: in 1924, 15 of 109 English MPs (13.8 per cent) were ILP-sponsored, in Scotland, 12 of 26 (46.2 per cent) were. In contrast, local Labour parties sponsored 22 MPs (20.2 per cent) in England, but a mere 2 (7.7 per cent) in Scotland.

Yet this clear picture has been increasingly obscured by research, so that it is possible to see 'Red Clydeside' as, at worst, a figment of the imagination, and, at best, only a partial explanation of the rise of Labour after 1918.[78] For a start, it is uncertain how far, and how many of those involved in these industrial disputes were militant socialist revolutionaries. Many, it appears, were skilled craftsmen worried at the erosion of their privileged status, and were striving to have their elite standing protected against semi- and unskilled labour (male and female) which threatened to undermine this in the exigencies of war production. Once the future employment prospects of these rather conservative-minded men were guaranteed, militancy evaporated. Again, it is not clear from the recollections of those at the core of the agitation how far there was a revolutionary socialist agenda; Manny Shinwell and Thomas Johnston, for instance, subsequently strenuously denied any such motives.

There is no agreement when the revolutionary socialist movement peaked: many stress 1915–16, others point to the growth in activity in the last two years of the war, others yet opt for January 1919. Another element sees the rents question, rather than the factory unrest, as vital: it mobilised a wider spectrum of occupations, and also propelled women to a prominence not hitherto accorded them. The ILP lay behind the rents campaign, and the electoral breakthrough achieved by Labour was a triumph for the ILP, whose greater strength in Scotland can be related to the housing issue. Moreover, the CWC did not reap political benefits: apart from the marginal Kirkwood and J. W. Muir, none of the shop stewards' leaders won a Clydeside seat, most instead ending up in the Communist Party.

There are additional difficulties in seeking to explain the rise of Labour by concentrating narrowly on developments in war-time Glasgow, over and above the incoherences among the advocates of a 'Red Clydeside'. It must be remembered that what applied in some parts of Glasgow did not operate elsewhere in the city, still less in the rest of Scotland. The rents question, for example, seems to have played no major part in the war-time rise of Labour in Paisley, nor was it very relevant in mining areas or the east of Scotland. Yet Labour's advance occurred in these places, as well as in Clydeside. The idea that the rise in the ILP's membership at the end of the war reflected a mass swing to anti-war socialism is misleading: the adherence of moderate miners union leaders like Harry Murnin and James Brown, along with ex-Liberals such as James Barr and E. Rosslyn Mitchell, demonstrates that the ILP was an umbrella organisation, with no narrow doctrinal basis. The setbacks suffered by the Maxton–Wheatley axis in the mid-1920s is much less surprising in this context. It is instructive to note that five of the six gains made in the 1918 election occurred outside the Clyde area.

Influences other than war-time tensions on the Clyde can be identified as helping Labour in the early 1920s. The victory in 1922 may owe more to the higher turnout, most of which seems to have been caused by the low numbers of military men casting their vote in 1918: only 22 per cent of the service votes were cast in East Fife. If this is a reason behind Labour's improved performance in 1922, it can have little to do with the domestic war-time events, as none were involved in these. It is argued in some places that after the collapse of the 1919 strike, many turned from revolutionary methods to parliamentary tactics, a device used to explain the 1922 surge. Yet the first signs of a new post-war mood came in July 1919, when Labour gained Lanarkshire Bothwell on a massive 18 per cent swing. This was a solid mining seat, a union not involved in the January general strike, and the MP was an ardent pro-war champion. Moreover, it is possible that Labour breakthrough owed more to post-war conditions: the government's failure to initiate social reform, mounting unemployment after the short-lived boom, and renewed uncertainty over rents levels were all highly significant in pulling voters leftwards in 1922.

A broader set of forces may be seen at work in propelling Labour forward after the war. These factors relate to a range of socio-economic trends, rather than to ideological ones. These contributory sources – which include the widened franchise system, the homogenisation of the working class, greater solidarity created by the growth of working-class institutions, and a diminution in the sectarian divide – also help to explain why Labour in Scotland was less socialist than the rhetoric of the Clydesiders implied.

The Fourth Reform Act of 1918 had arguably more impact in Scotland than in England, in that the increase in male electors was proportionately greater. This would very likely assist Labour. This was especially the case as many of the previously unenfranchised – primarily in unskilled occupations – were unionised during the war. Thus, in Edinburgh the war stimulated the enrolment in unions of workers in such industries as chemicals, rubber, hosiery and precious metals, as well as clerks, milliners and asylum attendants, and also saw a growth in unionisation among transport workers.[79]

Working-class solidarity was affected by altered social conditions which eliminated the deep divides within the working class before 1914. Unemployment before 1914 was primarily a problem of the unskilled: now it was endemic among skilled men too, as heavy industry floundered. The growth of council housing meant living conditions became more uniform, and generally began to improve, as the worst slums were cleared. Wage differentials narrowed between 1914 and the 1920s, so lifestyles became more shared.[80] The growth of mass entertainment – cinemas, dance-halls and spectator sport – was accompanied by the decline of the rational leisure activities in the pre-war era which had marked the skilled, self-improving worker apart from the rest of the proletariat. The rise in unionisation among less skilled strata contributed to a closer sense of identity, particularly through inter-union collaboration on various institutional levels, from the STUC down to trades councils.

The rise in trade union membership in Scotland was quite dramatic. A survey in 1925 revealed that 60 per cent of trade unionists – over

300,000 individuals – were affiliated to the STUC, against only 140,000 in 1911, and the entry of major unions previously outside the STUC, notably the Engineers, gave greater clout to the Congress. The STUC also became better organised and more coherent. A rash of amalgamations after the war increased the unity of the movement. An internal reorganisation of 1922 made the STUC more effective, with a General Council formed to give weight to the bigger, national unions, and a permanent secretariat was established under William Elger, the long-serving general secretary. The voice of trade unionism was thus clearer and more powerful after the war.[81]

War-time experiences meant that the case for state ownership of basic industries became undeniable in the eyes of unions. State control of mines, begun in 1917, was a major catalyst; by 1918 the Scottish coal-fields were staunchly in favour of nationalisation, and railwaymen and iron and steel workers took a similar position. The case for public owner-ship of a specific sector did not mean acceptance of the case for the wholesale socialisation of the economy: it could, as in the case of many miners and railwaymen, simply be a sectional demand. Edinburgh Labour Party politics after 1918 were dominated by trade unions, who saw Clause IV not as an ideological statement, but as a specific justifica-tion for public ownership of, for example, the railways. Nevertheless, the benefit to Labour of this attitude was enormous.[82]

Relations between trade unions and socialists had been edgy for most of the 1914–18 era. The war was initially very popular with the unions and the vast bulk of the working class. A small minority of the ILP opposed the war: only two of the 17 ILP Glasgow councillors did so. Miners enlisted more enthusiastically in Scotland than elsewhere, and anti-war individuals were robustly dealt with. David Graham, a Lanark-shire miners' leader who became a Labour MP in 1918, read an anti-war declaration by Ramsay MacDonald at a union conference, then tore it up, to the acclaim of the delegates. The Stirling miners' delegates with-drew for over two and a half years from the local Trades & Labour Council in protest at representatives of the anti-war Union of Demo-cratic Control being granted a hearing by the council.[83] This antagonism was not everywhere healed after 1918: in Edinburgh, the unions kept a firm grip on Labour politics in order to repulse any left socialist influences. It was a long-term fallible aspect of the ILP that it never managed to establish firm bonds with the unions.

The STUC had little truck in the inter-war years with militant stances, industrial or political. It had only a marginal role in the war-time unrest, and was a very reluctant participant in the 1926 General Strike, to the despair of the more militant grass-roots elements.[84] After the strike, the STUC moved in a centrist direction. It declined to affiliate the Communist-led Unemployed Workers Movement, and later it revised voting and procedural rules so that annual conferences would be controlled by larger unions to the detriment of trades councils, where more extreme elements were influential.[85] As noted below, it played a crucial role in eliminating Communist influences in Labour Party organisations.

A major bonus for Labour was the unqualified adherence of the Irish Catholic community. British policy in Ireland between 1916 and 1921 turned the Irish in Scotland against the Liberals: Churchill was unseated in Dundee in 1922 partly because of this.[86] The Irish nationalist party organisations in Scotland had collapsed in war-time and Sinn Fein never established itself as an alternative, so that Labour became the natural home for this intensely working-class grouping. In the 1918 election, 10 Roman Catholics stood for Labour, and the *Glasgow Observer*, the community's newspaper, was staunchly pro-Labour.[87]

The benefits accruing to Labour were increased because the Irish were heavily disenfranchised before 1918: one careful calculation suggested that under one half of them had the vote in the late nineteenth century.[88] Labour's support of the 1918 Education Act, which protected the Catholic schools, was less significant than is sometimes claimed in winning the endorsement of the hierarchy, who worked harmoniously on Education Authorities with Protestant Unionist majorities, as in Glasgow.[89] Moreover, the influence of the church upon voters can be overstated: John McGovern, fiercely anti-clerical and opposed by the hierarchy, was never in danger of losing his Shettleston seat.[90] The Irish Catholic population was heavily concentrated among the less skilled working class, the sector suffering most from unemployment and poverty in the inter-war era, so their adherence to Labour stemmed from socio-economic factors as much as from religio-ethnic ones.

The power of Catholics within the Labour Party between the wars was, however, minimal: only three sat as Labour MPs, yet there were two Catholic Unionist MPs, and there were no more than six Roman Catholic Labour councillors when that party controlled Glasgow in the 1930s. The close relations between Catholicity and Labour in the inter-war years reinforced the essential moderation of Labour. The church hierarchy was much exercised by fears of Communism and turned to Labour to best resist the menace of Bolshevism. The prominence in Labour of Patrick Dollan was reassuring; although a lapsed Catholic, he was

unshakeably anti-Communist. The moderate inclinations of the Irish
Catholic vote were demonstrated at Motherwell in 1923, when it appears
that many refused to support Labour's candidate, the Communist
Walton Newbould.[91] Thereafter less extreme candidates were put up in
the seat.

Labour also drew benefit from the other side of the sectarian fence.
With the position of Ulster settled by 1921, the working-class Orange
vote had less cause to identify with Conservatism. Some indeed blamed
the Conservatives, as partners in the Coalition government, for collud-
ing in the creation of the Irish Free State, and the consequent abandonment of Southern Unionists. The Tories, who, as we have seen, were
assiduously wooing the Liberal vote, were accordingly not over-anxious
to be perceived as close to the Orange order. The upsurge of a separate
militant Protestant political party in the 1930s is a testimony to the Tories' avoidance of rabid anti-Catholicism. To be sure, Unionists still
wooed the Orange vote in some seats, such as Motherwell and Coatbridge & Airdrie. But generally, Orangemen seem to have turned to
class-based voting: for example, Bridgeton, the Glasgow stronghold of
the movement, returned James Maxton with immense majorities for a
quarter of a century from 1922. Labour's focus on housing problems, as
noted above, united the working-class, as instanced by Govan, a Protestant heartland, the first post-war gain in Glasgow by Labour.

Lastly, the role of the co-operative movement is too often overlooked.
It had greater support in Scotland, where 13.6 per cent of the population
were members in 1918, against 9.5 per cent in England.[92] Moreover, the
Scottish movement had a stronger engagement in non-retailing activities: the men's and women's guilds were very popular, while educational
and recreational societies also revolved around the local store in many
communities. Links between the co-operative movement and Labour
were very strong between the wars, and in many constituencies the men
and women's co-operative guilds did important electioneering work for
Labour. In 1922 in Dunfermline, the women co-operators seem to have
worked almost alone to canvass and deliver the female vote for Labour.[93]
The Co-operative Party, formed in the later stages of the war, generally
worked pretty closely in Scotland with Labour, and bulked larger than
in England: in the 1918 election, proportionately three times as many
Co-operative Party candidates stood in Scotland as in England.[94]

As with the Catholic Irish, the support of Orangeism and of co-operators probably acted to dilute the pure socialist elements within Labour.
In Paisley, for example, the co-operative wing was in heated conflict with

the ILP over candidate selection in the early 1920s.[95] The essential task for moderates in the Labour leadership was to coalesce these diverse strands in order to contain more militant elements. Such was the strength and tactical skill of the latter that the issue was not effectively resolved until the later 1920s. But the costs in terms of a working organisational Labour Party structure were substantial, and were indeed not really repaired before the onset of the Second World War. Because the ILP bulked so large in Scotland, its internal dynamics were central to the outcome.

Although in the immediate post-war years the Clydeside left-wing group appeared dominant within the ILP, this steadily waned after the middle of the 1920s. Particularly after the 1926 General Strike débâcle, the Scottish ILP positioned itself in the centre within the spectrum of Labour Party opinion. It should be noted that this move away from the left seemed to have no discernible impact on membership. While Maxton and the 'Red Clydeside' faction had seized control of the national ILP in 1925–6, in Scotland, Patrick Dollan led the ILP in repeatedly rejecting far left policies. The Scottish party preferred the more modest demand of a minimum wage to the left-wing living wage which the ILP's 1928 manifesto, *Socialism in Our Time*, advocated. The Scottish ILP firmly repudiated the ultra-left Cook–Maxton Manifesto of 1928 at its annual conference. It is noteworthy that electoral support for Labour increased sharply in 1924, scotching the left ILP's argument that the timorousness of the outgoing Labour administration had alienated the working class. Similarly, the highly moderate manifesto on which Labour fought the 1929 election yielded the largest share of the poll in all inter-war contests.

The war did, however, have a significant impact in radicalising the Glasgow ILP leadership: Maxton, Wheatley and their associates moved sharply to the left. The rather ethical pre-war socialism of the ILP was replaced by a more militant variety, deriving a significant degree of inspiration from Marxist analysis. Although these tendencies were not widely shared in the Scottish party, the Maxton–Wheatley group's radicalisation carried important consequences for the organisational development of the Labour Party. These militants followed a doctrine of inclusiveness towards the Communist Party, and indeed in the immediate post-war era, they seriously considered affiliating the ILP to the Communist International.

The import of this stance was intensified by the extent of the Communist presence in Scotland in the 1920s: in Fife alone in 1926, there were 500 members, out of a British total of 10,730. Some recruits had been shaped by the war-time agitations on the Clyde: most of the CWC leadership – Arthur MacManus, Tom Bell, James Messer – opted for the CPGB, the pre-eminent example being Willie Gallacher. This Glasgow base was widened by the involvement of certain mining areas in Fife and Lanarkshire. Some of these were influenced by the classes in Marxist ideas run by John MacLean's Scottish Labour College. For others – frequently younger men – the changing nature of the coal industry in the post-war period impelled them to Communism. The emergence of larger, intensely mechanised pits, such as Bowhill in Fife and Blantyre in Lanarkshire, proved a fertile recruiting ground for the party.[96] There were other outcrops of Communist influence – notably the Vale of Leven and Greenock. The latter is interesting, since the Communists outpolled Labour in elections in the early 1920s, yet this Clydeside burgh was not greatly involved in the war-time shop-stewards' movement, even though it was a major shipbuilding centre. Additionally, in 1922, Motherwell returned a Communist MP, one of only two elected in all of Britain, and in Dundee there was a respectable vote for the party: in 1923 it got just under half of Labour's total.

This strong presence and the support among ILP elements for the incorporation of Communists into the Labour Party meant that for much of the 1920s the Scottish Council of the Labour Party was preoccupied with combating Communist involvement. In perhaps a dozen seats, the party hierarchy had to intervene, in many cases repeatedly, to insist that there be no links with the CPGB. The most extreme challenge was offered by the nomination of Communists as Labour Party candidates: this occurred at Kelvingrove in 1923 and 1924. The admission to Labour Party bodies of Communist delegates from properly affiliated societies posed difficulties, with Glasgow especially vulnerable. Again, bids were made to get CPGB-dominated bodies such as the Minority Movement affiliated to the Labour Party in Glasgow and Bannockburn. Trades & Labour Councils, which were effectively the Labour Party organisation in a great number of seats, proved highly porous when it came to Communist penetration: Greenock proved a serious headache in 1925, and Glasgow had to be reconstructed in 1927–8. A number of constituencies declined to expel individual members who were Communists, and a string of local parties were accordingly suspended or dissolved, including St Rollox, Springburn, Kelvingrove and Bridgeton in 1926–7.[97]

The concern of the Labour Party administration in Scotland to extirpate traces of Communism overshadowed the prosecution of normal business. In 1927, a member of the SAC complained about 'the time [which] was being wasted in dealing with Communist matters at every meeting and in submitting reports of Committees. They ought to spend it in dealing with Housing and Trade Union questions and propaganda.' The chair replied that it was 'impossible to escape' the issue of Communist infiltration, while another member added that this concern arose through 'no fault' of the SAC: 'the Party would never be healthy until it had been thoroughly purified by the exclusion of the Communist elements'.[98] The London-based NEC devoted much less time to CP permeation. It regarded the Scots as obsessed with trivial infringements, and on several occasions the latter complained about the indifference of the parent body to the situation in Scotland.[99]

With consequently little attention devoted by the Scottish Advisory Council to constructing an efficient party machine at constituency level, this responsibility devolved largely either to the constituency's ILP or to a locally powerful trade union. So, in the breakthrough general election of 1922, 41 of the 43 candidates were ILP members, 21 of whom were sponsored by the ILP itself, and 10 by the miners. In both cases, efficient permanent structures were rarely installed in the locality. The union with the greatest political involvement was the miners' union (SMF), in virtual sole unquestioned command of up to 15 seats. When a candidate vacancy looked like arising in 1926 in North Lanarkshire, the miners insisted that there should be no open invitation for nominations. Only a SMF choice should be considered, since the miners had an 'unchallenged right in a constituency in which they had previously expended large resources and had secured representation of the Party in Parliament'.[100]

Yet the miners frequently constructed no formal organisation in their seats: in 1929, the Labour Party's National Executive was told that 'the organisation of the Party in North Midlothian was in a very poor state and that the constituency has been very badly neglected'.[101] After the 1939 South Ayrshire by-election, occasioned by the death of the veteran miners' leader, James Brown, the Scottish party noted that 'it could be said the seat for the first time had been won on Labour Party policy'.[102] The fragility of this network of organisational sub-contracting was exposed in 1931. The miners, deeply riven between two camps – moderates and militants – decided in 1930 to withdraw their political agents from working Scottish constituencies. Labour was very alarmed at this decision, and rightly so, for the setbacks encountered in the 1931 election in mining sets were most severe: only one of fifteen stayed with Labour.[103]

The corollary of leaving seats to the ILP to manage was that individual Labour Party membership was normally minimal, as the ILP feared any alternative power-base might damage its position. Where the ILP was strong, therefore, the constituency party as a distinct entity – be it individual membership or the women's wing – was likely to be vestigial. A sample of the stance is revealed at a meeting held in Larbert to launch an individual members' section of the Labour Party, when the chairman explained that 'no-one could go into the Labour Party unless they first joined the SSP [the ILP's successor]'. When a campaign to recruit individual party members was initiated in 1932, there was stated to be general support, apart from a few who 'indicated an indisposition on their part from the ILP point of view'.[104] Dundee, not an ILP stronghold, boasted an individual membership of about 2,000 in 1935 and Aberdeen, also not an ILP bastion, had 1,400 in 1936. But in ILP fiefdoms, direct party membership was minuscule. The 'frequent opposition' of the ILP was blamed in 1925 for Scotland's low rate of development of women's sections.[105]

The influence of the Communists was increasingly held in check after 1926. The collapse of the General Strike had a bifurcated effect in Scotland. Those who saw the end of the strike as a betrayal by official union leaders were pushed to more urgent advocacy of left-wing policies, but for the vast majority the episode confirmed their aversion to extreme adventurist militancy. Unions were therefore more inflexible in opposing Communist infiltration. It was in these years too, that the ILP in Scotland, led by the staunchly anti-Communist Patrick Dollan, turned decisively against the far left, as outlined above. From the middle 1920s, moreover, the Scottish Labour College, previously a hotbed of ultra-leftism, merged with other similar institutions into the National Council of Labour Colleges, and came under the moderate influence of Arthur Woodburn and J. P. Millar. Marxisant analysis was replaced by a more empirical programme, epitomised by Woodburn's own work on finance in 1928, stimulated by his realisation that 'even then the practical problems of socialism had not intruded themselves on our vision and a vague utopian concept satisfied most propaganda'.[106] Under the tutelage of the new men, a stream of able working-class students emerged who, by the 1930s and 1940s, had secured positions of influence in local and parliamentary politics. Almost without exception, these were more moderate than the generation reared in the college in the previous phase. They included MPs like Peggy Herbison, George Lawson, Eustace Willis and Tom Oswald, as well as a spreading network of burgh and county councillors across Lowland Scotland.

Electorally, the Communists were in decline and Labour was expanding in the later 1920s. The total poll for the Communists was lower in 1929 (27,114) than in 1923 (29,427), despite boosting their candidates from three to ten, and even with an enlarged electorate after the 1928 Franchise Act: in the party's best hope, Dundee, support slipped 10,380 in 1923 to 6,160 in 1929, while Labour's rose from 23,345 to 47,602. Whereas in 1923, 38 per cent of Labour voters also backed the Communist in this two-member seat, by 1929 only 5 per cent did so. The intervention of Communists in seats where the Labour activists had been sympathetic probably additionally alienated many: Glasgow Springburn, where the CLP had been disbanded for its pro-Communist leanings in 1926, was lost in 1931 thanks to CPGB intervention.

The 1930s posed two exceptionally acute difficulties for Labour in Scotland.[107] First, the 1931 election was more disastrous than in England: the vote slumped by nearly one quarter, in England it fell by one sixth – and in Wales it barely budged. Dissection of the campaign by party officials disclosed three core areas of concern, which were tackled in the remainder of the pre-war years. Threadbare organisational techniques were pinpointed. The Scottish Council chair complained of inadequate canvassing, which meant, as another executive member lamented, that although cars were available on polling day, they were of little use 'for lack of definite lists of proper people to be called for'. Closer co-ordination with trade unions and the Co-operative bodies was also highlighted as vital. Lastly, it was accepted by many that Labour's alleged extremism had been skilfully deployed by the National Government parties. Councillor Brady, the Labour agent for Ayr Burghs, 'referred to the effect of the Post Office Savings scare, even Labour people having in some instances voted for the Government'. By implication, the Red Clydeside tradition and the high visibility in Scotland of the ILP had backfired, hence the particularly adverse electoral impact in Scotland. The drive to produce moderate, reassuring policies and the enfeeblement of the Labour left hereafter owed much to this post-mortem.[108]

The second challenge faced by Scottish Labour in the 1930s was that the ILP breakaway of 1932 was primarily Scottish-based: all the four ILP MPs elected in 1935 were in Scotland, with the party's total poll of 5 per cent compared with 0.1 per cent in England. By the end of the decade, Labour in Scotland had weathered the worst of the challenges and had established some electoral momentum, although even by the 1935 election it had not regained its 1929 support. On the other hand, Labour began to pick up control of town halls to a degree unknown in the 1920s. Glasgow Council fell into the party's hands in 1933, and by 1939, there were 17 burghs controlled by the party.

The electoral aspect of the ILP secession was not as serious as initially feared by Labour. Labour could not unseat the sitting ILP MPs, but the ILP, *per contra*, could not win anywhere else. The secessionists were a minority of the ILP in Scotland: 128 of the 147 branches declined to leave Labour. Only about seven of the 40 ILP members on Glasgow Council followed the Maxton line, and most of these were concentrated in the four city wards which formed the bedrock of ILP support. This suggested much of the backing was a personal vote for highly charismatic MPs like Maxton. Govan – the cradle of the ILP's political power in Clydeside – stayed Labour, along with its MP, Neil Maclean. The dwindling challenge offered by the ILP outside the East End of Glasgow was shown in Kilmarnock. At a by-election in November 1933 the ILP candidate (who had been the sole opponent in 1931 against the National Government candidate) got 20.9 per cent, coming close behind Labour's 27.4 per cent. By the general election eighteen months later, the same ILP candidate lost his deposit with 9.5 per cent, while Labour rose to 33.4 per cent.

One consequence of the departure of the ILP activists was to deplete the left wing in the Scottish Labour Party for the rest of the decade. The Scottish Socialist Party, formed by ex-ILPers loyal to Labour was of little importance; at best it had about 2,000 members, and by the outbreak of the Second World War it was as good as extinct. The left-wing campaign groups which flourished in the English Labour Party during the 1930s were barely present in Scotland. Scotland put forward only 12 of the 134 petitions submitted by constituency associations to the Labour Party NEC in 1939 opposing Stafford Cripps's expulsion for advocating radical socialism, whereas in strict proportionality, there should have been 17 or 18.[109] The NEC was informed in 1938 that there was little interest in Scotland in the Popular Front movement, apart from East Lothian, hardly a core Labour area.[110]

The 1930s revealed the Scottish Labour Party still striving to establish a meaningful organisation. It was acknowledged that, 'while wonderful spontaneous organisation seemed to arise at election times', permanent machinery should henceforth be put in place in the constituencies.[111] Particular attention could now be devoted to building up individual membership sections, and a succession of drives were launched during the decade. At the end of 1933, a special organiser was appointed to develop this field.[112] Widespread interest among members in improving organisation was reported to the NEC in 1935. Semi-defunct constituencies – several affected by the ILP schism, such as Glasgow Kelvingrove and North Lanarkshire – were revived, and local branches were set up in places like Jedburgh and Oban. By the end of 1934, county and regional federations had been established across Scotland to encourage collaboration between party associations.[113]

Glasgow offered a vivid indication of the changes occurring. In 1934 the National Agent rather wearily informed the NEC that 'our Glasgow people are much more concerned about the troubles of the whole world than in detailed organisation and propaganda in the city'. Early in 1939, however, the Scottish party secretary reported 'good progress' in establishing ward branches in Glasgow, and commended 'the development of a Labour Party spirit' in the city.[114]

Labour found it difficult to match the Tories in mobilising women and young people. Women's sections of the Labour Party were slow to form, but the way forward emerged in this decade by linking the party with the Co-operative Women's Guild and the STUC's women's wing. Under these joint auspices, a series of conferences were held to consider the low profile of women in the Scottish party. Labour women were now getting elected to local government councillorships in greater numbers: in 1932, Mrs Clarice Shaw joined Ayrshire County Council.[115] In 1926, there were a mere four branches of the youth wing in Scotland, against 172 in England. In 1931, a vigorous campaign was launched to build up Scottish involvement, yet by 1936 the respective figures were 23 and 472, and as late as 1938 it was reported that until quite lately there had been scarcely any active branches in Scotland outside Glasgow.[116]

As a result of the weak grass-roots base in the 1920s, routine party work had not been carried out. Canvassing, for example, was often not systematically undertaken at elections: instead, reliance was placed on broader propaganda work – a traditional ILP approach, as noted in chapter 1. A report to the NEC on the 1927 Leith by-election noted the contest as 'typically Scottish in character', with 'extremely successful meetings', but only a partial canvass was conducted, because 'Scottish traditions in the matter of canvassing are very hard to break down'.[117] Eight years later the Scottish party secretary recorded that at the Edinburgh West by-election, there had been 'great difficulties in persuading them [local party members] to canvass'. Only one third of voters were canvassed – 'and then only ineffectively'.[118] The beginnings of efforts to address this problem were indicated when classes on electioneering in 1938 drew audiences of 51 in Glasgow and 40 in Edinburgh.[119]

The great forte of the ILP had lain in providing highly effective publicists for the socialist cause, and Labour acted to produce its inhouse alternative. The Labour Speakers Association was launched in 1937 to deliver talks and spearhead rallies where requested. Twenty seven speakers were used in the first campaign, and about 14,000 people came to 75 meetings. A meeting held in Glasgow late in 1937, addressed by Clement Attlee, Dollan and Woodburn was deemed 'by far the best meeting which had been held for many years in Glasgow'.[120]

The party reinforced its links with allied bodies, such as the Co-operative movement and the STUC. In 1931 the Co-operative Party increased its representation in selected seats, and this greater unity was enhanced that year by the SCWS voting to engage in political activity. In the Dumfriesshire contest in 1935, the local co-operative society provided 70 cars for Labour on polling day. In the 1931 general election, a Co-operative Party agent assumed responsibility for running Labour's campaign in Greenock. By the end of 1931, consideration was being given to a joint Co-operative–Labour Party recruiting campaign. In 1937, 'complete harmony' between Labour and the Co-operative movement was intimated at the Scottish Co-operative Party's conference. Collaboration between these two and the STUC grew. In 1933, demonstrations in Glasgow and Edinburgh were held under the auspices of all three, and in November 1937 a tripartite division of responsibility for looking after working-class interests between the STUC, the Co-operative movement and the Labour Party was agreed.[121]

A main plank of Labour's strategy in the 1930s was to consolidate organisational decision-taking and policy discussion within the confines of the party, so marginalising affiliated entities. Effectively this required minimising the impact of the SSP, lest it acquire the influence enjoyed by its predecessor, the ILP. From the outset, the party hierarchy stamped on SSP pretensions. Glasgow Cathcart protested at the SSP setting up a youth section, to which the latter retorted it was merely following ILP practice, which Labour had not objected to before. The NEC insisted, however, that the Scottish Council was the only proper body to develop sections, and instructed the SSP to liaise with the SAC, which Dollan undertook to do.[122] Subsequently, complaints about aggressive SSP conduct were reported to the SAC, something very rare in the heyday of the ILP. So, Glasgow Partick objected to the SSP's efforts to thwart the formation of ward parties, and Motherwell CLP protested about the SSP's attacks on the local MP, which had infuriated local party activists.[123]

The limited scope allocated to the SSP was seen in the sponsorship of parliamentary candidates. Barely half a dozen seats had SSP-sponsored candidates; all the rest were the responsibility of trade unions or of the constituency Labour parties, with the latter taking the bulk. This of course was a marked shift from the preceding decade, when the ILP's sponsorship was a highly pronounced feature of Scottish Labour. Again, policy discussion was securely tied within Labour. Conferences convened by the Scottish Council to consider Labour policy became a feature of the 1930s. In 1938, meetings were held at the four main cities with the assistance of the Labour Speakers Association.[124]

Labour's developing self-assurance was highlighted by its inauguration of a rural campaign; since it had established itself quite well in urban-industrial areas, this was the next logical step. The capture of the Western Isles in 1935, followed by encouraging responses to subsequent by-election campaigns in constituencies as far apart as Ross & Cromarty and Dumfriesshire, and the decay of the Liberals, persuaded the Labour Party that such seats could be captured.[125] A van was acquired in 1939 and fitted with a loudspeaker audible at a distance of half a mile so as to tour scattered country communities, most of which had hitherto never heard Labour's message. In the summer of that year, 676 meetings were held in the 16 constituencies visited and 28,000 party leaflets handed out.[126] In fact these attentions, though claimed at the time to have made a considerable impact, do not seem to have borne many electoral benefits for Labour in either the short or the long run. The victory in the Western Isles probably owed much to local and personal factors, rather than portending a general rural breakthrough.

More success attended the other area concentrated on by the party in the later 1930s. This was the development of local government political work. The Scottish Advisory Council ran conferences in efforts to encourage constituency parties to build up their bases in council chambers, with a particularly large meeting held in 1935. Forty thousand leaflets were distributed during the 1934 municipal elections, and a major offensive against the Moderate and Progressive parties was declared in 1938.[127] In addition, conferences were also arranged for Labour councillors to assess policy issues confronting them; for example, housing legislation was discussed in 1935 and 1938.[128]

The concomitant emphasis on a pragmatic, almost managerialist approach to policy, which local government involvement seemed to necessitate, chimed in neatly with Labour's general shift away from the full-blooded socialism which the ILP continued to champion. Within

Labour itself, Woodburn was a strong influence towards more moderate policies, while Dollan and Johnston, the two dominant presences after 1932, were disengaged from any erstwhile radicalism. The development of closer association with Scottish Co-operative bodies and, above all, with the STUC stiffened this propensity. The latter had become quite intimately engaged in the corporatist movement of the decade. The Mond-Turner talks had been overwhelmingly approved of by the congress, and the STUC's decision to work with the Scottish Development Council, the creation of progressive big businessmen, was a further symptom of the new centrism of the labour movement. Its political wing, shorn of the left, was of course a willing partner in this process.

So, by the outbreak of the Second World War, while Labour in Scotland was not at the same organisational level as in England, it was making headway, even if the overall performance was patchy. It had made distinct progress in a number of areas in the 1930s, thanks in part to the firm unity and discipline created by the containment of the Communists and the departure of the ILP. Constituency structure and expansion were addressed, links with cognate parts of the organised working class were deepened. It had effected the transition to a more moderate political position, and it had identified local government as a vital area of activity. In this sense, the framework for the post-1945 Labour Party was more or less set up.

3

CONSENSUS AND CONVERGENCE?, 1939–59

I

If the period between the wars, and more particularly the 1930s, can be seen as one of general Conservative pre-eminence, the decade immediately after the Second World War served to stress the continuing strength of that party in Scotland. The swing in the first two general elections was better for the Tories in Scotland than in England, and in the next two almost identical:

Table 3.1 General election swings, 1945–55

	England	Scotland
1945	−12.1%	−8.2%
1950	+3.0	+3.5
1951	+1.2	+1.1
1955	+1.8	+1.3

Notes:
1 The swing is towards (+) or away from (−) the Conservatives.
2 For 1935, all 'National' votes are treated as 'Conservative'.
3 In 1935 and 1945, the ILP vote is included with Labour.

Moreover, in 1945 and 1950 the Conservative share of the poll in Scotland was very close to that in England, something never before or after achieved. Support for the Tories continued to grow until in 1955 the

70

party won over 50 per cent of the vote, the only occasion this century that a party has gained an absolute majority of the Scottish popular vote. It is also revealing that no Conservative seat was lost at a Scottish war-time by-election, but in England seven fell in a steady procession. Indeed, the only war-time defeat in Scotland for the incumbent party occurred when the SNP won Motherwell in 1945 from Labour, whereas no English Labour seats were lost.

The performance of the Conservatives is the more creditable in that key electoral reforms were detrimental to their interest. The business vote registration procedure was altered by legislation in 1945 which placed the responsibility for registering upon the voter, and not, as hitherto, upon the registration officials. The result of this, the Tories reckoned, was that only one third of those so qualified in 1945 were actually enrolled.[1] Thus, the loss of Glasgow Kelvingrove, where there were 591 registered business votes in 1945, and a Labour majority of 88, would presumably have been averted had the entire business vote been available. The complete abolition of the business vote by the 1950 election clearly cost the Tories the Glasgow Central seat, where the business vote was the second highest in Britain at 3,387, or almost 10 per cent of the total electorate. A Unionist majority of 1,516 was turned into a lead for Labour of 3,004.[2]

As in part of the inter-war period, the Liberal Party underperformed in Scotland. Compared to England, proportionately fewer seats were contested, and the party's share of the vote was normally lower.[3] Yet, as in the previous era, in terms of seats won, the Scottish party did better.

The striking feature of Labour's electoral effort is that it did not maintain its inter-war advantage over England after 1945, when in any event the latter had made greater advances from the 1935 starting-point. But 1950, 1951 and 1955 were the first elections since the First World War in which Labour was more popular in England than Scotland – a position

Table 3.2 The Liberal performance, 1945–55

General Election	Seats Fought (%)		% Share of Vote		MPs (No.)	
	Eng.	Scot.	Eng.	Scot.	Eng.	Scot.
1945	51.8	30.1	9.4	5.0	5	0
1950	81.4	57.7	9.4	6.6	2	2
1951	18.0	12.7	2.3	2.7	2	1
1955	18.6	6.9	2.6	1.9	2	1

Source: F. W. S. Craig, *British Electoral Facts, 1832–1987*, (Dartmouth, 1987), tables 1.28–31.

which only subsequently occurred in the two 1974 elections. We must be wary of assuming that the post-1945 settlement involving the Welfare State immediately and decisively established Labour's supremacy in Scotland.

II

The bases of the Unionist strength in this period may be attributed to three broad areas: organisation, policy and relations with the Liberals. It is also arguable that these advantages were not as permanent as they seemed, and that the roots of the subsequent problems faced by the party derived from inherent weaknesses which were gradually exposed after the mid-1950s.

Although in the post-mortems on the 1945 rout the Tories sometimes blamed the run-down in their organisation as a factor, this was at best only partly true for Scotland. In 1941, 10 of the 24 western area constituency agents were still in position. By 1943, the grass-roots showed clear signs of recovery: membership had risen by one quarter from 1942. A review of the party's position later that year accepted that there had been some organisational decline in rural areas, but little in urban areas. Moreover, in spring 1944, a good eighteen months before the election, a travelling organiser was appointed to build up local machinery. As a result, two-thirds of constituencies in the western area were served by an Organising Secretary at the general election.[4]

Political awareness was also sustained, for the party was much exercised throughout the war at the impact left-wing propaganda was felt to be having. The annual conference, shelved at the outbreak of war, was quickly resuscitated in 1941, since both the Labour and Liberal Parties had continued to hold theirs. Monthly meetings for women were held in a Glasgow restaurant, addressed by leading politicians on issues of the day, so keeping activists informed for political debate with opponents.[5]

The setback experienced in 1945 inspired the Tories to revamp their organisation. A drive to install agents in all seats was pretty well carried out by 1950, but it was acknowledged that more than professional expertise was still required. Party leaders stressed the need to inject new, and specifically younger, blood into the membership. They emphasised the vital importance of developing political education for the new recruits so that socialist propaganda could be effectively countered. Over the next decade, the results of this appeared impressive. Individual membership soared. The West of Scotland Council claimed 150,000 members in 1953 (a five-fold increase on the 1947 figure), suggesting perhaps a total of a quarter of a million for all of Scotland.[6] This meant that about one in five of all Unionist voters had joined the party then.

As building up a younger support base was central, in their own eyes, to the revivification of the Tories, the Junior (later Young) Unionists were restarted in 1946, and within five years about 200 branches existed. Early dividends were indicated in the 1950 election, when three Young Unionists were selected as candidates, albeit for impregnable Labour seats.[7] Women's sections were also encouraged to expand after the war. Political discussion was stimulated with day conferences, such as one in 1952 which attracted over 1,000 women.[8]

To foster the spread of new techniques throughout the associations, regular meetings were held from 1949 for top constituency officials and paid organisers in all the west of Scotland seats. At these, matters of common interest were discussed. New ideas on electioneering or organisational techniques were floated and views on policy direction were also aired. Thus, the committee considered setting up political education groups, involvement in municipal elections and recruiting trade unionists, as well as debating the party's agriculture policy pronouncements.[9] The quality of party propaganda was upgraded, for it had been a widespread complaint that the literature used in 1945 did not contain enough material of specific relevance to Scotland. This was carefully attended to in subsequent contests, and drew approving comments from activists.[10]

The results, measured in electoral efficiency, were formidable. One particular aspect fully worked by the Tories was the postal vote, introduced from 1950. In the average Scottish constituency, 1.8 per cent of voters had a postal vote, but in general, safe Labour seats were below the norm: Glasgow Bridgeton, with only 0.3 per cent, was the lowest in Britain in 1950. In marginal seats, the postal votes were more numerous and highly significant: in Rutherglen in 1951, 536 voted by post, and the Tory squeaked in by 352. Also in 1951, the Liberals lost Roxburgh & Selkirk by 829 votes in a contest where there were 1,373 postal votes: this was 950 more than in the previous election, when the Liberal majority had been 1,156. In at least five other seats the postal vote almost certainly helped the Tories to victory at various elections in the 1950s.[11]

The party was able to undertake electioneering with great proficiency. Canvassing was thorough: when Central Ayrshire was captured in 1955, a canvas of nearly 100 per cent had been conducted.[12] In the

Table 3.3　Election expenditure per Scottish constituency, 1945–55

	1945	1950	1951	1955
Con.	£660	£701	£709	£692
Lab.	505	628	564	531
Lab. % of Con.	76.5	89.6	79.6	76.7

Source: The Nuffield British General Election Surveys, 1945, 1950, 1951, 1955.

1951 election contest in Aberdeen North, one of Labour's safest seats, an academic survey found that the Tories canvassed as many voters as Labour. The Unionist association there had as many members as its Labour rival, which was one of the biggest in Scotland; the Tories had a full-time agent/secretary, while Labour had an inexperienced temporary agent; the Tories worked from smarter premises and spent more.[13]

One key element in the superiority of Tory machinery was the financial advantage enjoyed over Labour. The average amount spent per constituency in general election campaigns by the Tories was, apart from 1950, about 20 per cent to 25 per cent higher.

The policy position of the Unionists also contributed to their successes. Since the inter-war Unionist Party had seemed more socially engaged than in England, and given that post-1945 Conservatism in England is frequently portrayed as moving briskly to centrist, consensual policies, especially on economic, social and welfare issues, then clearly the Scottish Tories would be expected to adopt that stance with few demurrals.

There are obvious indications of a readiness among Scottish Tories to embrace the new ideas on economic and social policy. An instance of this came at the exceptionally early date of November 1941, well before the march to consensus is usually seen as starting. The MP for Renfrewshire West, Capt. Henry Scrymgeour-Wedderburn, gave a 'very thoughtful' address to Western Council Tories on post-war reconstruction. He observed that:

> all political parties would have to discard some of their former political prejudices in order to promote the spirit of goodwill and co-operation which would be essential if the immense post-war problems of reconstruction were to be successfully tackled. He envisaged a planned economy, involving some measure of a continuation of war-time controls. It was the lack of foresight in this matter of planning, he believed, which was responsible for many of the troubles which arose after the last war.[14]

Yet there are countervailing signs. Walter Elliot, the epitome of progressive Scottish Conservatism between the wars, was not particularly enthused by the Beveridge Report of 1942 on Social Security, which provided the basis of the Welfare State. Only one Scottish MP, Scrymgeour-Wedderburn, was a member of the 41-strong radical backbench ginger group, the Tory Reform Committee. Three of the seven members of the Progress Trust, a small semi-clandestine group of Tory MPs formed to oppose the implementation of Beveridge, sat for Scottish seats: indeed the chair, Sir Alexander Erskine-Hill, represented Edinburgh North.[15]

Among the constituency activists, there was a similarly blurred attitude. The Western Council voted in 1940 by a ratio of three to one against modifying means-testing of pensions. This suggests that the 'war-warmed impulse of people for a more generous society', in Titmuss's phrase, had encountered icier blasts in Scotland. The SUA responded cautiously to the Beveridge Report, concluding that there seemed to be no great public interest, because higher wages had altered perceptions, and a more important priority among the people was winning the war. The last war-time annual conference, held in March 1945, carried resolutions defining the party's position. 'Schemes of "social security"' appear as the tenth item, and it was stressed that these of themselves were not enough to raise the standard of living.[16]

On full employment, the party seemed less than wholly committed. The 1945 annual conference referred to 'steady' – quite distinct from 'full' – employment levels. The overriding determinants of economic policy would be a successful export record and protecting savings by avoiding inflation, both of which of course implied a different set of priorities.[17] Many manifestos in 1945 rather seemed to want to revert to pre-war economic and social stances. Thus, James Stuart, then Chief Whip and subsequently the first post-war Tory Scottish Secretary, effectively rejected Keynesianism when he counselled caution over hoping for full employment until market forces had restored Britain to economic stability.

In 1941 the SUA set up a committee charged with considering a post-war programme for Scotland. The main fruit of its labours was a pamphlet on local government reform, hardly matching R. A. Butler's wide-ranging New Conservative menu. What is equally remarkable is that there is virtually no allusion to the National Health Service by the party's central organisations either in the war or in the immediate post-war years.

The one social issue on which the party was positive was housing, identified by the 1945 conference as 'the most clamant need, outweighing all other demands for social reform'. Accordingly, there should be a full deployment of resources, with the public and private sectors both playing their part.[18] Yet, 94 per cent of English – but only 79 per cent of Scottish – Conservative manifestos in 1945 referred to housing (the respective figures for Labour show Scotland narrowly ahead: 97 per cent and 100 per cent). Nevertheless, housing was an issue which helped in the succeeding general elections. The failure of Labour between 1945 and 1950 to build anything like sufficient houses in Scotland was seized on by the Tories. It was no coincidence that a Glasgow MP, Thomas Galbraith, was one of the movers of the famous election-winning resolution at the 1950 (British) party conference which pledged the Conservatives to build 300,000 houses a year. For Scotland, this meant a commitment to put up 30,000 a year. This was achieved, and the pointed contrast with Labour was made much of in propaganda material in the mid-1950s.[19] As is noted in the next chapter, it was the perceived wavering of the party on housing in the later 1950s that seems to have contributed to the start of the fall in the Tories' popularity.

By the time the party won office in 1951, a more coherent and welcoming view on social policy had emerged. Party activists called for rises in pensions and the expansion of the National Health Service.[20] In its early years in office, the party seemed to be meeting its promises to the satisfaction of the electors. Much of the successes of the first administration were emphasised as building up the infrastructure: the Forth Road Bridge, the go-ahead for New Towns like Cumbernauld, heavy spending on roads and an increase in the rates support grant to local authorities, were all made much of in the run-up to the 1955 election. These were projected as indicative of how well the party was defending the interests of Scotland: Stuart was commended for successfully increasing Scotland's share of government spending.[21] Thus, the endorsement of the post-war consensus by the Scottish Tories reached its apogee in the mid-1950s.

As noted earlier, the Liberals performed less well in Scotland after 1945 than in England. In part this was because of the adroitness with which the Unionists angled for Liberal votes, primarily by the device of the continued, and indeed enhanced, profile accorded to the National Liberals. In England and Wales the electoral presence of the National Liberals declined, as they seemed a relic of the inter-war party system. In Scotland the number of Tory candidates who wove the word 'Liberal' into their party designation actually grew. The reason for the nomenclatural switching is perhaps the greater menace in terms of seats won by the Scottish Liberals. The innovation of 'Liberal-Unionist' is particularly interesting as an evocative throwback to before 1914.

Many of the relevant seats had been previously held by Liberals in the post-1918 era. Thus two-thirds of all National Liberal candidatures were in Fife and Angus, old Liberal strengths. But only one seat (West Renfrewshire) was fought in west central Scotland,[22] where the Liberals had been obliterated in the 1918–22 phase. This eagerness to accommodate National Liberal sympathies was evident in the North Angus & Mearns constituency. In this new seat, Colin Thornton-Kemsley, formerly the plain 'Unionist' MP for the Kincardineshire portion, changed to a 'Unionist & National Liberal' in order to assuage the National Liberals in the former Montrose Burghs, which had been added to the constituency shortly before the 1950 general election.[23]

With the unadorned Liberals the Tories were always ready to reach accommodations, as in the 1918–39 phase. The best instance of this was Dundee, where the previous two-member constituency was split into two single-member seats at the 1950 election. Hitherto, one Tory and one Liberal had fought for the two seats. Careful negotiations were conducted to avoid both parties running in each seat, so leaving Labour with two easy victories. A complicated agreement was reached, in which the Conservatives alone would fight both seats in 1950, but if they failed to win either, then in the next contest the Liberals would run in one, the

Table 3.4a Pro-Conservative candidates and MPs with 'Liberal' in their party designation in Scotland, 1945–55

	Lib.-U.	Nat. Lib.	Nat. Lib. & U.	U. & Nat. Lib.	Total
1945	0	8(5)	0	0	8(5)
1950	0	0	5(3)	5(2)	10(5)
1951	6(3)	0	6(3)	1(0)	13(6)
1955	8(4)	2(1)	2(1)	1(0)	13(6)

Note: Numbers not in brackets refers to candidates, those in brackets to MPs.

Table 3.4b 'National Liberals, etc' in Scotland and England, 1945–55

	England				Scotland			
	Cands	%	MPs	%	Cands	%	MPs	%
1945	46	9.1	8	4.8	8	11.8	5	18.5
1950	38	7.5	10	4.0	10	14.7	5	16.1
1951	39	7.8	12	4.4	13	18.6	6	17.1
1955	29	5.7	14	4.8	13	16.9	6	16.7

Tories in the other. The Tories failed in both, and a Liberal entered as the sole anti-Labour challenger in Dundee West in 1951.[24] It is noteworthy that the Tories in the post-1945 Dundee elections styled themselves 'Unionist and National Liberal', whereas before plain 'Unionist' had been used.

It is in this context that the significance of the stress placed by the Tories on protecting Scottish interests from centralising socialism can be fully understood. In opposition between 1945 and 1951, the party repeatedly emphasised the need to abolish government controls, resist nationalisation, liberate free enterprise and eliminate bureaucracy. This was a recurring refrain, as in England. But the decentralising concept was extended in Scotland to argue for more devolution of responsibility for Scottish affairs to Scotland. This had two central aspects: first, the ministerial team handling Scottish business would be beefed up. A minister of cabinet status would be appointed and would reside in Scotland, handling day-to-day policy, while the Scottish Secretary would remain, but now be primarily located in London, to protect Scottish interests at the policy-formulation and legislative stages. Secondly, the nationalised concerns would be compelled to devolve responsibility for their Scottish operations to boards situated in Scotland and directly answerable to Scottish opinion. But it did not fulfil its pledges on Scottish control of Scottish matters, except to a very limited degree.[25] Yet this breach of promise did not stimulate a nationalist backlash.

As well as marking out a distinct position in relation to Labour, the Tories used this anti-Whitehall posture to counter the threat of Scottish nationalism and pull back Liberals into the fold. This was certainly the angle which local parties were urged to adopt when pointing out this policy to voters. This concern was underscored by the Dundee poll in 1945, which indicated that 40 per cent of the Scottish Nationalist vote was shared with the Liberals, and only 30 per cent with the Tories (cf. Table 3.6).

Policy, however, contained hidden traps. The logic of adopting corporatist tendencies in government and the retention of the mixed economy with heavy welfare commitments created tension with the free-marketeering impulses of many rank and file supporters. They were uneasy at the abandonment of some of the anti-state rhetoric of the later 1940s, and found the increased role allotted by Tory Scottish Office to trade unions especially distasteful. On the other hand, the mounting emphasis placed by 1955 on the ability of Scottish ministers to work the Whitehall system in order to ameliorate Scottish economic and social conditions carried the danger that any faltering in this record would rebound against the Tories, and could in the longer run encourage the argument that withdrawal from the United Kingdom might be a better *modus operandi* than covert lobbying in the corridors of Whitehall. Lastly, the perpetuation of the 'Liberal' element in the Conservative alliance bore the risk that if there was discontent with the party, or if it rapidly tried to shed the Liberal connection, the alternative of abandoning the Tories was fresh in the minds of many voters.

III

For the Liberals, the post-war decades marked the party's lowest ebb in the whole century. In 1945, the party in Scotland had no MPs and the leader of the British Liberals, Archibald Sinclair, came third in the seat he had represented since 1922. The 1950 election was the Liberals' biggest effort: the number of candidates was doubled, from 23 to 41, but their vote rose by a mere one third, and 29 deposits were lost. The disintegration after the high expectations of 1950 was rapid and total: by 1955 a mere five candidates stood, and the total vote slumped to one third the 1945 figure. Even in places with a longstanding Liberal tradition, the party vanished: in Banffshire, a Liberal seat until 1935, no Liberal ran after 1950. Where Liberals did fight, their vote plummeted. In Caithness & Sutherland, Sinclair's old seat, they secured only 15 per cent of the poll in 1951.

The peripherality of the party is highlighted by the five seats it chose to fight in 1955: Orkney & Shetland, Caithness & Sutherland, Invernessshire, West Aberdeenshire, and Roxburgh, Selkirk & Peebles. Where the party did have some profile in urban-industrial constituencies, it was usually because of an understanding, explicit or implicit, with the Conservatives; for instance, Dundee, as discussed earlier, and Greenock. Even the high point of the early 1950s, the party's double near-capture of Invernessshire at a by-election in 1954 and the general election the following year, simply offered on closer analysis reinforcement of the party's weaknesses. It confirmed the party as strongest in the remoter rural areas, for in the other four by-elections of this parliament – all in the urban Lowlands – the Liberals did not fight.[26] Moreover, much of the success at Inverness was attributable to the personality of the candidate, rather than the policies of the party. J. M. Bannerman was always a highly charismatic electioneer, but as one of the pillars of the Gaelic community, he was able to mobilise a large cultural vote in a seat with the second largest number of Gaelic speakers.[27]

The Liberals' problems lay both in organisation and policy. The already threadbare inter-war central organisation was badly affected by staff losses during the war. It was an ageing party: two of its leading officers were so deaf by 1945 that they could not discharge their respons-ibilities.[28] It seemed that virtually the sole person working at national level in the war and immediate post-war periods was Lady Glen-Coats. She attempted almost singlehandedly to keep grass-roots spirits alive, zig-zagging across Scotland continuously, trying to find potential can-didates and then persuade constituencies to accept them. The young John Junor was 'spotted' by her and taken to numerous places to help build up party morale. He was a candidate three times between 1945 and 1951.[29]

The quality and numbers of the party's activists in the constituencies deteriorated after the war. Lady Glen-Coats wailed in 1947:

> The truth is that England is beating us hollow both in the spirit and letter of the Liberal cause. When I go South I am ashamed of our Scot-tish Liberals and their lack of application to the spade work of organisation . . . We have too many old people. I found that in Paisley and it ruined organisation. Now I have got rid of them and in a matter of weeks things began to perk up.[30]

The Dundee Liberals' secretary bemoaned the change in the member-ship: whereas between the wars there had been distinguished citizens in their ranks, now these were inactive. The inertia and apathy corroded even those who had resumed political activity after the war. Early in 1948, a leading woman office-bearer in Dundee resigned, explaining graphically the despair experienced by loyal activists:

> I personally feel that I have sacrificed my household and my duties there on a good many occasions for the Liberal Club. In the past the results were perhaps worth it. During the last years and months I cannot feel that anything has been achieved – other than a feeling of frustration – by anything I have tried to do . . . Our efforts are nullified by indifference on the part of Association officials.[31]

The enfeebled state of central organisation left the Scottish Liberal Association (as it became in 1946) unable to control local parties, thereby adding to the lack of direction. The SLA's efforts to stop the deal reached between local Liberals and Tories in Dundee in 1950, as described in the previous section, resulted in humiliation for the national body. It insisted on running a Liberal, but few local members worked for him. His share of the poll (1.9 per cent) was the lowest of any Liberal in a very bad year for the party. Several constituency associations had no links with the SLA; for example, Ross & Cromarty had been outside since the 1930s, while in Invernessshire three different organisations claimed to be the authentic Liberal association in early 1945.[32] As a small highly devolved party, the Liberals had few institutional filters to exclude the occasional dubious adherent, adding little to their reputation as a serious party. An active fascist in the 1930s, W. W. Gilmour, stood in Midlothian & Peebles in 1950, without having completely abandoned his previous views.

By the early 1950s the Liberals were in serious disorder. The vibrant Lady Glen-Coats had quit, two of the rising hopes were also effectively inactive: Junor had entered Fleet Street, John MacCormick had put his efforts into the Covenant, and after its collapse, had little heart for further mainstream politics. Jo Grimond, shuttling between his northern islands fastness and Westminster, seemed rather marginal to Scottish politics, so that sometimes only J. M. Bannerman appeared enthusiastic and committed in this period, fighting elections everywhere. The precipitate decline at a lower level was revealed in the Dundee Liberal Association. Members' subscriptions between 1947–8 and 1950–1 averaged £79, and in the following three years they fell to £60. Quite dramatically, in 1954–5, subscription income plummeted to £25 and for the rest of the decade averaged £27.[33]

Equally important, there was little ideological space in which the Liberals might establish a coherent identity. The Tories, as we have seen, had presented themselves in the 1950s as a centrist party, able to woo those who wished above all to keep Labour out of government. This left little scope for the Liberals to make a distinctive pitch. Adjusting to the issues of the mid-twentieth century seemed hard: the party's war-time reconstruction committee advocated the old pre-1914 standards – taxation of land values, wider access to smallholdings and free trade; but it did not say much about social reform, beyond endorsing Beveridge's proposals – which hardly differentiated it from the other two parties. Significantly, a meeting addressed by Beveridge at the Scottish Liberals' AGM in late 1944 was only half-full, while the non-party meetings held by Beveridge to expound the ideas in his report were far better attended.[34]

The party continued to stress one issue very firmly: Scottish Home Rule was reiterated as essential in the reconstruction report, and the British leadership were warned that Scottish Liberals would not dilute this position.[35] But Liberals found themselves in an acute dilemma thereafter. On the one hand, with the repositioning in 1942 of the SNP (as discussed below), and more so after its by-election success at Motherwell in 1945, there was now a serious and credible political alternative. On the other hand, the fate which befell the Scottish Covenant petition in the late 1940s carried bleak implications for the Liberals. Despite securing an alleged two million signatories, the movement failed completely to influence either of the two main parties to legislate for Home Rule. Liberal morale was accordingly exceptionally low in the early 1950s, and Lady Glen-Coats cited the disarray among Home Rulers as a central factor in her decision to withdraw from active politics in 1952.[36]

On many issues, the post-war Scottish Liberals were anti-Labour. At the 1946 AGM, the SLA expressed its concern at the 'grave danger' posed by a 'so-called planned economy', urged an end to restrictions on enterprise, production and trade and opposed the reintroduction of contracting out of the trade unions' political levy.[37] Archibald Sinclair felt disinclined to run again after his defeat in 1945 in part because he was unhappy at the tendency of the Liberal MPs (none of whom were Scottish) to support the Labour government. Certainly the drift to merge or associate with the Unionists became apparent at various levels after 1945. The SLF itself opened up discussions with the Scottish National Liberals, the Tories' allies. This move, made in 1944, was ahead of England, whom the SLF hoped would be stimulated to similar action by their example. The initial talks were described as 'very friendly and cordial', but eventually faltered, and a second tentative feeler in 1945–6 also came to nothing.[38] Some constituency parties, as noted earlier, reached electoral accommodations with the Tories. Elsewhere, more drastic events occurred. A section of the Kincardineshire Liberals entered into negotiations to merge with the Conservatives in 1952, even though in 1945 they had narrowly lost to the latter.[39]

Movement into the Tory camp also took place at an individual level: J. A. Stodart ran as a Liberal in 1950, but in the 1955 contest he was elected as a Tory, and went on to hold junior ministerial office. The only Liberal MP other than Grimond elected between 1945 and 1963 wound up as a Conservative councillor in London. The legacy of this period of over-close relations with the Tories would reverberate to the Liberals' disadvantage in the succeeding period of rapid political change.

IV

For the Scottish National Party, the war and post-war decade revealed elements both of progress and of stagnation. The party entered the war as a rather ill-coordinated amalgam of disparate nationalistic tendencies. Its strength was that by the end of the war it had acquired a more coherent identity and programme, with a firmer organisational framework. It also enjoyed somewhat greater electoral credibility than heretofore. On the negative side, there was no decisive establishment of the party as the authoritative vehicle for securing self-government for Scotland, and at the same time, the early hopes of a permanent electoral breakthrough were not sustained.

The inter-war period witnessed the formation of a distinctive Nationalist party, but the electoral impact was minimal. The original pressure group for self-government was the Scottish Home Rule Association, formed in 1886. Liberal and Labour *prominenti* were identified with the SHRA, which in turn had seen its role as a pressure group seeking, like other classic late Victorian radical lobbies, to influence Liberals or Labour. In the 1920s it became apparent that, with the Liberals destined for oblivion, hopes had to be pinned on Labour. But by about 1928, it was evident that a Home Rule measure would not easily win a Commons majority, and Labour politicians turned away from this policy as the attractions of a more centralised socialism grew.

While the influence of literary nationalist currents in the 1920s and 1930s were obviously integral to the rise of Scottish nationalism, other factors were as significant. Many radicals and left-leaning individuals came together to form the National Party of Scotland (NPS) in 1928. R. E. Muirhead, a Fabian, ILPer and erstwhile Young Scot, was instrumental in launching the NPS, accompanied by Thomas Gibson, another with left-wing credentials. The NPS thinkers were concerned to combat economic and social distress with collectivist solutions. But the Scottish Party, formed in 1932, embodied a more right-wing approach. The key players here included Professor A. Dewar Gibb, the duke of Montrose and Sir Alexander MacEwan. For them, the nefarious influence of centralising socialistic trends, together with more ethnocentric ideas of Scottishness, were influential. In 1934, the two merged into the Scottish National Party, with John MacCormick emerging as the driving force. Electorally, nationalist candidates before 1939, under whatever flag, fared abysmally. Deposits were rarely saved, and even slightly eccentric candidates could outpace them: in Fife East in 1933, an 'Agricultural' candidate attracted four times as many votes. The SNP remained uncertain whether it should continue as a sort of lobby, or act as a fully self-standing party, and this left it incoherent.[40]

During the war, a decisive resolution of the ambiguities in the SNP's approach was reached. At the outset, the leadership supported the war, but there was a groundswell of opinion among the rank and file against this position. A number of fundamentalist nationalists refused to fight for the British state. Some did so on the constitutional grounds that they did not recognise the British government's right to commit the Scots to military involvement. Others adopted the socialist internationalist line also espoused by the ILP. A few SNP members – notably Douglas Young, a rising younger activist – who failed to win the status of conscientious objector wound up serving jail sentences.[41]

Discontent at the leadership's acquiescence in the British government's policies produced a revolt at the 1942 annual conference. Young led a majority which defeated the existing position and pledged the SNP to contest elections and reject any remnants of the old pressure group approach. This element insisted on adherence to the concept that the SNP was a fully fledged free-standing party. MacCormick and many of the pro-war wing quit the party, and through the Scottish Convention maintained the pressure group approach. The remaining members proceeded to reconstruct the SNP. Organisational matters were placed under the control of Dr Robert MacIntyre, who proved pretty effective in dealing with disruptive and dissident elements, and a tight disciplinary code was enforced. Next, membership was built up: in the rest of the war years, this grew by 60 per cent. Thus the SNP acquired a larger presence on the ground, and also demonstrated that its new stance was gaining recruits. Finally, an effort was made in 1946 to draw up a coherent policy statement which would give added depth and a broader perspective to the party. In general the party moved somewhat to the left with this declaration of aims.[42] It espoused a sort of old-style radicalism, rather than flirting with socialism: diffusion of property, not concentration in private or state monopolies, was seen as vital for democracy. It also unequivocally espoused full independence, rejecting MacCormick's intermediate status approach.[43] Finally, its insistence on exclusive membership, barring those from other parties who sought cross-party co-operation, emphasised its distinctive electoral identity.

The extent to which the party's new line was popular seemed confirmed in the run of by-elections held during the war:

Table 3.5   SNP war-time by-election results

Date	Constituency	SNP % Poll
10 April 1940	Argyllshire	37.3
28 April 1942	Glasgow, Cathcart	5.5
17 February 1944	Kirkcaldy	41.4
12 April 1945	Lanarkshire, Motherwell	51.8

The climax of course was MacIntyre's triumph at Motherwell, where a seat which had been highly marginal in the previous two general elections was narrowly won for the SNP in a straight fight with Labour.

Motherwell notwithstanding, the overall record of the 1939–45 years and, even more, the succeeding decade, suggests that the SNP had not yet reached any position of electoral momentum. In other by-elections where the SNP did not run, anti-incumbent party candidates performed at more or less the same level. In the North Midlothian contest, held in February 1943, the Commonwealth Party candidate won 48.1 per cent of the vote, failing by only 689 to topple the Tory. This comfortably exceeded the SNP's 41.4 per cent gained at Kirkcaldy a year later. Similarly, when other options were available, the charms of the SNP were less pressing. At Glasgow Cathcart in April 1942, an independent Nationalist came a bad fourth, well behind the ILP and a maverick aristocratic pacifist. In other words, support for the nationalists in the war was part of an undifferentiated anti-incumbent vote, as much as a positive endorsement of the SNP.

At general elections the party made no headway. The 1945 election results were virtually identical to 1935. In each election, eight seats were fought, and in each the poll share was 1.3 per cent, but lost deposits rose from five to six. A psychologically serious blow was that MacIntyre lost his seat, although he did come second ahead of the Tory. At Kirkcaldy, a by-election near-miss eighteen months before the 1945 election, the share of the vote gained by the same candidate dropped from 41.4 per cent to 17.0 per cent. By 1950 the SNP seemed quite unable to mobilise support. Only three seats were fought, and all the candidates lost their deposits, including MacIntyre at Motherwell. In both 1951 and 1955, a mere two seats were fought, the lowest general election presence since 1929, and the total poll in both years was below 0.5 per cent. The party's record at by-elections was equally abysmal, interventions simply producing a trail of lost deposits across Scotland from Glasgow Cathcart in 1946 to Dundee West in 1952. Significantly, no nationalist ran in the Motherwell by-election of 1954, less than ten years after MacIntyre's triumph.

Perhaps the most disturbing feature from the SNP's viewpoint was that one important aspect of the much-vaunted gambit adopted as part of the 1942 revolt did not seem to be producing dividends. This was the shift to a more left of centre stance, so rejecting any leaning towards Liberal and Tory standpoints, because the proponents of the 1942 *coup* argued that wooing the working-class voter was the best way to success. Motherwell, of course, as well as Kirkcaldy, had looked to be early fruits of the new stance. But the next best performance in this period came at West Perth & Kinross in 1955, scarcely the stereotypical proletarian heartland. Analysis of the 1945 voting patterns in Dundee offered few signs of progress along these lines. The distribution of votes was as follows:

Table 3.6   Cross-voting at Dundee, 1945 general election

	Lab.	Lib.	SNP	Con.	Total
Lab.	47,519	1,384	1,402	354	50,659
Lib.	1,384	969	3,264	27,613	33,230
SNP	1,402	3,264	668	2,442	7,776
Con.	354	27,613	2,442	1,900	32,309
Total	50,659	33,230	7,776	32,309	

Source: D. G. Southgate, 'Politics and Representation in Dundee, 1832–1963', in J. M. Jackson (ed.), *The City of Dundee : the Third Statistical Account* (Arbroath, 1979), table 12.5, p. 321.

These results demonstrate how limited were the inroads the SNP had made on Labour. Three per cent of Labour voters also voted SNP, but 7 per cent of Tory and 10 per cent of Liberal votes went to the Nationalists. In other words, Liberal cross-overs constituted nearly half (43 per cent) of the SNP total, while the Unionists at 33 per cent were about double Labour's 19 per cent contribution. So, despite the high hopes of the SNP, Nationalist voters identified overwhelmingly – exactly three-quarters, in fact – with the centre and the right of the voting spectrum. As subsequent decades were to reveal, this was not a unique peculiarity in the SNP's electoral experience.

This failure in the post-war era reflects a number of difficulties. First, in the early years of peace, the Covenant campaign may have suggested to many that petitioning still had potential. Yet in 1951 and 1955, when MacCormick's preferred approach had been demonstrated to be impotent, the SNP could not woo disgruntled signatories of the Covenant, even though the Liberals languished in the electoral depths. It may be that the fissiparous and sometimes eccentric tendencies of the nationalist movement led voters to regard the SNP as lacking real weight. The schisms and purges meant that several prominent, well-respected individuals found themselves outside the official SNP fold, yet to themselves and to a wider audience these expellees embodied the nationalist cause. MacCormick's switch to the Liberals was perhaps especially difficult. For long the genius behind the SNP, he now seemed to be conferring nationalist credentials upon the Home Rule party, and his near-success at the Paisley by-election of 1946 only added to the confusion. At the same time the antics of the likes of Wendy Wood simply encouraged a tendency to view nationalists as entertaining but frivolous political figures, even though she had no formal links with the SNP.[44]

In addition, there were problems in convincing voters of the SNP's policy coherence. Some expert commentators regarded the policy statements of the party as vacuous and unconvincing. The Scottish co-author of the Nuffield 1945 general election survey was scathing, roundly dismissing the SNP's manifesto for being 'vague on the constitutional side to the point of frivolity'.[45] So long as the procedures by which independence would be gained and the subsequent parliamentary system were ill-defined, the party was going to have trouble in persuading voters of its general competence. Most of all, there was little interest by the voters in the cause of self-government. The Labour government's betrayal of its 1945 pledge to introduce a measure of devolution, and its contemptuous dismissal of the Covenant petitions, reaped the reward in the 1950 and 1951 general elections of the highest popular votes the party has ever won in Scotland.[46]

By the end of the 1950s the SNP seemed pretty well where it had been a quarter of a century earlier: a small party whose supporters were undoubtedly dedicated, but still had the aura of marginality around them.

V

Labour faced less acute internal strains between 1939 and 1945 than during the First World War. Few party members opposed the war: most of those who might have had probably already joined the ILP. When by-elections came, the electoral truce was usually observed by Labour activists. Where this (very rarely) broke down, the results were reassuring

Table 3.7a Individual CLP membership per constituency, 1939–51

	England	Wales	Scotland
1939	732	605	410
1942	388	438	225
1945	814	914	460
1951	1,424	1,110	810

Table 3.7b Size of individual membership of CLPs, 1951

	England		Wales		Scotland	
	No.	%	No.	%	No.	%
Under 1,000	139	28.0	15	41.7	52	73.2
1,000–2,000	221	44.5	18	50.0	15	21.1
Over 2,000	136	27.4	3	8.3	4	5.6

Source: Labour Party, *Annual Reports*, 1939–54.

for the official party: in the Stirling East & Clackmannan by-election, held in October 1939, a pacifist run by dissident local party members against official Labour polled 6.8 per cent, and independent left-wingers and ILPers rarely threatened to win – unlike the SNP and the Commonwealth Party.[47] This internal unity and dearth of support for more left-wing alternatives in and after the war makes Labour's weaker electoral performance in Scotland when compared to England in the first decade of peace puzzling.

Labour's organisation, chronically enfeebled between the wars, did improve, but not sufficiently to bring it up to the levels attained either by the party in England and Wales or by the Scottish Tories. Thus, membership recruitment languished for most of the war, and it was not until October 1944, a good six months behind the Conservatives' launch of their electoral preparations, that Labour began to revivify constituency actvity in readiness for the forthcoming election.[48]

But the most serious obstacle lay with the failure of Labour to build up a mass membership in Scotland, in comparison to England and Wales. Scotland had an inordinately large number of CLPs with under 1,000 members. The consequences of this lack of numbers were considerable. For one thing, the low volume of funds generated militated against effective grass-roots machinery.

The experience of the Stirling & Falkirk constituency party is instructive. In 1950, a scheme to appoint a part-time agent/organiser was abandoned, as the CLP could not meet the wage bill of £300 per annum.

Efforts to finance an agent through a football sweepstake foundered because not enough volunteer collectors came forward. Even after the Scottish headquarters promised up to £200 a year to underwrite the cost of a full-time agent in 1950, the local party's financial position was too precarious for the post to be filled.[49]

Again, there were not enough bodies on the ground to carry out routine political operations. These problems were most acute in Glasgow, and came to the NEC's attention in a post-mortem on the loss of the Camlachie seat in a by-election in 1948. Until six days before polling, there were never more than twelve party workers out canvassing the constituency. As a result just over 70 per cent of the electorate was canvassed. On polling day itself, a mere 30 workers turned up, most of them present only after 7 p.m. Labour failed in the evening to get working voters out to the polling stations because of understaffing and inadequate canvass returns.[50] By contrast the Tory machine was able to organise three full literature deliveries and a total canvass in this contest.[51] A study of the 1950 election contest in Glasgow confirmed that canvassing and general electioneering duties were carried out far more systematically by Conservatives than by Labour.[52]

The NEC was so disturbed by the 1948 Camlachie revelations that it despatched Emanuel Shinwell and R. T. Wardle (the British National Agent) to report on the situation in Glasgow. They found things – in something of an understatement – 'far from satisfactory', and called for the appointment of a full-time organiser to deal with the whole city.[53] Yet the subsequent reports of the Glasgow City party suggest little progress occurred. Individual membership, which, it was estimated, should have been about 25,000, was just over 5,000 in 1951, when seven of the 15 CLPs were on minimum affiliation (i.e., 240) and a further five affiliated under 500. A membership drive in 1952 did double the membership, but Bridgeton only managed 30 recruits, while Gorbals added 759. Also in 1951, it was felt that 'there are too few women's Sections in Glasgow', while a year later the finances of the city party gave 'great cause for alarm'.[54] This parlous condition contrasts vividly with the Scottish Tories who, as we have seen, had a massive membership and were financially strong.

The draining impact of low active individual membership on wider areas of organisation is again plainly illuminated by the example of the Stirling & Falkirk CLP. The individual members averaged about 400. But many of these were paper members, displaying little activism. Efforts to initiate membership drives failed to take off, partly because not enough existing members were willing to do this work. The CLP's Honorary

Organiser resigned in 1949, protesting at the lack of support he received in his efforts to develop the party's structure. While no doubt some of these problems were the result of apathy, it should be noted that in the analysis of the 1950 election, comments were made on the presence of many helpers on polling day who were not paid-up party members.[55]

In the cases of women and youth recruitment and organisation, Labour in Scotland toiled feebly, again well behind not only Labour in England and Wales, but also the Tories in Scotland. A survey in 1951 for the NEC revealed that there were proportionately five times as many Scottish constituencies without a women's section as in England or Wales.[56] The fund-raising importance was clear: in 1949, the women's sections contributed between £3,000 and £4,000 to Scottish party funds. But involving them beyond this was a slow process. It was noted by the Scottish Executive in 1950 that 'women are now as interested in politics as men, and in some cases more so'.[57] There was then a sustained campaign to expand the movement, but this sputtered out by 1954. In the early 1950s, efforts were made to inculcate greater political awareness: in 1954 there were six advisory councils, seven conferences, three day and two weekend schools specially for women. Too frequently, however, women were not given key posts in election campaigns. Instead, 'all too often Women's Sections are only recognised and thought useful when money is needed'.[58] These difficulties were evident at grass-roots level. In the Stirling & Falkirk constituency, despite repeated efforts between 1943 and 1950 to build up the women's wing, the constituency party secretary observed that the women's organisations 'functioned mainly in the social sphere'.[59]

The Labour League of Youth was slow to take off in Scotland. In 1949 there were 13 Scottish branches out of a British total of 415, but by 1951, Scotland had 86 out of 777 branches. But from then on, decline in Scotland set in: by 1952 only 35 branches existed and over two-thirds of constituencies had no branch. In 1955, after consideration by the Labour Party's Scottish Advisory Council, the movement was disbanded in the face of Trotskyite permeation and discord.[60] However defective the Tories' Young Unionists may have been, they were never as feeble and distracting as the Labour League of Youth. Labour's tensions with the youth wing were of course not unique to Scotland but the need to recruit younger people in Scotland was very acute. The party, at both parliamentary and municipal levels, was an elderly to middle-aged movement. Only three of the 35 MPs who were first elected between 1943 and 1951 were under 35 years, but five were over 60.

Part of the cause of Labour's weakness lay at their Scottish headquarters. During the war, illness and death left the central office seriously understaffed, but after 1945, matters improved, and the forceful presence of Will Marshall gave direction. Yet misjudgments at the top undoubtedly meant that Labour struggled in the post-war years to operate effectively in key constituencies. The Scottish leadership in the immediate post-war years seemed euphoric beyond reason about the party's electoral hopes. It was decided in 1946 that a newly appointed organiser should concentrate on the Highlands, since Labour had supplanted the Liberals as the main challengers to the Unionists in all four of the northern mainland seats in the 1945 election.[61] Seats like Invernessshire were marked as a 'possibility' for capture by Labour. Enthusiasm for and interest in Labour's policies was stated to be intense in these Highland seats: a conference on party policy held at Inverness in 1947 drew 251 delegates.[62]

Despite these auspicious omens, the electoral outcome was disappointing. No Highland seats were gained in 1950 or 1951 – if anything the party seemed to lose ground there. After the 1950 contest, the party administration in England wondered if the energies of the Assistant Scottish Organiser should not be switched from the barren north, given that all except two of the marginal Scottish seats were located in the Lowlands. But of course, many of these had been rather neglected while resources and energy were invested in the Highlands. For instance, the Stirling & Falkirk party, struggling to build up its organisation in a fairly marginal seat, received a visit from Marshall only in November 1950, after the election of that year. His offer of financial assistance towards appointing a full-time organiser in the seat came too late to have any significant impact on the May 1951 election.[63]

In the realm of policy, Labour in Scotland was not particularly radical, and in some areas it was arguably more circumspect and centrist than in England. A good measure of this distinctive tone was forged in war. It is frequently stated that the standing of Scottish Labour received a boost in war with the appointment of Tom Johnston as Scottish Secretary in the coalition administration. Johnston was acclaimed on all sides of the political spectrum as highly successful in office. But it may be that his legacy to Labour was more ambivalent. Johnston was by 1940 no longer a radicalising force. His views on the reform of the health service were no more progressive than those of the English Minister of Health. His Education Act could not compare in terms of the social revolution it engineered with R. A. Butler's English Education Act; instead it was regarded as disappointing by most figures in Scottish education.

Johnston, far from moving enthusiastically down the road of partisan socialist change, sought to operate by establishing a broad consensus, including the great and the good of the Scottish establishment. This was exemplified by his creation of an advisory committee on Scottish economic and social matters, composed of all former Scottish Secretaries. This meant, as Willie Adamson had died in 1936, that none were Labour. The grandly titled Council of State proved to be ill-focused, incoherent and generally irrelevant to solving post-war problems. But the council did, by its existence, pre-empt any more dynamic innovations by government.[64] In looking for a non-partisan approach, Johnston may have diluted the credit for any progressive plans given to Labour, whereas in England Labour was identified more unequivocally with forward movement.

In the approach to the 1945 election, Scottish Labour placed importance on its policies as the only solution to the country's domestic difficulties, and this reflected the perspective at the constituency level where there was considerable interest in improving social conditions. But there was no particular emphasis laid on what many might regard as the two pillars of the Welfare State (Beveridge and the NHS), which are often seen as the base for the ascendancy of Labour after the mid-1950s. The Nuffield study of the 1945 election found that the major issues stressed by Scottish Labour manifestos were housing and pensions.[65] The Stirling & Falkirk constituency association, at this time a centre-to-left-leaning local party, convened two special conferences in 1944 on housing, while in 1943 the constituency MP focused more on old age pensions than on Beveridge when addressing activists. Only after the 1944 White Paper – two years after the Beveridge Report appeared – did the CLP decide to hold a conference on social security. The main points emphasised in the 1945 adoption speech made by the sitting MP – soon to be the Scottish Secretary – in his general pledge that Labour would carry through socialist legislation were (in order): housing, education, the nationalisation of 'the Mines, the Transport Industries, Gas, Electricity, Land, Banking'. He was then interrogated by party activists on water, housing, foreign policy, education, finance and India. There is strikingly no reference here to Beveridge, the NHS or full employment.[66]

In office, Labour is frequently depicted as disappointing expectations in Scotland. It is particularly notable that the housing programme was well below target. Again, recent writing has stressed the repudiation by the Attlee adminstration of earlier pledges to bestow greater control of Scottish affairs to the Scots. The relentless logic of central socialist planning led many, notably Herbert Morrison, to consider self-government for Scotland at best a distraction from and at worst detrimental to the goals of a socialist society. Hence the most that Arthur Woodburn could wring from his Cabinet colleagues was to enhance the role of the Scottish Grand Committee in 1948.

Woodburn's struggles inside government demonstrated the importance of the calibre of Scottish Secretaries in shaping policy outcomes. The first two post-war Labour Scottish Secretaries, Joseph Westwood and Arthur Woodburn, were worthy and dull, in the tradition laid down between the wars by Willie Adamson. No major pieces of legislation to benefit Scotland fell from their hands, and Westwood's dismissal by Attlee for inadequacy was brutal but not unfair. The third Scottish Secretary of the Attlee governments was more dashing. Hector MacNeil showed a lively interest in restructuring the Scottish economy. His persistent and persuasive efforts secured the arrival of IBM at Greenock, the first major post-war multinational inward investment to locate in Scotland (and, by chance, in MacNeil's constituency). MacNeil's early death in 1955 was a great misfortune for Labour in Scotland, and perhaps in Britain, too. He was a brilliant orator with dynamic ideas and managerial abilities whose departure left Scottish Labour looking somewhat lacklustre for a generation.

Yet it is worth noting that in 1950 and 1951, Labour's record appears to have lost the party few voters. The actual number of votes given to the party was well in excess of 1945: 10 per cent higher in 1950, and 15 per cent in 1951. Indeed, 1951 marks the numerical apogee of Labour's support in Scotland, despite the subsequent extension of the franchise. This suggests that voters were pretty pleased with Labour, at least in the party's traditional areas: jobs and public ownership gave material and ideological contentment. With a large share of the Scottish economy based in those sectors taken into the state's hands, it may be surmised many workers were highly satisfied. Moreover, while the electorate did not seem to actively disapprove of Labour's achievements in office, there was also very little protest from MPs and by implication the active membership, who selected the parliamentary candidates.

The weakness of the individual membership section of the party carried important implications for the balance of power within the post-war party. With an enfeebled organisation, Labour drew very heavily upon the commitment and support given by the trade unions throughout this period. It was their delegations at constituency level which helped the party to maintain an identity, and much of the propagandising and

disciplining of the party's natural supporters seems to have been conducted as much through union channels as formal Labour Party ones. In
addition, it was the funding supplied by the unions which permitted any
Scottish central administrative and organisational framework to survive.
Unions paid affiliation fees on their members in Scotland, but also put
up additional sums at elections. They also frequently released their Scottish officials to assist Labour in contesting elections, serving as agents in
constituencies where the local party could not provide. Above all, since
numerous constituencies could not finance running a candidate, it was
not unusual for a member of a prominent local trade union (frequently
an official in the union's bureaucracy) to secure the nomination through
the guarantee of sponsorship. The Scottish miners' union was the most
significant beneficiary of this relationship. In the 1955 general election,
when Labour slipped back electorally, unions gave £3,641 to the party's
election fighting fund. But in 1959, a year of marked advance in Scotland, £8,449 was donated by unions for the fight. Also after the 1955
election, the Scottish Labour Party council upbraided unions for their
lack of commitment to constituency party work, and it would appear
that by the next election, this deficiency had been remedied.[67]

The most significant source of candidate material was, however, local
government. This again was not new: a number of inter-war MPs, from
Wheatley onwards, had this background. Now there seemed to be almost
a career pattern of moving from council chambers to the palace of Westminster. There were at least a couple of reasons for this influx. First,
there were more Labour councillors; whereas in 1939, 17 burghs were
Labour-run, the wake of the 1945 tidal electoral wave resulted in
37 Labour-controlled burgh councils. Most of these remained firmly in
Labour's hold and where the party was toppled – as in Glasgow in 1950 –
recovery was normally quick and long-term.

Moreover, the claims of the councillors were in a sense irresistible.
The rise of Labour from the nadir of 1931 was achieved primarily in the
municipal arena: by 1935 or so the party had for the first time securely
established itself as the ruling party in a swathe of councils: Glasgow,
above all, stayed Labour from 1933. The paradox was not lost within the
party: in the height of the ILP socialist age – 1918–31 – municipal electors remained fairly impervious to Labour's message; in the post-1931
phase, they flocked to Labour. In part this was in protest at non-Labour
councils imposing cuts in benefit and increased rents, thereby consolidating Labour's claim to be the protectors of working-class interests in a
way which had previously eluded them. These were the circumstances

which gave Labour control of Clydebank in 1935.[68] After 1945 the discordance between municipal and parliamentary voting prevalent in the inter-war years diminished. In other words, there was a spill-over from the municipal successes for Labour into parliamentary contests. It was natural for councillors to seek to cash in on this success.

As a result of these two factors, candidates and MPs after the war were overwhelmingly middle-aged men with a background in trade union office-holding and/or service in local government. Few individualistic MPs were returned in the post-war decade: John Strachey in Dundee West was almost unique in this respect. The consequences were significant. With union sponsorship, and a career in local politics, the bulk of Labour MPs were immensely loyal to the party leadership, and not identified with subversive policies, as in the heyday of the ILP nominating candidates. The years of council service, where the work was more managerial and administrative than in the past, may have meant a lowering of ideological horizons among MPs.

Henceforth, Labour MPs in Scotland were characterised by their deep loyalty to the party and their eschewal of left-wing tendencies. Hardly any Scottish MPs were identified with the various internal left-wing revolts of the era – Victory for Socialism, the Bevanites and the Tribune Group. During the Attlee administration, Scotland was underrepresented among the left-wing rebels. Only 11 of the 145 MPs who voted against the Attlee government on left-socialist issues held Scottish seats; and of these 11, eight opposed only once, the other three on two occasions. Again, Bevanism in Scotland had remarkably few MPs. Only the odd quixotic maverick like Emrys Hughes could be consistently placed in the left opposition, along with the increasingly erratic McGovern. Others were from time to time to be found endorsing Bevanite positions, but these were mostly one-off stances.[69]

Ferocious loyalty to the leadership was the norm instead, as conveyed by Jean Mann in her memoirs. A former ILP street orator, by the late 1950s her devotion to Gaitskell was unswerving. It is perhaps no coincidence that a number of left-inclined Scots wound up holding English seats: Jennie Lee and John Mackie being the obvious examples. In this respect, it is rather similar to the pre-1914 era, when left Labour candidates had little prospect of getting nominations for Scottish seats.

By the mid-1950s Labour was well established in its heartland, being represented by rather stolid local political figures. Labour was not only identified with traditional industrial activities, as a corollary it was also seen as the party of central Scotland. Although after the war it did

supplant the Liberals as the main opposition party in several rural constituencies, this was frequently more because of the latter's weaknesses
than through any rising tide of socialist sentiment in the small towns and
the countryside.[70] In Kincardineshire, for example, the emergence of
any non-socialist alternative to Toryism would not encounter any great
resistance on the part of Labour.

The trade union and local government background of many MPs con-
formed to a static class model which was becoming increasingly out-
moded. Here the early death of MacNeil was significant. A university
graduate and a journalist, he represented something of new social force
which, with his death, was not built on at the time. It was another ten to
fifteen years later that a clear detectable presence of professional, highly
educated and extremely articulate Labour MPs began to emerge from
Scotland. But this arrested progress may have played a part in leaving
Labour in the mid-1960s and early 1970s looking rather old-fashioned
and out of touch with social trends in the country.

VI

The Communist Party performed reasonably well in 1945: five candidates got an average of 6,500, Gallacher retained West Fife against a
determined Labour push, and two other deposits were saved. By 1950,
decline was apparent: 15 of the 16 candidates somewhat ambitiously
entered lost their deposits, with the average vote slumping to 1,700.
Worst of all, West Fife fell to Labour as Willie Hamilton battled – sometimes literally – to topple Gallacher, who actually finished in third place.
A year later the Communist candidate in this seat lost his deposit.

The turning point for the CPGB seems to have come in the late 1940s,
and it is likely that, as in the rest of Britain, the decisive factor was a reaction to the intensification of the Cold War in these years. The Catholic
Church also played a role in undermining Communism. The existence
of a shop-floor Catholic Workers' Guild, begun during the war and
persisting afterwards, provided a nucleus of organised opposition to
Marxist influence in factories. Hamilton's successful campaign in West
Fife against Gallacher owed something to the activities of Roman
Catholic shop stewards in the seat.[71] The high percentage of Scots who
were Roman Catholics – and were still overwhelmingly working-class –
would certainly make the guild highly influential.

After the electoral rebuff of 1950, the Communists switched from mainstream electoral endeavours, other than retaining a presence at a very few selected constituencies. More energy was directed into industrial and labour issues, where the party's influence outstripped its electoral popularity. Their dominance in the Scottish NUM was central to their role: a large union (around 60,000 members in the mid-1950s), it carried particular weight at the STUC. An apostolic succession of Communists led the union, the two most important in this period being the brothers Alec and Abe Moffat. Other unions with a pronounced Communist presence included the engineers and the boiler-makers. It is, however, remarkable how few of the CPGB trade union notables offered themselves at parliamentary elections, although some did enter local government contests.

The other main left party, the ILP, had been in steady decline since it seceded from Labour in 1932, and this decline intensified in the war. As discussed above, the ILP performed unimpressively in war-time by-elections compared to other parties, suggesting that it could neither reach nor convert public opinion, unlike in the previous world war.

The return of three ILP MPs for Scottish seats in 1945 was little more than a nomenclatural fiction. A deal was brokered with Labour before the election campaign opened. It was accepted that neither side would put up candidates against the other, and moreover that the ILP would confine its electioneering to the seats it already held. With Maxton's death in 1946, the ILP crumpled. The party did win the Bridgeton by-election against Labour, but by the 1950 general election the MP, James Carmichael, had himself joined Labour. Now he trounced his ILP opponent, who lost his deposit. The veteran ILP MP Campbell Stephen died shortly after Maxton, having just negotiated his re-entry into the Labour Party, and the ILP again came nowhere in the 1950 general election in his old seat, Camlachie. John McGovern, the third ILP MP returned in 1945, had attached himself to Labour well before the 1950 election, part of a bizarre political and intellectual odyssey that ended a decade later with him, by now a fervent member of the Oxford Group (founded by Frank Buchman and identified with virulent anti-communism), giving his support to the Conservative Party in the 1959 general election.[72] In effect by about 1950, the two left-wing parties which had plagued Labour's life between the wars had been completely eviscerated. Labour was now in a virtually unassailable position on the political left.

4

THE DOMINANCE OF LABOUR AND THE CHALLENGE OF NATIONALISM, 1959–79

I

After nearly a third of a century in which electoral politics in Scotland followed a pattern relatively similar to that obtaining in Britain, from 1959 the trend in Scotland deviated quite sharply, and since then has never fully returned to running parallel with Britain as a whole. While in 1959 there was a swing of 1.4 per cent to the Tories in England, in Scotland it went, also by 1.4 per cent, to Labour. In all but one of the following six general elections down to and including 1979, judged by the swing measurement, the Tories never performed as well in Scotland as in England. Their share of the Scottish poll declined from the high-water of 50.1 per cent in 1955 to 31.4 per cent in 1979, while the change in England was from 50.4 per cent to 47.2 per cent. More significant per-haps was the disproportionate decline in MPs returned to parliament: for all of the 1960s and 1970s, the figure hovered around the low twen-ties, or markedly less than one third of the total. The credibility of the party was thereby badly damaged.

The beneficiaries of the Tory collapse changed across time. Labour made the initial breakthrough in the 1959 and 1964 elections, picking up nine seats, nearly all in the industrial west, but only capturing two more in the 1966 and 1970 elections. The setbacks of the middle 1960s mostly occurred in the outlying fringes of Scotland, and the losses leeched to the Liberals, who won five seats in 1964 and 1966, but none in the 1959 or either of the 1974 contests. In the 1974 elections it was primarily the Nationalists who profited: seven of their eleven MPs in October held former Tory seats. The recovery of the Conservative vote in 1979 translated into retrieving seats most recently lost: those casualties of the pre-1974 phase were not, generally, recouped.

Labour's support was, like the Tories, also less certain: in the four elections between 1959 and 1970, Scotland was pronouncedly more pro-Labour than England, but in the two 1974 polls, England led. In 1979, Scotland outstripped England, but in absolute terms the level of support was markedly below 1970, which itself had been the poorest for Scottish Labour since 1935. But with a skewed electoral system, the party emerged with the overwhelming majority of MPs throughout the 1960s and 1970s. In a mirror image of the Conservatives, the upshot was to create a picture of Labour's impregnability north of the border: certainly the return of Labour governments in 1964 and in 1974 – twice – owed a great deal to the Scottish contingent.

The Liberals continued to run in fewer seats and to poll less well in Scotland compared with England, yet managed to be more effective in winning seats: in two parliaments (1964 and 1970), there were more Scottish than English Liberal MPs. The weaker levels of support in Scotland cannot be ascribed entirely to the presence of the SNP. Between 1959 and 1970, even adding the Nationalist poll to the Scottish Liberal vote, the third party total fell short of the Liberals' share in England.

The most dramatic aspect of these electoral processes was the advent of the SNP. After over thirty years of forfeited deposits and humiliations at the count, the party advanced at breakneck speed. From 1961–2, when the SNP gained a creditable 18.7 per cent and 23.3 per cent of the poll in the Glasgow Bridgeton and West Lothian by-elections respectively, the fortunes of the SNP grew steadily. The remarkable by-election victory at Hamilton in 1968 rocked Scottish and British politics. One of the safest Labour seats in Scotland was lost to a complete novice candidate fighting in virgin territory for the SNP. Municipal advances coincided with and followed the Hamilton result: in 1968, the SNP topped the popular vote in the Glasgow council contest. But the 1970 general election represented a setback: on the lines of Motherwell in 1945, Hamilton was lost. The sole victory – in the Western Isles – was perhaps the product of local rather than national factors.

Yet this setback seemed temporary, for the 1974 elections marked a high point for the party: in October, 11 seats were won, the share of the popular vote came to 30.4 per cent, whereas the Conservatives had 24.7 per cent. For a period after this second 1974 election, opinion polls placed the SNP as the biggest party in Scotland and it looked poised for further advances – the party was second in 46 seats, with 18 of these winnable on a swing of 5 per cent. However, the apparent forward march of Scottish nationalism soon proved to be a chimera: from July 1977 support began to dip alarmingly, a trend confirmed by three poor by-election performances, followed by a collapse of the parliamentary party in 1979 from eleven to two, and a halving in its share of the vote to 17.3 per cent – albeit still ahead of its 1970 position.

II

This period saw a profound realignment in the political proclivities of the national institutions. For nearly half a century from the end of the First World War, as we have seen, these were to a greater or lesser degree sympathetic to the Conservatives. But in this period they either became neutral, or in certain instances shifted to a pro-Labour stance.

From the late 1950s there was a pronounced political reorientation in the alignment of the Scottish press, hitherto overwhelmingly pro-Tory. As the circulation figures show, the indigenous titles in the four main cities had very high saturation readership figures for their localities, and all were Conservative supporters in the 1950s. Likewise, the two Sunday titles, the *Sunday Post* and the *Sunday Mail*, were both Tory and universally read throughout Scotland. Of the London-based 'nationals', only the pro-Conservative *Scottish Daily Express*, selling at its peak about 650,000 copies, had made any impact in Scotland.[1] The *Daily Mirror*, with by far the biggest circulation in England, sold only 100,000 copies in Scotland. Labour's relatively poor performance in the four elections between 1945 and 1955 may have had some connection with the more adverse press balance in Scotland.

The initial change came in 1956 when the ailing Kemsley Press group sold the *Daily Record* to the Mirror Group. Under the new owners it was transformed from a lacklustre, rather lower middle-class organ into a Scottish version of the *Mirror*. The new, more demotic style alienated its stuffier former readers, but instead the *Record* established a major niche:

it became the staple reading diet for the working-class, particularly in the industrial Lowlands. Its circulation rose sharply from around 350,000 under Kemsley to 668,000 twenty years later.[2] Like its new English stablemate, the *Record*, hitherto solidly Tory, strongly supported Labour, as did its Sunday sister title, the *Sunday Mail*.

The second stage came in the 1960s and early 1970s with a slew of newspaper closures. In 1960, the *Bulletin* folded. This was a Tory sympathiser (but with nationalist undertones) whose contents can be described as something of a daily version of the *Sunday Post*, but possibly not quite as intellectual. The *Record* seems to have absorbed most of the *Bulletin*'s largely west of Scotland circulation of around 200,000.[3] The shut-down in 1974 by the *Scottish Daily Express* of its large Scottish office had a massive impact. The paper's autonomous Scottish component, which had been considerable, was pretty well eliminated, and circulation plummeted.

Many of the disaffected *Express* readers seem, somewhat surprisingly, to have turned to the *Record*, whose sales rose steadily throughout the 1970s. Between 1961 and 1974, it increased circulation by 31 per cent, while the four Scottish regional dailies rose by only 12 per cent. This pre-eminence attained by the *Record* in the 1960s and 1970s marks a clear divergence from England. There, the *Mirror* lost out to the *Sun* as the preferred choice of the working-class readership in the 1970s. The political implications were profound: the *Sun* through the 1970s grew increasingly hostile to Labour, while the *Mirror* diluted its traditional unquestioning backing of Labour – sometimes seen as decisive in the 1945 election – until it seemed almost semi-detached from the party. The *Daily Record*, however, was unswerving in its backing for Labour: in the 1979 election, one of its senior writers, Harry Conroy, was seconded as Labour Party press agent for the campaign.

The Tories lost more friends among the press in the 1970s when both the *Glasgow Herald* and the *Scotsman*, the two heavyweights of the Scottish press, moved from almost a century's solid backing for Unionism. Both

Table 4.1 Scottish newspaper sales, 1961–74

	1961	1974	% Change
Press & Journal	96,000	110,000	+4.6
Courier & Advertiser	130,000	128,000	−1.5
Glasgow Herald	83,000	96,000	+15.7
Scotsman	68,000	87,000	+27.9
(Sub-Total)	(377,000)	(421,000)	(+11.7)
Daily Record	489,000	640,000	+30.9

journals advocated devolution with remarkable enthusiasm, given their unwavering approval of Unionism since the Irish Home Rule crisis of 1886. As the 1970s progressed, the two papers broadened their critique of the Tory Party into other areas, and although neither ever endorsed Labour, certainly the Conservatives received a much more hostile reception in their columns than previously. In the second 1974 election, the *Scotsman* recommended a vote for the Liberals or the Nationalists. So, while the balance of the metropolitan press between 1945 and 1979 tilted heavily away from a sort of equipoise to a very strong bias to the Tories, in Scotland the process was reversed.

The underlying preference towards Conservatism which the Church of Scotland displayed from the end of the First World War shifted in the later 1950s. In 1950, George MacLeod's public support for Labour produced a furore of adverse comment in Glasgow.[4] By the 1960s this was less of a rarity. An episode seen as portentous at the time came in 1959. A General Assembly committee report strongly criticised the Conservative government's policy towards African nationalists in the Central African Federation, an area in which the church had a longstanding missionary involvement. This suggested that while the laity were still disposed to vote Tory, as voting behaviour studies indicated, the clergy were moving in a more liberal direction, as the moderatorship of MacLeod in 1957 indicated. MacLeod had until then been seen by many in the Kirk as virtually a Communist and/or a Roman Catholic, but now he was the dominant influence in the deliberations of the General Assembly.

Concern at the persistence of Scottish social problems, unease at the ethics of nuclear deterrence, and generational change, as ministers radicalised while students and trainees during the 1930s and the 1940s grew to be the majority within the clergy – all contributed to the altered outlook. The Gorbals church group of the 1960s epitomised many of these features. Among this religious team's members was Geoff Shaw, who came from a comfortable Edinburgh middle-class background and was jolted out of complacency by missionary work in the Gorbals. Shaw entered politics as a Labour councillor in 1970, becoming in 1974 the first leader of Strathclyde Regional Council.[5]

This radicalisation of the Church of Scotland can be linked to the phenomenon of a rising generation of Labour politicians heavily influenced by Protestant social thinking: centred initially on MacLeod's Community House in Glasgow, they included Bruce Millan, Dickson Mabon, George Thomson and Gregor MacKenzie, who all became Labour ministers in the 1960s and 1970s. A succeeding generation similarly influenced included John Smith and Donald Dewar, while Gordon Brown was a son of the manse. This created a left Protestant grouping which had perhaps been less present in Labour since the period before the First World War.

Whether because of the apparent drift from its older stance, or because of wider social changes, the influence of the Church of Scotland in Scottish society dwindled in any event from the later 1950s. Membership entered into a period of steady decline from then; local government reorganisation in 1974 reduced the numbers but increased the politicisation of councils on which clergymen had previously sat; the ideology of personal liberation prevalent left the Church marginalised on moral issues. In the later 1970s, a highly sympathetic writer observed:

> The Church was seen to be in decline, no longer attracting men and women who could hold their own intellectually in any company; it was relegated to a private 'religious' sphere inhabited by those timid and nostalgic souls who liked that sort of thing.[6]

Until the 1960s the Tories continued to benefit enormously, as in the inter-war era, from attracting those seeking legal preferment, whose debating skills were highly advantageous to the party. Thereafter, this stream of talent became parched, and after Norman Wylie joined the bench in 1972 it ceased completely. There were still a few advocates sitting as MPs, but these (notably Malcolm Rifkind) were seeking political, not legal, careers. The reasons for this marked change, so deleterious to the Tories, are not clear. It may be that the great growth in business in the courts from the 1970s meant that judicial salaries were not tempting to highly paid advocates. There was also unease expressed from the 1960s within the profession at the unedifying prospect of law officers in parliament appointing themselves to judgeships, and this may have had an impact.

Likewise, education became less of a natural Tory area of support. The well-supported pre-war Glasgow Unionist Teachers' Association seems not to have survived, and by 1958 it became very difficult to find teachers prepared to join the Conservative Education Advisory Committee. The profession had tilted to a more pro-Labour stance. In 1954, the Labour Teachers' Society became an affiliated society of the Labour Party,[7] and in 1971–2 the two main teachers' unions joined the STUC. Part of the shift in the allegiances of schoolteachers may have been attributable to the tightening grip on local government enjoyed by Labour.

Promotions and transfers in the school system were notoriously said
to be an important area of patronage for councillors. There was also a
pronounced inflow of teachers into the ranks of Scottish Labour MPs.
Between the wars, four teachers and lecturers sat as Labour MPs, but in
the comparable period 1945–66, there were fully 13, including Willie
Ross, Peggy Herbison, Norman Buchan and Tam Dalyell.

III

The steep decline in the fortunes of Conservatism in Scotland had two
main causes, with a third consequential one.[8] First, the party's policies
were seen as moving out of touch with Scottish opinion and the objective
needs of the country. Secondly, the social context which boosted the
party in England was less present in Scotland. Thirdly, organisational
defects which were partly related to the preceding two factors, but had
also lain immanent from the previous phase, became very severe.

In the later 1950s, the divergent paths of the two economies became
incontrovertible: while England boomed, Scotland stagnated. In Scotland, unemployment rates were half as high again, emigration continued at high rates, yet England faced an acute labour shortage.
Traditional industries were declining in Scotland, and few new sectors
were emerging as alternative job providers.[9] The Conservatives' slogan
in the 1959 election carried a degree of crass insensitivity to the situation
north of the border: 'You've Never Had it So Good' was not inaccurate
in England but in large tracts of Scotland it was disastrous. The Scottish
Tories' post-mortem on the 1959 election remarked with trenchant
mordancy: 'It was pointed out that while the poster "Life's Better with
the Unionists" had been extremely effective, there were certain areas
where it could not have an impact.'[10] Between then and the 1964 election, the themes of unemployment and economic difficulties were
stressed time and again in internal party discussions as the obstacles to
success. The setting up of large new industrial developments like the
Ravenscraig strip mill and the Bathgate and Linwood car plants had not
produced a significant impact on job opportunities by 1964. Having
stressed in the earlier 1950s the skill of the Scottish Secretary in securing
from the Treasury a better than par deal for Scotland, the party now
suffered for the patent failure of this approach.

The economic record of the next Tory administration, 1970–4,
was, from a Scottish perspective, not very beneficial. Edward Heath was

elected on a platform of hostility to the state sector and the threat of assaults on the welfare system. But this approach was hardly attractive to Scotland, in view of the high share of employment in the public sector, while the poverty prevalent in urban Scotland placed great reliance on welfare. Moreover, the crisis at Upper Clyde Shipbuilders in this period had a very negative impact. It underlined the apparent indifference of the Tories to systemic Scottish economic problems, while the mass campaign of the shipyard workers against closure galvanised popular support in the west of Scotland against the government.

The party compounded the electoral weakness which its economic failures created by alienating support in other areas. The decision taken in the early 1960s to try to enter the Common Market had a greater appeal in England than in Scotland. The 1975 referendum on entry to the EEC showed that Scotland (58.7 per cent in favour) was less enthusiastic than England (68.7 per cent). There were two significant reasons for this greater Scottish scepticism. First, her heavy industry base was geared to international staple trade, rather than to the internal market of the EEC, which was more relevant to the new industries, mostly located in England. Secondly, agriculture, which was proportionately larger in Scotland, was very hostile to the Common Market. Moreover, upland and marginal farmers, strongly represented in Scotland, were seen as at greatest risk from the EEC's agriculture policy. Eight of the seats lost between 1959 and 1964 were urban-industrial,[11] but 11 of the seats lost between 1964 and 1974 had a sizeable farming vote.[12] It was perhaps no accident that the major beneficiary in 1974 of the Tory decline should prove to be the Nationalists, who were the only party unequivocally opposed to the Common Market. In a number of these rural seats where the Nationalists made headway, the main issue pushed by the SNP was withdrawal from the Community, with Scottish independence barely alluded to.[13] The Conservative recapture in 1979 of several of these seats may indicate reassurance among farmers that the Common Market was not going to jeopardise their livelihoods (indeed, quite the contrary).

The Tories also pursued policies which seemed to make sense at a British level, but in a Scottish setting served only to antagonise natural supporters. A good example is the implementation in the early 1960s of the Beeching Report, which meant the closure of unprofitable railway lines, with serious implications for rural Scotland, both Highland and Lowland. Several Tory county associations identified worries about the rail service as a factor in the party's ebbing of support in the 1964 election.[14]

Another important area where the pursuit of a British-wide approach backfired badly in Scotland was in housing, and here the impact was more evident in urban constituencies. The Tories owed much of their return to power in 1951 and their consolidation in 1955 to their emphasis on house-building. But thereafter, this skilful touch was blunted in Scotland. The 1957 Rent Act, and the 1961 property revaluation exercise, had dire consequences. The first, by immediately ending rent controls on better-quality private rented accommodation[15] hit the middle class severely, as the party itself noted: 'many of our supporters were having to pay very high rents and resented having to subsidise people in corporation houses where the rents were low'.[16]

An added adverse ingredient was the rates revolt of the later 1950s and early 1960s. Compared to England, rates bills in Scotland were high because there was a larger subsidised public housing sector and, moreover, rental levels were kept low, so that a higher subsidy element than in England was imposed on rate-payers.[17] Property revaluation meant that many house-owners faced steeply increased rates charges, for although the aggregate value rose by 50 per cent after the revaluation exercise, average rates fell by only 20 per cent (from 23s.9d. [£1.19p] to 19s.4d. [97p] in the pound). In other words, the revenue from rates went up from £77,370,000 in 1960–1 to £93,650,000 the following year, and the Tories carried the blame for this. Revaluation was not carried out in England, so there was no outcry there. It was in an attempt to avoid a renewed political backlash against a projected revaluation in the mid-1980s that the poll tax was devised.

Yet the party also suffered because cut-backs on spending on public housing meant fewer houses were built: the average annual total fell by one-third between 1952–6 (32,005) and 1957–62 (22,459), with the 1962 tally, 18,977, just half of 1953's 37,155. The state subsidy element was pruned, so pushing up council rent levels; thus in Glasgow in 1959 (an election year) SSHA tenants faced a hike from 5s.2d. (26p) per week to 8s.5d. (43p). Labour exploited this systematically from their capture of Glasgow Kelvingrove in a 1958 by-election, while the Glasgow SSHA tenants held rent strikes in 1958–9. Labour made great propaganda play with this multiple squeeze on housing, and the whole issue was identified by Tories as a leading factor in the 1959 election setback.[18]

Over a decade later, the error was repeated. The 1972 Housing Act, which forced much higher council house rent levels, provoked massive protests in Scotland, where again its implications were more widespread than in England. This measure was cited as a major factor in the collapse in support for the Tories in the New Towns, where the other parties organised a tenants' rent strike.[19]

The Tories floundered to find alternative policies which might appeal. The revival of the commitment to devolution, after Heath's Declaration of Perth in 1968, did little to win voters over. It seems probable that this was never a high priority for the electorate in the 1970 election, as it had not been in 1950 or 1951. Nevertheless, a firm impression was created among Scottish voters of Conservative duplicity and opportunism, thanks firstly to the absence of any serious endeavour by the 1970–4 Tory administration to implement constitutional reform, and secondly to the back-tracking after the accession of Mrs Thatcher away from full-hearted commitment to devolution to a strident advocacy of the status quo.[20]

The organisation of the party became less overwhelmingly superior from the mid-1950s. There is evidence of a decay in Tory Party efficiency, certainly compared to England. These problems manifested themselves both at the centre and at grass-roots level.

Propaganda seemed less effective than previously. There were constant complaints about the failure to bring forth material which had a Scottish slant to it, and some efforts were seen as inept and even unhelpful. Part of the blame for the 1964 election defeat was pinned on the comprehensively poor quality of the Tory literature: 'The Scottish manifesto was the wrong colour; it was a mistake to put Sir Alec's [Douglas-Home, the prime minister] photograph on the front; it was too verbose and not sufficiently constructive.'[21] The more astute exploitation of the press and other media by the SNP in the later 1960s was pointed to by party members as a worrying development.

In the wake of the 1959 and 1964 election defeats, the central structure was reshaped. The intention was to bring Scotland up to English levels of competence, mainly by greater concentration of power at headquarters, with new regional bodies given less autonomy than the old Eastern and Western Councils. These changes did not prove effective in stemming the deterioration in the party's position, electoral or organisational. By 1974, central staff had been cut from 20 to 14, and a subsequent reorganisation reduced this further to five. At the 1979 election, this had risen to seven, the same headquarters manning level as the SNP.

Disarray at the centre mirrored political etiolation in the constituency associations. The most graphic statement of the problem came during the internal dissection of the 1964 general election. It was disclosed that in 1959, 600 offers of help were received in the eastern region during the campaign, of which 300 were from people under 45 years of age. In

1964, however, a total of only 200 individuals offered help, of whom 17 were under 45 years.[22] At the root of this difficulty were a range of interlocking ingredients, amongst which may be pinpointed: the calibre of the membership, mounting financial commitments and a changed social terrain.

It is difficult to establish the exact numbers of party members. There are indications that a recruitment campaign in 1958 was not very productive: 'from the point of view of numbers this could not be considered an outstanding success'. Central Ayrshire Tories recorded a disappointing response to a membership drive initiated in 1975, although no details are available.[23] The problem, as suggested in previous chapters, lay in part in determining how politically involved these subscribing members were. Evidence for notional commitment rather than dedicated involvement is available. There is a rather despairing call from the Western District chairman in 1959 for associations to submit resolutions to the Annual Conference, 'thus demonstrating that their organisation was alive'. Yet in 1963 and 1964 a bare one quarter (11 out of 39) seats in the Western area submitted resolutions.[24] Declining interest in the party was shown in poor attendance at meetings, a topic of comment from the later 1950s. This may be ascribed to shifting social customs, but the falling off in attendance at the Scottish party's annual conference was symptomatic of deeper problems. In the early 1950s, over 2,000 representatives would turn up, but by the start of the following decade, halls were being booked with a maximum capacity of only around 1,000.[25] An effort in 1966 to raise funds, the National Subscription Campaign, sought an annual 10 shilling (50p) payment by party members. In Central Ayrshire, which had one of the largest local associations with around 5,000 members, after learning that the campaign had met with 'little or no success, it was decided that no further attempt should be made with this scheme, which lacked appeal'.[26]

The organisation of women and young people, two areas previously seen as Conservative strong points, became sources of concern. As early as 1956, prominent Tories were musing on the need 'to increase the amount of political activity for women'. The apparent prejudice against them holding high office within the party's organisations, or standing for elections, whether parliamentary or municipal, was also noted.[27] Between 1945 and 1979, the Tories had in total a mere two women MPs, and they overlapped only between 1959 and 1966.[28] Yet three women Unionists had sat between 1931 and 1935, and two in the succeeding parliament. Labour had three women MPs throughout the 1950s and two in the

1960s. As noted later, the SNP's three women MPs did much to enhance the party's image. The problem of getting more women into parliament was of course exacerbated by the dwindling Tory representation.

The Young Unionists also began to falter in the early 1960s. In 1963 plans for a new structure were discussed, as it was felt desirable to 'increase the political activity' of the youth wing. This had been prompted by a dearth of resolutions submitted to the movement's annual conference. But in 1964, problems still persisted, as 'the overall Young Unionist membership was still too low'.[29] This repeated threnody of a party which was failing to win the rising generation was most extensively expounded in the aftermath of the 1964 election. The Western district's youth organiser lamented the party's inability to attract under-30-year-olds, or to hold those between 30 and 40. There had not been produced a corps of younger people who were sufficiently interested and politically aware to make an impact on their own generation. Above all, it was necessary to develop a cadre of Young Unionist leaders and to formulate a programme of special interest to those aged between 25 and 40.[30]

A cameo of this problem can be etched from the Central Ayrshire Tories. As early as 1956, this constituency had troubles: only two Young Unionist branches existed, while in 1971, the Tory stronghold of Troon had only five or six members. In 1976, the constituency annual report alluded to 'our depleted Young Unionists', who were stated at that year's AGM to be 'at rock bottom'. In December 1979, it was decided that: 'The Agent would try to find out if the Branch was still operating, what programme was being followed and exactly when meetings were supposed to be taking place.'[31]

The Tories' difficulties had significant financial implications. On the one hand, as noted above, the local associations could not raise adequate funds by appeals to members. As a consequence, alternative sources of revenue bulked large in the activities of the grass-roots. Also, changing social patterns made some of the more hallowed financial expedients less beguiling: by the mid-1970s summer fêtes were no longer money-spinners.[32] The difficulty was intensified by the growing demands to spend. The most important of these was the spread of direct intervention in local government contests by the Tories, rather than, as heretofore, camouflaging themselves as 'Moderates' or 'Progressives', labels which were virtually extinct by about 1970.[33] The result was a sharp rise in the outgoings of constituency parties. The Central Ayrshire association spent £4,205 on the three parliamentary elections between 1974 and 1979, and in four local elections (including a by-election) between 1974 and 1980, £3,161. The latter, plus a contribution of £950 to the European parliament election in 1979, represented new demands. The total of £8,216 compares with the total election expenditure between 1964 and 1970 (a period which also covered three general elections) of £2,781.

The response was to cut back on other expenditure, and in Central Ayrshire this involved closing offices and sacking staff. By 1980, the party could not afford to replace its agent, and agreed to share with the neighbouring North Ayrshire association. Yet exactly a year later, this joint appointment was terminated because of the heavy deficit the Central Ayrshire association was carrying. The abandonment of the practice of wherever possible having an agent, which went back some 60 years, served to underline the gravity of the decline of grass-roots Conservatism, and of course to accelerate its further enfeeblement.[34] Across Scotland, the pattern was repeated. As shown below, by the 1970s election expenditure in Scotland was significantly less than in England, and no higher than Scottish Labour. In the 1970 contest, the Conservatives had agents in 60 per cent of English seats, but in only 40 per cent of Scottish seats.

The lack of financial wherewithal and a membership with low political commitment stemmed from a crucial difference between Scotland and England. In the former the organisational reforms introduced after 1945 by Sir David Maxwell-Fyfe and Lord Woolton did not apply. In particular, Scotland did not adopt the English requirement that local parties should make quite substantial contributions to central party funds. In Scotland, this local party quota was set by the Eastern District Council at 'approximately half' the English level, while the Western Council had no system whatever.[35] Only four associations out of 37 in the west contributed: Central Ayrshire's £50 was about one-third of the grand total. The central aim of the English scheme was therefore lost: substantial quota sums necessitated a large and very active membership in the constituencies, so providing a wider social background than the pre-war party, and also affording a large army at elections. These attributes Scotland signally lacked.

Hence the repeated Scottish refrain that the party workers were not very politically active, and were socially restricted. In a survey of Central Ayrshire branches in 1978, it was reported that in Dalry, 'although the committee works well on social events, there was little enthusiasm otherwise'. In the Dumfriesshire by-election of 1963, it was discovered that Dumfries burgh had not been canvassed for many years, and that no local workers would make themselves available for this work, so that canvassers had to be drafted in from Edinburgh and Glasgow.[36]

The reluctance of ordinary party members to operate in working-class housing schemes or to seek trades unionists as members became ever more apparent in this era, and contrasts sharply with the Tories' success in England. Paid missioners, usually female, were hired through party headquarters and sent into council housing estates to canvass support, but the regular membership did not participate in these recruiting drives. So the Central Ayrshire Organising Secretary suggested that a missioner be sought to 'break new ground' in the council housing areas of Garnock, because 'it would encourage the local Committee in that rather difficult area to follow up and enrol members when it was established that there was support'.[37] In the grim reading of the entrails after the 1964 election, some officials stressed that the increased use of missioners had led to a belief that there was no need for members to canvass.[38] Cathcart, revitalised in the late 1950s by Teddy Taylor and John Young, showed thereby the deficiencies existing elsewhere. A missioner had been parachuted into the vast Castlemilk council estate in the mid-1950s, visiting 360 households and reporting that there were 'a number' of Unionists there, but no follow-up effort occurred. However, the Taylor-Young regime established a Castlemilk branch in 1964 which 'a number of wives of local firemen and police officers joined', and in 1970 another housing estate, Toryglen, also had a branch.[39]

Trade unionists were not seriously wooed by the Tories until very late in the period. Efforts in the early 1950s to emulate the successful English precedent by setting up a Unionist Trade Union association met with little support among party activists. A brief experiment initiated in two Stirlingshire constituencies in 1951 was pronounced a success, but no major efforts were made to extend the scheme elsewhere. It was reported to the central administration that opinion in the constituencies was 'overwhelmingly' hostile. Not surprisingly, there were complaints in 1954 about the difficulties in distributing party literature among trade unionists.[40] Central Ayrshire Conservatives did not manage to establish a Conservative Trade Unionist section until the late 1970s, and even when formed its membership was a feeble fourteen.[41]

The efforts in the later 1960s of the party to build up support in the five New Towns illuminated the Tories' struggle to reach new social groupings. The Tories had seen the New Towns as an ideal context in which the working class, removed from their traditional, socialist-influenced environment, could be wooed away from Labour.[42] The SUA set up a special committee in 1967 to collate organisational lessons and tactics across all the New Towns. But the Conservative New Towns campaign proved unsuccessful. One common complaint was the lack of contact between Tory branches in the older parts of these communities and the rawer newly built areas. So, in Irvine, the existing branch had 'little link' with the New Town, and it was agreed by the co-ordinating committee that there was in all the New Towns no affinity of interests between the two component communities.[43] By the early 1970s the New Towns initiative was wound up by the central party, leaving Labour and the SNP to fight for mastery of these symbols of the new Scotland.

Social stasis was accompanied by low levels of interest in policy and ideology. Political education committees struggled to interest members in the party's message. In 1961, it was reported that while some constituencies in the western district still had such bodies, in many they were defunct. Efforts that year to suggest that all seats should have political debates at meetings met with a poor response.[44] Central Ayrshire showed this pattern. The branch reports for 1961 disclosed that virtually all activity was centred on social events, and although the association chairman urged that politics should resume a pivotal role, there was little real commitment to this.[45] Yet in England political study groups had been vital in building up involvement and bringing on a leadership cadre.

Cathcart was the main exception to this inertia. It is of interest because under the dynamic MP Teddy Taylor, the Tories retained the seat until 1979, by which time only one other Glasgow seat (out of 15) was Conservative, against the seven held by the party in 1955. Taylor demonstrated that it was possible to cope with the changing social complexion of a constituency, caused in this case by the injection of a large working-class vote through the building of the Castlemilk estate. Taylor's brand of demotic Toryism and the organisational skills of his local party made Cathcart the model for the rest of Scotland, offering the glimmer of an opportunity for the Scottish Tories to emulate the social and cultural adjustments which in England laid the foundations for success. Indeed, Cathcart Tories were brought to party headquarters to explain to other constituency officials how an energetic and effective organisation could flourish.

When one of the key figures, J. H. Young, joined the Cathcart party in 1962, at the age of 31, he was at once made assistant to the Treasurer, who was 80 years old and needed help to count money. The party was inactive: after six weeks on the executive, Young was 'fed up, because all they talked about was whist drives'.[46] Taylor and Young rallied the local party: new branches were opened in council schemes; by 1974 the Young Unionists numbered over 100; supper and luncheon clubs were set up to mix social and propaganda events; a 200 Club meant that funds were generated independent of large donors, several of whom had withdrawn their support when the sitting MP was elbowed aside after machinations by the new influx.[47] No other association was remotely able to match this. As we have seen, the pattern was rather that of Central Ayrshire: a genteel but quite precipitate deterioration to near-extinction.

The unbalanced basis of party membership fed through into the choice of candidates. In England after the war the Conservatives recruited MPs from the less exalted ranks of the solid and lower middle classes – Edward Heath, Reginald Maudling, Enoch Powell and Margaret Thatcher being the most prominent beneficiaries of this revolution. But this trend was almost non-existent in Scotland, where of course the Maxwell-Fyfe reforms, designed to democratise candidate selection, did not apply. The party in Scotland never fully adjusted to accepting the new class echelons as fit to fight under the party's label. Its candidates remained stubbornly upper class in an age when aristocratic and landowning characteristics were increasingly seen as contrary to the meritocratic values of the new society. The choice in both 1950 and 1951 for the intensely urban and industrial Stirling & Falkirk constituency of the local landowner, William Forbes of Callendar, was not atypical.

Scottish Tory MPs appeared more upper and middle class than their English counterparts in the 1970s. Of the 21 MPs elected in February 1974, only five had been to Scottish state schools, against 14 educated in English public schools – in fact more (six) had gone to Eton than to the entire Scottish state sector. A mere two had taken their first degree in Scotland, against 11 at Oxbridge. Only three of the 21 were in anything below upper-middle class occupations, and these were an accountant, a computer consultant and a personnel manager. There was absolutely no sign of the self-made, lower-middle-class type of MP then emerging in England. Once again, Cathcart pointed the way which no one followed: the choice of Taylor as MP was inspired – lower-middle class, a product of the Scottish state school and university systems, articulate and dynamic, with a Scottish accent (which he had to moderate when he migrated to Southend after 1979), he was far removed from the languid public school types preferred elsewhere in Scotland. When Taylor won the nomination in 1964, his rivals were an identikit parade of this outmodedness: he defeated the son of a former Lord Advocate, an Edinburgh QC with an upper-middle-class background, and the Hon. George Weir, heir to Viscount Weir and the eponymous engineering concern.[48]

Moreover, the calibre of Tory MPs declined steeply. The loss in 1958 of two MPs who had a popularity beyond narrow partisan confines was symptomatic of the trend: Walter Elliot died, while Robert Boothby became a life peer. Elliot was an irreplaceable urbane and elegant expounder of liberal Toryism. Boothby's maverick views (he opposed the Suez invasion of 1956) made him immensely popular across a wide band of opinion. His replacement at East Aberdeenshire reflected the social archaicism of the party: Patrick Wolridge-Gordon, brother to the chief of clan MacLeod, had been educated at Eton and Oxford and was a local laird. There was a feeling among the party that the quality of those offering themselves for selection was not very high, as a comment made at a West Stirlingshire party meeting in 1962 indicated. In marginal Central Ayrshire in 1967 a new candidate, Ian Lang, was selected. He was local and showed ability, although, as it was noted, he had no 'deep' political experience as yet.[49]

The problem facing the Conservatives can be seen to have two dimensions. First, the core middle class were less present in Scotland than in England, and where it was found, it had different perspectives. Secondly, the basis for working-class Toryism – Essex man and his various neolithic predecessors – was absent in Scotland.

There was lacking in Scotland a burgeoning middle class with a commitment to the values of enterprise and individualism, again unlike England. The indigenous Scottish business middle class, who had played a key role in the running of the country and in maintaining a sense of Scottish identity over two centuries, became a diminishing breed. It was this demographic feature as much as a change in the political complexion of the solid middle classes that eroded the Tories' natural support.

The managerial class was less well developed in Scotland, and moreover, much of what there was worked in the state, rather than the private sector. The nationalisation of the basic industries, on which Scotland was more reliant than England, created one difference. In addition, the greater prominence of the public sector generally in Scotland had an influence on voting behaviour. Thus, local government employment grew more rapidly in Scotland after the reform of the structure: between 1960 and 1975 local government jobs grew by 47.5 per cent, but in England by only 32.2 per cent.[50] Again, greater spending on health and social security services per capita in Scotland had an impact. The vast majority of Scots tended to use state provision rather than private: fewer children went to private schools, and with greater spending on health the attractions of privatised medicine were lower.[51] So, both as employees and customers, middle-class professionals had a greater involvement with public sector provision in Scotland.

Secondly, very few home-grown entrepreneurs emerged in the post-1945 era in Scotland: self-employed small and middling businesses were less common than in England. In England, the growth of new industries encouraged a penumbra of supply and service firms catering to the needs of the growth points, and at the same time the spread of higher living standards through several strata of society generated more demands for businesses to meet. For instance, estate agents and property and building services mushroomed to slake the aspirations of the new house-purchasing classes, whereas in Scotland, as we have seen, this trend was not nearly so prevalent. In the latter, where the old staples were in decline, there was little opportunity for small new businesses to start up. When new industries did enter Scotland, they almost invariably originated outside Scotland – frequently emanating from north America or Europe. These firms tended to have a class of international, highly mobile managers who would move in with their corporation and move out again after a spell of duty: Scots tended not to be dominant in the managerial cadres of these multinationals. Between 1939 and 1964, immigrants to Scotland were overrepresented in the professional and management sectors, and significantly underrepresented among manual workers.[52]

There was a distinct lack of employers and self-employed people in Scotland, the sort of class who formed the backbone of English Conservatism, and most significantly, the adverse gap was widening:

Table 4.2 Employers and self-employed as a percentage of employees in employment, Scotland and the United Kingdom, 1966–74

	1966	1970	1974
Scotland	6.4	6.7	6.6
UK	7.2	8.5	8.4

Source: *Scottish Economic Bulletin*, 13 (1977), table 4, p. 32.

A later study pinpointed Scotland as underperforming in the creation of new firms by about 36 per cent below the British average, a shortfall primarily ascribed to the lack of an entrepreneurial infrastructure, with the loss of Scottish potential business people to England cited as a key element.[53]

Emigration, a recurring feature of Scottish demography in these years, may also have discriminated harshly against the Conservatives. It is likely that those who left the country included a large number with skills, professional and technical, who realised that there was little scope at home for career development; while many with entrepreneurial abilities would look elsewhere for opportunities. A larger than proportionate share of all men emigrating to Canada in 1965–6 and 1975–6 were in the professional and higher managerial ranks.[54] Forty-four per cent of Scottish-born university students graduating between 1966 and 1969 left the country to find work, nine out of ten of these relocating within the United Kingdom.[55] It is notable that in the post-1945 era several Scots Tories sat for English constituencies, most with modest middle-class backgrounds, as distinct from the more upper-middle class origins of Conservative MPs in Scotland itself, e.g., John MacGregor, a chartered accountant, Robert McCrindle, an engineer, and David Knox, a print manager. These men are different from the refugees who flooded south in the 1980s under the impact of Scotland's vigorous repudiation of Thatcherite Conservatism. The first group had settled in England and emerged, so to speak, from their grass-roots involvement in politics.

Social change moved at a slower pace in Scotland compared to England in this period, especially in the working class. There was no equivalent in scale to the workers in the motor and other newer industries who seemed to provide a new base of Conservative support by rejecting the instinctive class-based voting of previous generations. On the whole, the Scottish working class remained more tied to the traditional heavy industries and their ancillary sectors. The trappings of affluence penetrated Scotland later and less thoroughly than England: holidays abroad, car ownership, consumer durables – all these touchstones of the newer working class, with their concomitant implications for voting behaviour, were less prominent.[56] After attending a Labour Party function in West Lothian in 1965, the cabinet minister and MP for Coventry, R. H. S. Crossman, reflected on the contrast:

> Looking down from the platform on this audience, I realised it was exactly the same audience I addressed in Coventry when I first went there as a candidate in 1936. But under the pressure of affluence Coventry Labour has changed whereas Scottish Labour remains much the same as thirty years ago – this is one of the reasons why it is so much more reliable and easy to manage than Labour Parties in the South. Sophistication has undermined the solidarity and the simplicity of Midland Labour Parties, whereas in Scotland one can make the old traditional speeches and the audiences are content to sing the old traditional songs which Coventry would laugh out of court.[57]

Most distinctive of all, of course, was the lower level of house-owner-ship among the Scottish working class. As noted earlier, public sector rented housing was the norm for the vast bulk of Scots families: in 1974, 54 per cent of Scottish housing was public sector-owned; in England, only 29 per cent was. The implications of this for community identity, class solidarity and political identification are readily apparent and not bene-ficial to the Conservatives: it has become a psephological truism that type of house occupancy is an even better vote predictor than class. Equally relevantly, home ownership and the start-up of small firms are intimately linked, as property is frequently used as security for loans to start up in business.[58]

III

On the surface, the revival of the Liberals in Scotland in the 1960s mir-rored the simultaneous successes of the party in England, initiating a long period of erratic but generally positive return to electoral signific-ance. But there were differences in Scotland. First, the expansion was short-lived: by 1970 four of the six seats gained in the 1964–6 surge had been lost. While English Liberalism sustained similar reverses, the difference was that in Scotland there was no resurgence in the 1970s. Secondly, Liberals in Scotland tended to do well in different sorts of seats: there was no headway in suburban, middle-class seats over these years – the protesting commuter was not a Scottish phenomenon. The Scottish party performed creditably in seats which had a strong recent tradition of Liberal (even if sometimes National Liberal) representation, most of which were rural outlying constituencies. Here the decision by the Tories from the 1964 general election to drop all 'National Liberal' etc. trappings, and instead stand as Conservatives pure and simple, could well have boosted the Liberal recovery in these very areas. Elsewhere the party remained dormant and was unable to galvanise support: this was especially the case in the western Lowlands, where the party had been virtually extinguished soon after 1918.[59]

As well as historic traditions, however, the Liberals' advance was per-haps assisted by other factors. First, there was much discontent in the remoter parts with the Conservative government's policies, as it was felt their economic and social well-being was being neglected, for reasons already discussed. Thus, the Conservative MP for Caithness & Suther-land, Sir David Robertson, resigned the party whip in 1959 in protest at the plight of his constituency. The Tories ascribed the Liberal inroads in the Highland area in the mid-1960s to the latter's production of a plan for the regeneration of the Highlands and Islands region. This gained much support in the area, 'where there is a built-in feeling of regret', as the Tories rather sourly commented.[60]

The party's growth was frequently impressive but febrile: in Kincardineshire (nearly a Liberal win in 1945), the party's association had been moribund from 1952 until about 1961. Then its membership soared from 600 to 2,600 in three years, closely rivalling the constituency Conservative Association. The Liberals attracted over one third of the poll in the 1964 election. Equally precipitate was the subsequent downturn: in the 1970 election, the candidate, despite being Jo Grimond's son, came fourth, losing his deposit, after a slipshod campaign in which he had only a handful of party workers. By 1972, the Kincardineshire Liberal Party had shrunk to about 50 members.[61]

The Liberal Party itself had changed: the pre-war group of upper-class long-standing Liberals – the Glen-Coats, Aberdeen, Lamont and Cowdray types – had either died or moved across to the Conservatives. Although the Grimond clan kept the links with Asquith–Tennant line of grandees, a new type of Liberal was emerging, usually from more modest middle-class occupations – David Steel's father was a clergyman, Russell Johnston was a schoolteacher, Alasdair MacKenzie and George Mackie were both farmers. The claim sometimes made that the Liberals failed in Scotland in the later 1960s because they were perceived as too English seems hard to sustain.

The party was unable to establish a broad base in local government which other parties found indispensable for sustained political growth, and which gave English Liberals a springboard for parliamentary success in many places. In most of the constituencies where the Scottish Liberals notched up Westminster representation, there was a long tradition of non-partisan local government. Although even in the Highlands and the Borders Labour fought under its own flag, the term 'Independent' was borne by councillors who were otherwise openly Conservative or Liberal (it should be added that there was the odd genuine non-party independent). The most glaring instance of this was John M. Bannerman, the leader of the Scottish Liberals, who served on Stirling County Council as an Independent. It is significant that Greenock, a perennial Liberal prospect, was virtually the only town with a bloc of Liberal councillors. The SNP fought under their own colours, and this may well have been a factor in their greater success in this era.

Again, outside of the core Liberal areas, where the party had a long-standing presence and identity, the misfortune of the Liberals was to be identified too closely with the Tories, or to have no recent profile in electoral terms. As the Unionists declined in favour so the Liberals were also tarred – this would be applicable to urban seats like Dundee and Paisley, where deals had long been done between the two, and where disgruntled voters turned instead to the SNP. Perhaps the other causes for the party's retreat were policy-related. As already noted, Liberals were whole-hearted proponents of entry into the EEC, and as this became clearer to voters it may have damaged them – and benefited the nationalists, as noted above. Also, the party was less interested in pushing for Scottish Home Rule in the 1960s, as it found other issues to stress. The newer figures in the party seemed less eager to emphasise this issue than the previous generation: John Bannerman looked at times to be a Home Ruler who happened to be a Liberal rather than vice versa. But endeavours to reach an electoral accommodation with the SNP around 1964–6 foundered on the opposition of Russell Johnston and George Mackie. This was a catastrophic decision, and perhaps reinforces the impression of the isolation of the Liberals from the political context of central urban Scotland.

IV

The Liberals' back-pedalling on devolution for Scotland proved tactically inept, since the major beneficiary after 1966 from disaffection with the two main parties proved to be not the Liberals but the Scottish National Party, hitherto little more than an engagingly eccentric fringe party with few serious electoral pretensions. The dramatic electoral triumphs achieved by the SNP were matched by a spectacular organisational expansion. The number of branches rose from 40 in 1962 to nearly 500 in 1968, while party membership, up in the same period from 2,000 to 120,000, comfortably exceeded that of Labour.

It would appear that the support garnered by the SNP came from a mixture of sources. A degree of support at by-elections undoubtedly came from protest-voting, with the poll at subsequent general elections falling sharply back, as in Hamilton in 1970 and Govan in 1974. But the SNP vote at general elections was not heavily dependent on this. The success or near-success of the Nationalist challenge was not usually based on a decline in the vote of the party holding the seat; most notably the Tory vote held pretty firm in their seats in 1974. Moreover, since much of the backing for the SNP came from younger, often first-time, voters, this cannot fit the protest-vote model, which is predicated on a revolt by long-standing partisan electors.

It seems probable that the increase of votes between the two 1974 elections owed something to tactical voting, as supporters of other parties swung behind the SNP as the second party in constituencies. This trend was more pronounced among Labour than Tory voters; in February 1974, the largest swings in all of Britain away from Labour occurred in about half a dozen seats where the SNP prospered mightily. Similarly, Liberals appeared to turn to the nationalists to oust the party in control. With this reinforcement, the SNP toppled sitting MPs in some seats and elsewhere positioned itself very handily for one more push to victory at a forthcoming contest.[62] By 1979, many tactical voters, it would seem, reverted to their 'natural' party, arguably in dismay at the SNP's conduct either in propping up Labour or in bringing down the Callaghan ministry and so risking a Conservative government, depending on the tactical voter's real partisan proclivity. Certainly in its 1979 campaign guide, Labour emphasised this, pointing out that in parliament the Nationalists had voted with the Tories against the 1978 Budget to protect the wealthy. Labour further alleged that while in Clydeside the SNP had loudly supported the Upper Clyde Shipyard workers' bid to keep their jobs, in Westminster Nationalist MPs had torn up telegrams from the shop-stewards urging backing for legislation to nationalise shipyards and so protect employment.[63]

Yet this does not explain why the SNP was seen as the third party, instead of the Liberals, who had achieved that status in the earlier 1960s. The electoral relationship between the two parties was intriguing: in February 1974, the Nationalist vote rose by 18.6 per cent where no Liberal stood, but by only 4.8 per cent where they both ran. In 1979, as the SNP collapsed, the Liberals in Scotland experienced a 3.6 per cent rise, against a 5.3 per cent drop in England and Wales.

In most Nationalist strongholds there was only an emaciated Liberal presence before or after the Nationalists' high peak: Argyllshire is perhaps the sole exception. The SNP could not dent the Liberals in the mainland Highland seats, while the Liberals had long failed in the Western Isles. The south-eastern borders, where David Steel was secure, resisted the Nationalists. But the SNP prospered in the eastern agricultural belt running from Nairnshire to the upper Forth, and in urban-industrial areas in the Scottish midlands, particularly around Stirlingshire – much of this being terrain which the Liberals had rarely contested regularly in the decade or so before 1974. The stance of the SNP as a radical, but not overtly socialist, party probably tapped in to the traditional political leanings of the rural Lowlands which had lain inert since the disintegration of the Liberals, and which Labour had never managed to relate to. Further, the cry of a vote for the Nationalists being a 'Vote for Scotland' was compelling, and did not require any broader ideological commitment. To many only peripherally engaged in politics, this appeal to Scottish identity was sufficient cause. However, it reiterated the shallow level of engagement with SNP philosophy and strategy.

But significant though these components may be, they do not explain all of the support given to the Nationalists. The SNP finally managed to persuade many who saw themselves as Scottish to perceive independence as the best means of preserving and promoting Scottish identity. Two reasons may be adduced to account for this upsurge in Scottish consciousness. Some new element may have occurred to make it sharper, or an existing feeling may have been redirected from other parties. There is no obvious explanation for a heightening of Scottish identity in the middle 1960s and after. It seems clear that a strong feeling of Scottishness had long existed among people of every and no political complexion. There was no major literary, artistic or linguistic nationalist tide to stimulate these feelings in the 1960s and 1970s. After all, the cultural 'Scottish Renaissance' of the 1920s had not galvanised the Scots to support nationalism, and the movements of the 1960s were arguably less impressive artistically – indeed many of those involved were much less committed to the concept of independence. In any case, the SNP of the 1960s tended not to emphasise this aspect, and pitched its appeal to other quarters.

The end of Empire is occasionally highlighted as a motivating force: no longer able to play a part in a large world power, Scots did not wish to stay with the diminished British state after the withdrawal from the Indian sub-continent and the African colonies, a process virtually complete by the early 1960s. The chronology is difficult here. In reality, it was the white dominions with which Scots identified – mainly because so many had relatives there as a result of continuing emigration. But the dominions had enjoyed a high degree of self-government since the 1920s. The retreat from Africa and Asia after 1945 evoked little protest in Scotland at the dissolution of the Empire: indeed, the Church of Scotland criticised the government for not ceding independence in Central Africa sooner. It is striking that in the 1945 election, the manifestos of Scottish

Tory candidates referred much less frequently than English counter-parts to the Empire – or indeed to defence and foreign policy generally. It will be remembered that, relatively, the Tories in Scotland outper-formed those in England in 1945, so imperialistic feelings cannot have been pertinent. Scottish Labour candidates were also less inclined to men-tion the empire, and cognate policy areas, than their English comrades.[64]

Perhaps a more weighty ingredient was the loss of faith by the later 1960s and early 1970s in the ability of the two Westminster-focused par-ties to deliver economic and social policy benefits. Neither party when in office had succeeded in bringing demonstrable gains: Labour's applica-tion between 1964 and 1970 of its much-vaunted planning apparatus could not avert rising unemployment, steady emigration and the per-petuation of acute social problems. The succeeding Conservative admin-istration presided over the symbolic collapse of the Clyde shipbuilding industry and incipient troubles in the vehicle-making sector lured (or rather pushed) north in the 1960s.

In these circumstances, the SNP was able to galvanise this unease, especially when the world price of oil rose nearly fourfold after the Arab–Israeli conflict in 1972. The SNP skilfully argued that the North Sea oil revenues should be applied not to Britain as a whole, but should be treated as under the sole proprietorship of Scotland, in whose waters the finds lay. By using the huge predicted revenues, the Nationalists contended, the serious economic and social problems of Scotland, which the two unionist parties had laboured so long and so vainly to address, could be swept aside and a new, prosperous footing provided. The oil issue thus allowed the Nationalists to position themselves as the guar-antors of the maintenance of the Welfare State and full employment, just at the time when Labour's traditional pretensions to this role seemed highly questionable.

The SNP's skilful advertising and propaganda work on North Sea oil clearly struck a response from those disillusioned with Labour and the Tories. Equally significantly, it gave the Nationalists a far more positive and concrete appeal than the alternative third party, the Liberals, as only with outright independence, it was argued, could Scotland expect to reap the full benefits of oil.[65] Additionally, it allowed the party to acquire an image of credibility and economic competence, shaking off any remnants of its past representation as a colourful but impractical body. It is perhaps significant that the SNP tended to do better on the eastern side of the country, where there would be a greater appreciation of the oil potential.

However, the economics of nationalism are not a fully comprehensive explanation of the party's advance: in the most depressed and deprived areas, where one might expect the 'Oil plus Independence' argument to make headway, the SNP stalled in the 1974 elections. In the industrial Lowlands Labour retained most seats and only occasionally looked vulnerable to the Nationalists. The seats where the SNP had most success here were those where appreciable social changes had occurred: for example, East Dunbartonshire, which included the new town of Cumbernauld, and the three Stirlingshire seats. In these areas two processes were at work: the traditional industrial bases – primarily coal – were almost extinguished, and a population influx had also taken place. The result was the erosion of the bedrock working-class communities on which Labour relied for support, and the emergence of both a new working class and of first-generation white-collar and lower professional groupings. All of these had moved from the solid working-class regions of old Labour support: the very act of so doing constituted for many a break with the past traditions. These were usually younger people, and it squares well with the high amount of support among the under 35s and those in the intermediate social classes which the SNP seemed to win in 1974.[66]

Linked to the social groups who turned to the SNP were the important organisational skills deployed by the party. The party applied sophisticated techniques of propaganda and electioneering derived in part from North America. Posters and party political broadcasts were bright and snappy, where the other parties seemed stuffy and old-fashioned: at a simple level, the party's logo was much more recognisable and understandable than either the Conservative or Labour efforts. The SNP introduced up-to-date methods at election time, such as the noisy motor cavalcade winding through every part of the constituency, and quick flesh-pressing tours of selected areas to derive maximum publicity for candidates instead of formal meetings. The choice of young, articulate candidates who were usually rather classless added a new tone to Scottish politics.[67] The prominence of impressive, forceful women – especially Winifred Ewing and Margo MacDonald – lent a distinctive modern image to the Nationalists, as none of the other parties then had much of a female presence at the top. The SNP injected a sense of fun, novelty and drive into the contests in 1974 and many electors responded positively.[68]

Yet given these positive forces flowing with the SNP in the early and middle 1970s, the subsequent decline of the party in the latter years of the decade is perplexing, especially as the economic condition of Britain, which had been acute in 1974, seemed nearly terminal by 1979. North

Sea oil, now in full production, should have been an even more compelling card to play than in 1974.

One reason for the retreat of the Nationalists may be that, once elected, they seemed to lack expertise and political sophistication. In local government, whether holding power or as the main opposition party, the SNP frequently proved inept and incompetent. Many of the party's candidates were recent recruits with no background experience: 57 per cent of parliamentary candidates in 1970 had been members for less than five years. Internal rows and faction-fighting broke out, with a spectacular episode, worthy of the Labour Party in its bitterness, taking place at Cumbernauld. In parliament, the SNP leaders were neither dynamic national spokespersons (in one survey, a majority of SNP voters could not identify the Nationalists' leader) nor adroit Westminster operators, as the party's conduct after the defeat of the devolution referendum indicated. The parliamentarians sent out muddled signals: they included some who were social democrats and others with Thatcherite leanings.

Worst of all, on the central plank of party policy – independence – there was disagreement: some were essentially Home Rulers, whereas others were whole-hog for independence. Labour's proposed devolution legislation deepened these chasms. While it was a straightforward task to demonstrate the benefits of North Sea oil, arguing the superior benefits of independence to Home Rule was more complex. Public opinion polls indicated that only about 20 per cent of Scots wanted outright independence, so intensifying the obstacles faced by the SNP. Whereas a number of the party's MPs were ready to assist Labour's legislative proposals, the dedicated rank and file activists were prone to reject halfway houses as a dilution of and distraction from the true aims of the movement. Hence between 1976 and 1979 the cohesion of the Nationalists became increasingly ragged.

If the electorate were confused by these conflicting messages, so were the SNP's grass-roots. On several occasions, the party activists felt themselves at variance with the MPs both on policy and on tactics. This was compounded by the lack of membership overlap between the parliamentary group and the national executive (usually only one MP sat on the twelve-strong executive), so that co-ordinated responses were often absent. As a result, disillusion set in not only among voters but also among the SNP membership.[69]

The SNP suffered from not having any permanent institutional backing which would ensure funding, personnel and continuity, as well as indirect influence. Labour had the unions; the Tories had business. The Nationalists were obliged to rely on the enthusiasm of party members, and when these faltered, the party was bereft. Indeed, there were central tensions in the SNP's organisational expansion, which were gradually unravelled as the 1970s progressed. For one thing, many members were little more than paper adherents. A survey in 1973 indicated that two-thirds of branches had not paid their dues to the centre, and that at best only 5 per cent of the enrolled membership were active.[70] Two studies of the party in the north-east, its stronghold, confirmed that only a handful of the members engaged in regular political work. Moreover, there was little discussion of political affairs at meetings, so that as the SNP leadership developed positions on a range of matters, friction and dissension was inevitable.[71] The support won from the younger groups in the electorate may not have been a long-term maturing strength. These are probably the most volatile sections of the electorate. Many of these voters, along with the protest and tactical voting contingent, may well not have agreed with the Nationalists' key demand for independence, and as this issue gained in saliency after 1974, may have switched parties in 1979. Surveys suggested that as much as two-thirds of SNP voters did not approve of independence. Nationalist voters felt least close of all in identifying with the party they voted for, again indicating a febrile and mercurial attachment: only 25 per cent of SNP voters saw themselves as 'SNP', while 41 per cent still identified with 'Labour' and 31 per cent with 'Conservative'.[72] Furthermore, while the approach to political campaigning identified with the SNP was undoubtedly fresh in the early 1970s, by the end of the decade it no longer looked novel, as the other parties borrowed from, and indeed extended beyond, the SNP's ploys.

It is significant in this connection that the downturn in the fortunes of the SNP came well before the 1979 general election. Three decisive by-elections in 1978 illuminated this: perhaps the most significant result was at Hamilton, where in 1968 the Nationalist breakthrough had occurred. Now, even with the most charismatic SNP politician, Margo MacDonald, as candidate, Labour won quite comfortably. The first of these by-elections, at Glasgow Garscadden in April, set the tone. Labour attacked the SNP unrelentingly over its independence policy and this seemed to turn round what had initially been regarded as a certain SNP triumph. In October, the SNP was routed in Berwickshire & East Lothian, a semi-rural Labour-held seat which shortly before would have been viewed as a prime Nationalist target. In the May 1978 regional council elections, the Nationalists were also in retreat, sustaining a fall of nearly

25 per cent in the popular vote in seats fought in the previous elections held in 1974. But in the district council elections of May 1977, the SNP's support had still been pretty much at the levels reached in 1974.

The decline of the SNP is clearly related, as is discussed below, to the regrouping exercise carried out by Labour. The idea that the loss of support for the Nationalists was connected with the failings of the Scottish team in the football World Cup in 1978 is surely unfounded. The erosion of the SNP's position had begun before the humiliation on the football field. In any event, the working-class west-central male, the archetypal Scottish football supporter, was the social segment whom the Nationalists had made least headway with. The areas of major SNP electoral impact were not great footballing territories. Additionally, following football was primarily a male pastime, yet the fall in women backing the SNP was more pronounced than men by 1979.

Given these open pointers to a dwindling of electoral support, the decision of the SNP to precipitate a dissolution in early 1979 is all the more bewildering, and set the seal on the Nationalists' collapse. The backing of the Conservatives' No Confidence vote also compounded the sense of a party out of its depth, for it was clear that an election held in spring 1979 could only produce a Tory government, so pushing the prospect of any measure of Scottish self-government further away.

V

From the end of the 1950s until the late 1960s Labour had prospered in Scotland by portraying itself as the party both of promoting economic development, so guaranteeing high levels of employment, and of defending the Welfare State. However, this was followed by a protracted period of intense disquiet and internal incoherence, caused by a blend of policy failure, organisational decay and a sclerotic adjustment to rapid social and cultural changes. But the 1978 by-elections heralded the recovery of Labour, as the party more or less simultaneously re-established its policy credentials, modulated its institutional and social supports to meet new circumstances, and revamped its organisation. The outcome was a confident party which in the 1979 election recovered – and indeed advanced – on ground lost between 1967 and 1977.

The most apparent reason for the party's faltering performance in the decade after the mid-1960s was the loss of confidence among voters in

Labour's capacity to bring about the much-promised improvement in economic and social conditions. These were the same factors which had lost the Tories support in the previous decade. The damage inflicted on Labour's overall growth strategy by the devaluation of 1967 had a serious impact in Scotland, where government cutbacks and the abandonment of expansion were felt very severely, an adverse impact compounded by the imposition of wages limitation and the threat of legal curbs on trades union powers. Glasgow Labour Party remarked on the downturn in receipts from trade unions' political levy fees in 1968, caused by 'discontent with some of Labour's policies, particularly Prices and Incomes Policy'.[73] Even though it is possible now to note that some progress was made in boosting jobs in modern industries and in attracting overseas investment, by the yardstick of the expectations aroused by the party before 1964 these seemed inadequate. Again, the failure to eliminate inadequate social provision at the end of six years of Labour administration made the party's early mockery of Conservative indifference look like a double-standard. This loss of credibility was still apparent in the 1974 elections when, as discussed above, the SNP's cry of 'It's Scotland's oil' struck home because it apparently carried a more realisable opportunity for economic recovery and social improvement than Labour's approach.

A fundamental pillar of Labour's appeal from the 1930s had been its effectiveness in local government, primarily in building council houses. But by the later 1960s, Labour's municipal image grew to appear negative, while social change, often initiated ironically by housing improvements, also had an adverse impact. For too long in too many places the party had enjoyed a monopoly of office: Labour had controlled Glasgow uninterruptedly, apart from a single brief interlude, from 1933 until 1968. A number of cases of corruption, nepotism and favouritism among Labour councillors came to light, resulting in prosecutions and adverse publicity in the later 1960s and 1970s.

In the older compact working-class communities there had been a natural Labour culture, associated with the workplace, trade union branches and working-class social and leisure activities. In the new council housing schemes, this framework of almost automatic Labour identification was weakened, and the network of party connections diluted – as noted above, the New Towns represented this trend in a pronounced degree, and proved fertile recruiting ground for the Nationalists. Establishing new bonds was much less straightforward for Labour.

The result of these factors was that in the later 1960s the Labour Party no longer seemed impregnable in town and county halls. The loss of control of Glasgow in 1968 was an exceptionally severe blow. The first council elections, held in 1974 after the reorganisation of local government act of 1972, confirmed the weakness of Labour: it performed badly in several traditional strongholds, controlling only Fife and Strathclyde regions.

A further index of the disintegration of Labour's long-settled culture was the decline of the Co-operative movement's political and social wings, which paralleled the enfeeblement of the retailing side in the face of competition from multiple stores and supermarkets. The men's and women's guilds were less numerous and, where they survived, less active. By 1955 the male version was almost extinct, with 600 members across Scotland. The Women's Guild was more successful, but at 28,000 in 1955, it had been reduced by one-third from its 1947 level, and in 1975 had only 290 branches, against over 500 twenty years before. The range of activities had narrowed: Co-operative music festivals, drama clubs, sports societies, still well supported in the 1950s, were folding everywhere in the 1970s. The Scottish movement's journal, the *Scottish Co-operator*, closed in 1974. The impact of the break-up of the old communities was partly to blame: very few new branches were established in the new council estates or in the New Towns; partly too, they were a victim of changing economic and social patterns, especially among the younger age group. The Women's Guild stressed the rise of the working mother as a cause of dwindling involvement.[74]

Associated with these difficulties on a range of fronts, the organisational strength of Labour had been badly sapped in the 1960s and early 1970s. As Scotland's constituency activity had always been lower than in England, this meant in some places the near-demise of any grass-roots activism. The party's fortunes in Glasgow, its heartland, may be taken as typical. Here individual membership, never very numerous, fell steeply. In 1952, 5,200 new members were enrolled in the party across the 15 constituencies in the city, thereby doubling the total membership. Attempts to stimulate membership served only to highlight how precarious the position was. After several years of trying to raise finance and promote interest among members in a social club, which would yield revenue from the bar and provide a venue for activists, the Glasgow Labour Party executive abandoned the enterprise in 1968. Equally disastrous was a bid in 1967 to generate cash by running a monthly prize draw in Glasgow: the venture was an abject failure, despite all executive members being urged to recruit strenuously: 'The result: *almost total failure*. In the whole city of Glasgow only FOUR persons have been recruited by and for the City Labour Party' – this in a city where nearly 275,000 people had voted Labour in the 1966 general election.[75] So dilapidated was Glasgow Labour that in 1969 – when the average constituency membership was 120 – the London headquarters ordered its disbandment. The loss of Govan in the 1973 by-election was ascribed as much to threadbare organisation as to policy discontent.

In Scotland in February 1974 there were seven Labour agents, in England, 131, a ratio to seats of respectively 1:10.1 and 1:3.9. At the head office in Glasgow, administration was creaking: in the February 1974 general election, no distinctively Scottish literature was produced to challenge the Nationalists' propaganda; instead material was brought up from London. There was no Scottish party research officer until the summer of 1974. The Scottish executive itself explained that headquarters had been too preoccupied with the first reformed local government elections to focus adequately on the snap February 1974 parliamentary election.

The reassertion of Labour's electoral position came, just as with its weakening, from a complex interaction of causes. To a degree, as we have seen, the loss of focus on the part of other parties in the middle 1970s was a bonus. At the core, nevertheless, was the restoration of the party's reputation as defender of the Welfare State and the promoter of economic and social improvement. But first, the constitutional question, on which in the later 1960s the party's stance was perceived to be electorally highly negative, had to be addressed.

When the first wave of SNP support came in the later 1960s, Labour had for nearly 20 years been indifferent to any commitment to Home Rule. It had been a core demand in the first quarter of the twentieth century, but after this it was eclipsed by the belief in a centralised command economy as the means to achieving socialism. Labour's drift from Home Rule was facilitated by the evident lack of reprisals exacted by the electors for not implementing declared policies. As noted before, 1950 and 1951 did not suggest voter revenge on Labour for dropping its 1945 pronouncements. By 1958, the party had formally abandoned even a nominal commitment to Home Rule.

Two forces conspired to change this. Labour thinkers in Scotland started to press for devolution as desirable in its own right, irrespective of political tactics. The publication of J. P. Mackintosh's *The Devolution of Power*, which appeared in 1968, was a seminal event in this rediscovery. He incisively linked the increased concern at the inability of Westminster to deal adequately with the specific needs of Scotland to the desire for greater democratic control of the executive. By the early 1970s these ideas had been taken up by the rising generation of modernising Labour figures in Scotland: most notably, John Smith, Jim Sillars, Harry Ewing and Gordon Brown.

This intellectual reorientation was intensified by the political exigencies faced by Labour at the end of the 1960s, and specifically, the need to respond to the Nationalist momentum, which seemed to pose a massive threat to Labour's Scottish support. Harold Wilson's reaction to the loss of Hamilton and the mounting defeats in local government was to defuse the issue by setting up the Kilbrandon (originally Crowther) Commission to investigate the case for self-government. If, as many suspected, Wilson hoped the whole question would disappear, the publication of the Kilbrandon report could not have been less timely for him, coming as it did on the eve of the 1974 elections, and substantially endorsing the case for devolution.

Initially, the *ancien régime* of Labour leaders in Scotland, most prominently Willie Ross, the Scottish Secretary, had remained determined not to budge from outright resistance to any degree of self-government.But the STUC had long championed devolution, and since 1968 had been advocating it with increased vigour. At a special Labour Party conference in summer 1974, the union leaders, notably Alex Kitson and Gavin Laird, acted to induce a somewhat reluctant Scottish party to revive Home Rule as party policy, so that by the October election the party had moved, however grudgingly, to embrace devolution.

The first attempt to frame a devolution scheme was produced by the government in 1976, but it was not well received in Scotland, as it was deemed not radical enough. The second effort, as noted, seemed to do the trick. Having outlined their devolution proposals, Labour responded to survey findings which suggested only a part of the Nationalist voters endorsed outright independence. Party propaganda from publication of the second White Paper until the general election highlighted the SNP's independence policy. As noted above, Labour's victory at Glasgow Garscadden owed much to the stress placed by the Labour candidate, Donald Dewar, on this. Under this further assault, support for the Nationalists fell away steadily.

The settling of the Assembly question coincided with an upturn in Labour's poll ratings across Britain. This seems related to an improvement in economic and social circumstances for many working-class voters as much as to the resolution of constitutional problems. To a considerable degree, the Labour governments of 1974–9 were more effective than their predecessors in the 1960s in delivering economic and social dividends. State subsidies kept the ailing heavy industry sector tottering on: Scottish shipbuilding, steel and coal survived. The car plant at Linwood was also underwritten by the government to stave off closure. The continuing inflow of multinational branch plants encouraged the view that the diversification of the Scottish economy was well in train. Labour hailed the creation of the Scottish Development Agency in 1975 as a major factor in this process. By the time of the defeat of James Callaghan's government in 1979, differentials in pay and employment levels between Scotland and England had narrowed. In addition, expenditure on welfare had on the whole been protected: in particular, on the all-important matter of housing, rents were reduced in real terms between 1973 and 1977, and the 1972 Housing Act had been scrapped. As the result of a Labour drive in the mid-1970s, Scotland had a higher ratio of hospital beds than England.[76]

Thus Labour was able to build on this return to bread and butter issues which were highly potent vote-winners and on which it was traditionally stronger and more appealing. The Nuffield 1979 general election survey notes that the campaign, unlike October 1974, had little of a distinctively Scottish agenda, for instead the key issues were unemployment, trade unions and the economy.[77]

As significant as the social and economic amelioration contrived by Labour was the medium through which these were generated. So, many of the new jobs established in the 1970s were in public-sector employment. Local government reorganisation spawned a multiplicity of additional posts. In Scotland, council employment rose by 29.8 per cent between 1971 and 1975, against 13.8 per cent in England.[78] By the later 1970s it was Labour local administrations who were presiding over this expansion. Also, with the Conservatives committed to reducing public expenditure, it seemed highly likely that these new state jobs would disappear. Therefore there was a strong vested interest in these voters seeking to perpetuate Labour in office in Westminster. It is not unfeasible to surmise that the significant growth in Labour's middle-class vote in 1979 (it grew from one-fifth to one-quarter of the class) was drawn from public sector managerial employees.[79] What is incontrovertible are the exceptionally close ties between public employment and Labour party activists: 52 per cent of Glasgow councillors worked in the public sector, whereas the figure for all British councillors came to only 36 per cent.[80]

The reconstruction of Labour in the 1970s was also dependent on the public sector employment phenomenon in another way. The adhesion of such trade unions to the Labour Party in this decade enabled Labour to recover its organisational vitality. Table 4.3a reveals the changing balance of trade union involvement in the Labour Party. The increase in affiliations in the 1970s was especially marked, easily compensating for the diminution in the traditional heavy industries. Between 1952 and 1969, total union membership affiliations to Labour rose by 23.7 per cent – an annual rate of about 1.4 per cent – but between 1969 and 1978, the increase was twice as fast at 3.0 per cent per annum – or 26.8 per cent in total. The vast bulk of the surge in the latter period came from unions either mostly recruiting among public sector workers or in white-collar occupations. The only traditional unions to rise were the Engineers and the Boilermakers.

The end of the 1960s saw the union movement somewhat disenchanted with Labour, but gradually a rapprochement was arrived at. The industrial relations and economic policies of the 1970–4 Conservative administration pushed the unions back to Labour, and the subsequent Labour governments did much to reassure and indeed enhance the status of unions. But between 1974 and 1977, with Labour adopting a policy on devolution in alignment with the STUC viewpoint, and then legislating for self-government, a further area of discord was removed. The rise of the SNP additionally pushed the unions to back Labour wholeheartedly, as they overwhelmingly rejected any flirting with outright independence. Lastly, the STUC's efforts in 1970–4 to forge a stand independent of Labour came to rapid grief: the assembly on unemployment summoned by Congress was bedevilled by faction-fighting. The STUC's call for resistance to the 1972 Tory Housing Act was largely ignored by the Scottish people and local government authorities, so the unions were compelled to acknowledge that only by working with and through Labour would reforms be effected.

From the mid-1970s, the annual reports by the Executive of the Labour Party in Scotland are particularly replete with references to the

Table 4.3a Trade union affiliations to the Labour Party in Scotland, 1952 and 1978

	1952		1978		% Change
	No.	%	No.	%	
Heavy Ind.	217,386	45.9	234,191	32.5	+ 7.7
Pub./Non-Manual	179,015	37.8	444,057	61.6	+ 248.1

Note: 'Heavy Ind.' comprises: Engineers, Boilermakers, Railwaymen, Miners, Foundry Workers, Iron & Steel and Textile unions.
　　　　'Pub./ Non-Manual' comprises: Public Employees Union, Transport Workers, General and Municipal Workers, Scientific and Technical, Shop Assistants, Health Workers and Clerical unions.

Table 4.3b Increases and decreases in union affiliations to the Labour Party in Scotland, 1969–78

	Increase			Decrease	
	No.	%		No.	%
NUPE	41,000	178.3	NUM	6,830	29.1
GMWU	39,000	59.1	EETPU	3,467	8.0
ASTMS	27,183	263.4	NUR	3,288	16.5
TGWU	26,000	23.2	Scot. Carpet Weavers	2,797	41.4
USDAW	17,387	39.2	ISTC	1,941	16.7
COHSE	9,326	69.7	NU Sheet Metal Workers	1,400	23.3
Total	159,896		Total	19,723	

close co-operation with and support offered by the STUC, including day-to-day contact and regular liaison meetings. Each had representatives on the other's working parties in order to minimise areas of discord; one result being a joint approach by the STUC and the Scottish Labour Party Council to the trade union group of MPs to discuss devolution. With individual unions, Labour claimed that by 1977 there was a realisation on both sides that they should collaborate to spread the political message widely. These processes climaxed in the 1979 election, when the party reported that unions with offices near Labour's Glasgow HQ – notably ASTMS and GMWU – gave clerical assistance during the campaign. The Transport & General Workers' Union distributed a broadsheet to its members urging them to vote Labour, while the Confederation of Shipbuilding Unions arranged for a government minister to address a mass meeting of shop-stewards. The STUC itself assisted with the production and distribution of leaflets, and several unions agreed to have their full-time officers placed in key constituencies for the duration of the election to work for Labour.[81]

In the midst of social fluidity, a long-standing pillar of Labour's electoral power remained relatively aloof from the surrounding changes. The Roman Catholic Irish community showed persisting commitment to the party. All voting surveys confirmed that those most impervious to the SNP were Roman Catholics, while Protestants were strongly Nationalist: in February 1974 7 per cent of the former and 48 per cent of the latter voted SNP.[82] This was of particular import because the Catholic Church was shedding adherents more slowly than the Church of Scotland, whose membership was historically more Tory-disposed, so that by the mid-1970s the two churches were becoming quite comparable in size.[83] The role of Roman Catholics in the Labour Party was, nevertheless, less than is sometimes painted: a mere eight became MPs between 1945 and 1970. On the other hand, fully one-quarter of Glasgow Labour councillors in 1968 were Catholic.

The most visible aspect of Labour's altered stance was in the choice of new MPs in the post-1970 period. The trade unionist and local councillor strand declined appreciably. More and more the typical member of parliament elected for the first time in this decade was from a middle-class occupation – lawyers like Smith, teachers and lecturers, trade union researchers, rather than those with shop-floor experience. Fewer of these new individuals had any council background: of the 15 elected for the first time in 1979, only six had been councillors. Even in Glasgow, the slowest place to modernise, change took place: between 1945 and 1970, 83 per cent of the city's Labour MPs had prior municipal experience, but by 1987 this had fallen to 63 per cent.[84] New Labour MPs had close connections with the growing employment areas within Scotland, and struck a chord with voters which had perhaps been lost lately.

The decline in councillors ascending to parliament had various causes. One was the radicalisation of younger people in the later 1950s through CND, then Vietnam and university unrest in the 1960s. This pulled in to Labour a pool of talent which bore fruit from the middle 1970s, such as Robin Cook, Gavin Strang and Gordon Brown. In addition there was the impact of the reorganisation of Scottish local government in 1972 following the Wheatley Report. The creation of very large regional councils with wide-ranging powers and *tabula rasa* for initiatives was very tempting to many. Strathclyde Region, after all, had a larger population than all of Northern Ireland, and was the largest local government unit in Western Europe. More could be achieved, many calculated, by working in local government than being a back-bencher in Westminster. Geoff Shaw, the hugely influential first leader of Strathclyde Region, harboured no parliamentary ambitions.[85]

In addition, the quality of councillors improved markedly in the 1970s, so helping Labour's credibility. The crumbling of Labour's support in the aftermath of the Hamilton by-election in 1968 meant that a swathe of elderly and rather ineffectual councillors was buried in the Nationalist municipal landslide at the end of the 1960s. Their replacements were pronouncedly younger and normally abler than their predecessors. Shaw, elected to Glasgow council in 1969, was one of a wave of younger councillors emerging then. These newer people often staged *coups* against the relics of the old guard, and sought to eliminate the closed, dictatorial caucus methods traditionally used by Labour to run its councils. Instead Shaw and his acolytes stressed openness, consultation and wider democracy. This gave Labour a cleaner image and matched the greater self-confidence felt by a newer, less deferential electorate.[86]

The party machine was radically revamped in the mid-1970s. The aim was two-fold: to increase efficiency and to remould the public image of the party. The first was assisted by the fact that, relative to the rest of Britain, Labour's membership in Scotland – both in the individual and trade union components – was less affected by decline, with the divergent paths showing up in the mid-1960s. Between 1952 and 1978, individual membership fell by 3.9 per cent in Scotland but by 35.6 per cent in England and Wales. From 1964 to 1969, British Labour Party individual membership fell by just under 20 per cent, but in Scotland the drop was only 9 per cent. As a result, whereas in 1952, Scottish individual membership constituted 7 per cent of the British total and in 1960 it had marginally improved to 7.7 per cent, by 1970 it had risen to 10.2 per cent and by 1978 it stood at 11.1 per cent – a far higher ratio than at any previous period since 1918. This may suggest that in Scotland either the Labour government's record was felt to be more successful, or that the party was more to the right, and so less alienated by alleged betrayals of socialism.

Equally striking is the steady rise in union affiliations in Scotland relative to England and Wales: over the period 1952 to 1978, the latter rose by 17 per cent but the former by a remarkable 48 per cent. The gap opened up in the early 1970s. Between 1970 and 1975, there were 102,271 extra Scottish trade union affiliations, but in the rest of Britain the increase was a mere 27,177. Indeed, in 1971 alone, union affiliations rose by 52,171 in Scotland, but actually fell by 11,320 elsewhere. In consequence, as with individual membership, the Scottish component of total trade union membership increased markedly: in 1952 and 1960, it was 9.4 per cent, growing to 10.8 per cent in 1970, and reaching 11.9 per cent in 1978.

Two weighty consequences flowed from this. First, Scottish Labour retained in a more intact form its core institutional support base, namely the unions. The party thus would be expected to perform better than in England from the 1960s, when the deviations between England and Scotland developed. Secondly, the rise of union membership of course meant a great accession of cash and assistance for the party, which enabled it to respond combatively to the SNP challenge. The Scottish party's affiliation fee income rose from £1,309 in 1970 to £4,223 in 1975 – admittedly boosted by an increase in fee levels. It is revealing that in election spending in the 1970s, the gap between Labour and Tory was much narrower in Scotland than in England.

At party head office, improvements were also put in place. A research assistant was appointed in May 1974, and in the following year a network of sub-committees and research groups was established. Policy seminars, day schools for key organisers and detailed guides for branch officials followed in 1977. Marginal seats became the focus of greater attention, and it was announced that in-depth canvassing would be used in future as 'a more scientific way' of working.[87]

It was also remarked by the executive that 'in many instances the Labour Party creates the impression of being a middle-aged dull organisation', and this would have to be changed. The first harbinger came in 1976, when a *coup* replaced the person pencilled in to chair the Scottish Executive, a stalwart of the Shop Assistants' Union. The time-honoured

Table 4.4a   Election expenses per constituency, 1970–9

	England		Scotland	
	Con.	Labour	Con.	Labour
1970	£974	£828	£854	£854
Ratio	100	85.0	100	100
1974 (Feb.)	£1,234	£1,123	£1,010	£1,054
Ratio	100	91.0	100	104.4
1974 (Oct.)	£1,307	£1,163	£1,167	£1,137
Ratio	100	89.0	100	97.9
1979	£2,262	£1,876	£1,802	£1,958
Ratio	100	82.9	100	108.7

Table 4.4b   English and Scottish Labour Party election expenses per constituency, 1950–79

	England	Scotland	Ratio
1950	£706	£628	89.0
1951	760	564	74.2
1955	620	531	85.6
1959	714	639	89.5
1964	767	690	89.7
1966	735	675	91.2
1970	828	854	103.1
1974 (Feb.)	1,123	1,010	93.8
1974 (Oct.)	1,163	1,137	97.8
1979	1,876	1,958	104.4

principle of Buggins's turn was swept away, and in came George Robertson, as part of a new Labour identity. He was young – just 30 – a university graduate and research worker. In 1977, the Party Secretary resigned. His post was split in two: the new post of Party Organiser went to Jimmy Allison, but the Secretary's office was filled by Helen Liddell. Not only was she a woman, a rare creature among the Labour hierarchy, but she was young – in her middle twenties. She was from a working-class background, but like Robertson, was a university graduate. Moreover, her previous post had been as a television journalist. Labour was learning fast from the SNP, and adroitly exploited the changing fortunes which occurred in 1977–8.

The newfound strength and confidence of Labour was revealed when a secession was staged in 1976, the dissidents leaving to form the Scottish Labour Party (SLP). At first glance this seemed to pose a damaging challenge to Labour. The SLP's advocacy of greater self-government than Labour was willing to countenance suggested it might tap the semi-nationalistic undercurrents which were supposedly swelling among Scottish left-wingers. The SLP leader, Jim Sillars, was widely regarded as one of the ablest of the rising generation of Labour politicians, with a reputation as an effective platform speaker. In the event, the SLP proved to be short-lived and had no discernible impact on Labour. Beyond Sillars's own South Ayrshire constituency base, the SLP attracted mainly university undergraduates, and a smattering of intellectuals – notably journalists and lecturers – hitherto somewhat aloof from the mainstream Labour Party. Only one other Labour MP defected, the eminently forgettable John Robertson, and no trade union organisation or leader identified with the breakaway. Sillars rapidly fell out with some of his party activists, and the SLP disintegrated in 1977 amid bitter recriminations and a tidal wave of expulsions and resignations. By 1979, Sillars was en route to the SNP, and Labour entered the election with no fear of a split vote with the defunct SLP. The loyalty of party rank and file to Labour and, perhaps more importantly, the refusal of the electorate to respond to the message of the SLP, confirmed the extent of the recovery achieved by the Labour Party.[88]

At any rate, Labour plainly appealed to Scottish voters. The party's vote rose from 36.3 per cent in October 1974 to 41.6 per cent in the 1979 general election. This was a virtually perfect inversion of the English position, where Labour declined from 40.1 per cent to 36.7 per cent. These Scottish results seemed particularly surprising, inasmuch as the referendum on the government's devolution legislation, held less than three months prior to the general election, failed to produce the requisite amount of support. Although a majority (52 per cent) of those voting endorsed the proposals, the threshold requirement (imposed by a revolt of Labour back-benchers) of approval by 40 per cent of the total electorate was not overcome, as those actually voting in favour constituted a mere 33 per cent of all voters. It might have been anticipated, given the perception that Labour's troubles in the mid-1970s stemmed mostly from its insipid approach to devolution, that it would be punished by the electors for failing in the end to deliver self-government. On the contrary, it was the SNP whose support evaporated at the general election.

Thus there was a paradox: the ending of the Nationalist challenge, as heralded by the 1979 election, did not signify a return to the pre-1959 period of electoral congruity between England and Scotland. Nor did the lukewarm commitment shown in the March 1979 referendum by the Scottish electorate to devolution necessarily mean that the issue had effectively been removed from the political menu. The next two decades were to underscore the centrifugal forces at play.

EPILOGUE: SINCE 1979

I

The course of politics in Scotland after 1979 showed an accelerating deviation from the pattern in England, and also in Wales. The Conservatives went into free-fall. By 1987, the proportion of Scots voting Tory was one half that in England, and this remained the case in the succeeding two elections. But the deterioration in support for the party seemed greater because the electoral system worked relentlessly against them. In 1997, when 17.5 per cent of the nation voted for the party, there was not a single Tory MP returned.

Support for Labour was invariably higher than in England, and in particular while the latter wilted under the impact of the SDP–Liberal assaults in 1983 and 1987, Scotland remained more buoyant. Interestingly, the two elections of the next decade showed Labour in England catching up with Scotland in popular support. But by the criterion of seats won, Scottish Labour did exceptionally well, notably in 1997, securing 56 of 72 constituencies. This was achieved with less than half of the total poll.

The Liberals failed to attain sustained take-off in Scotland, and always performed less well in terms of votes than in England. Yet, as in most previous periods, the rewards by the yardstick of MPs elected put the former well ahead. There was a close relationship between the rise and fall in support for Liberals with their allies and the ebb and flow of votes for the SNP. In the 1983 and 1987 contests, Nationalist difficulties gave the Liberals scope to attract higher levels of support. But in the two elections in the 1990s, the SNP re-established itself as the bigger of the two. Yet the scale of the Nationalist recovery in the 1990s should be kept in perspective. At around 21–22 per cent in both elections, support for the SNP was still substantially below the October 1974 poll of over 30 per cent. Moreover, the steady build-up of support at successive contests from 1979 seemed to falter in 1997, when the share of the poll was little altered from 1992.

II

The crisis for the Tories continued unabated. The social and economic doctrines so ardently espoused in England ran into incomprehension and hostility in Scotland. The speedy abandonment of corporatism may well have alienated even some in the business community, for, as we have seen, this approach has long and deep roots in Scotland. The entrepreneurial ethic had limited appeal in a country of large-scale production units, with a heavy slant to publicly owned corporations and multinational concerns. The run-down of steel and coal prior to privatisation disturbed many in Scotland, not just left-leaning individuals. A prominent defector from the Tories in the early 1980s was Iain Lawson, previously touted as the leading paragon of the new demotic Tories who, it was hoped, would propel the party along to a revolution in its social composition on the lines of English Conservatism. However, Lawson, appalled at the economic and social implications posed by the prospect of the end of Scottish steel-making, joined the SNP.

Many of the disparities prevalent in the preceding decade remained in place to render the policies and slogans of the New Right less compelling in Scotland than in England. The withdrawal of many of the multi-nationals who in the 1970s had been hailed as the salvation of the country, added to the sense of decline. There was not the surge in consumer- and service-generated wealth and growth experienced in England. With so many houses publicly owned, the spiral in property prices affected far fewer people in Scotland. With lower per capita income, spending in the high streets was lower, so service sector job formation, so significant in England, was much less pronounced in Scotland.

As heavier users of public sector services, the Scots found the programme of privatisation and cut-backs inconsistent with their economic and social interests. The sale of council houses to sitting tenants was slower to take off. This may not have been because of a strong ideological commitment to the concept of public housing, but for practical reasons. Rents were lower than in England, so the benefits of buying were less marked. With no escalation in house prices, the prospects of making sizeable capital gains were fewer. Lower incomes and job insecurity meant that the gamble of taking out a mortgage appeared to offer steeper odds. Additionally, much of Scottish council housing stock took the form of high-rise flats, which had much less attractive resale potential than traditional styles of housing.

The process inaugurated by Teddy Taylor after his defeat in 1979 had serious implication for the party's calibre and morale in Scotland. After his rejection at Cathcart, Taylor soon found a safe seat in England. Over the next decade, other defeated MPs crossing the border in order to revive their parliamentary careers included Michael Ancram, Gerry Malone and Iain Sproat. Not all were successful in winning an English seat, as the case of Anna McCurley demonstrated. Almost all of these carpet-baggers were serious politicians with promising ministerial careers ahead of them. Those MPs left behind were at best a mixed bag. Some very able and politically adroit people kept the Tory administration in some sort of presentable shape: each of the four Scottish Secretaries showed, in markedly different ways, outstanding qualities, certainly superior to the other Tory Secretaries since Elliot in the 1930s. But the abilities of junior ministers were highly variable, and the back-benchers, particularly in the recent past, were of distinctly poor timbre. The fact that a former junior minister, almost into his seventies, was recalled from the back-benches because not one of the rest of the non-minister-ialists was deemed fit for office, is a telling indictment.

As a result the Scottish Tories were stripped of their high-flyers which left the cause badly defended in Scotland in the realms of public debate. The sight of these refugees can have done little to encourage a rising generation to think it worthwhile to seek seats in Scotland. A number of recent instances of younger Scottish Tories, most notably David MacLean, going directly to seats in England, added yet another category of exiled Scottish Tory MPs.

The paucity of credible advocates of the Tory cause gravely imperilled the party's appeal, since many of the measures introduced or imposed by the government since 1979 were counter-productive. The repudiation of the commitment to devolution, effectively acknowledged in the imme-diate pre-1979 period, created confusion among Tories, many of whom had endorsed a measure of Home Rule, especially since the widely revered Lord Home had been identified with the proposal. As discon-tent with the centralising tendencies of the Thatcher government spread in Scotland, the party's unyielding commitment to full unionism alienated many. Moreover, the introduction of the poll tax in Scotland a year ahead of England was multiply disastrous: the unionist position was seriously subverted; the tax bore especially heavily on the poorer Scottish population; its repeal was a consequence not of protests in Scotland, but only because it posed serious problems in England. The Conservatives appeared hostile to Scotland and its special circumstances. This ineptitude was particularly damning because in reality the Scottish ministers had for the most part endeavoured to modify the full rigours of the New Right regimen when shaping Scottish policy. So, public spending per capita remained higher, while reforms in education, local government contracting out and so forth were either ignored or introduced very belatedly.

Local government posed another difficulty for the Tories. They retained control of very few councils. This had two causes. In some of the party's heartlands, the tradition of 'Independent' labels persisted, so that a full grass-roots structure was always fragile. In the more central areas, the impact of government policies after 1979 generated extreme hostility, resulting in low levels of support at council elections. Moreover, the structure of Scottish local government made it hard to develop flagship councils like Westminster, Wandsworth and Kent, where the radical right's agenda could be implemented. The region-district councils set-up meant that the former had the wider role, unlike in England where unitary authorities existed. Both Strathclyde and Lothian proved durable Labour councils, and their judiciously non-controversial but broadly progressive policies left little room for Tory cries of socialist extremism à la Greater London or Liverpool Councils.

Cathcart, previously the beacon for hopes of a Conservative recovery, now epitomised the problems of the party in Scotland. Decline was both electoral and organisational. The council seats within the constituency, which had long been in the hands of the Tories, slipped away, so that nine years after Taylor's defeat, only one councillor was Tory, against eight in 1979. The choices of candidate and agent for the 1983 parliamentary election were unhelpful; the former was an Edinburgh advocate not entirely popular with constituency activists, while the latter had no local knowledge. The local association began selling off its offices to meet financial needs: in the 1970s it had had four different sets of rooms across the constituency. Lastly, as a long-standing constituency party official remarked, a contributory factor to the Tories' difficulties was the 'unpopularity' of Mrs Thatcher and her policies.[1]

Most of the agencies of political culture in Scotland were, unlike England, impervious to the blandishments of Toryism in the 1980s and 1990s; indeed, if anything they moved in a contrary direction. The weight of the press grew ever more hostile to the Conservatives. The *Glasgow Herald* and the *Scotsman*, initially under the impetus of their endorsement to devolution, severed most residual sympathies with Conservatism. As the 1980s wore on, they broadened their critique to a denunciation of government policy on a range of economic and social issues. In 1992 both papers backed the Liberal Democrats, and in 1997 the *Scotsman* opted for Labour. The continuing preference exerted by Scots to read home-based broadsheets meant that the *Daily Telegraph* and *The Times*, the two leading heavyweight apologists for Thatcherism, could not secure a bridgehead. The *Daily Record* kept its circulation levels more successfully than the *Daily Mirror* managed to do in England, so the *Sun* remained the underdog in Scotland. In 1992, the circulation of the *Record*, at 760,000, was three times that of the *Sun*'s 290,000. The Tories were further afflicted when the *Sun*'s Scottish edition switched from them in the early 1990s to endorse the SNP.

The churches maintained their leftish leaning of the previous era. Mrs Thatcher's decision in 1988 to address the Church of Scotland General Assembly, choosing to deliver a sermon on the biblical basis for profit-making, was widely regarded as highly counter-productive. Perhaps she should have been told of the historical record of Scottish Presbyterianism's response to being lectured at by heads of government. The General Assembly's influential Church and Nation Committee produced a steady succession of reports in the 1980s highly critical of the impact of Conservative social and economic policies on Scotland. The involvement of the churches in the movements to secure devolution and in campaigns to oppose factory closures intensified this attitude.

The Scottish universities, on the whole, resisted the intellectual enchantments of the New Right. It is true that St Andrews could lay claim, if any university in Britain could, to being the begetter of the New Right economic thinking. But apart from a very few exceptions, most Scottish academics have not joined the dominant intellectual trends found in England: no radical right revisionist schools in history, political science and sociology have emerged.

III

The Liberals remained marginalised: their MPs represented rural fringe areas, and the party could not drive into urban Scotland, as it managed to do in England. Partly this was because the SNP had to a great degree established itself as the alternative receptacle of votes from those disenchanted with the two main parties, as Sillars's victory at Govan in 1988 indicated. Partly too, it was because there were fewer seats in Scotland with the sociological profile which provided the ideal hunting-ground for the Liberals in the south: the weakness of the Scottish middle class had implications not solely for the Tories, but also for the Liberals.

The formation of the Social Democratic Party in 1981 did not, it is reasonable to state, make the same impact in Scotland as in England. The SDP held only three Scottish seats in the 1983 election, and Robert MacLennan's success in switching from Labour to SDP, yet retaining his Caithness & Sutherland seat, merely reinforced the importance of personality in these outposts. When the SDP was formed, two Scottish Labour MPs (Dickson Mabon and MacLennan) signed up, along with a prominent party official and some councillors, but more significant was the refusal of right-inclined figures like Donald Dewar and John Smith to defect. The average SDP membership per constituency in Scotland (33) was the lowest of any region in Britain: in the south-east of England, it was 125, and in the Midlands, the lowest English regional figure – 59. Only Wales, with 40 members per seat, was akin to Scotland.[2]

The most intensive study of the SDP stressed that the prime motivating factor behind its support was antipathy to extremism on the part of both Labour and Tory, and certainly Scottish Labour did not meet this image.[3] The absence of the varieties of left-wing jacobinism in Scotland so prevalent in England meant the SDP did not have the oxygen of beleaguered Labour moderates in which to prosper. No Labour MP in Scotland was under serious threat of deselection from left-wing activists in the early 1980s, unlike in England. The Militant Tendency was essentially confined to two Glasgow seats, Pollok and Provan, and here they were successfully contained by the attentions of the Scottish organiser, Jimmy Allison, acting with some powerful local political figures.

Local authorities in Scotland equally avoided ultra-left stances. No regional council entered into conflict with central government by defying guidelines on spending and taxing levels. Only two of the less powerful district councils – Stirling and Edinburgh – adopted a confrontational stance, and in both internal *coups* removed those ardent for martyrdom, replacing them with more moderate leadership. In addition, the claret-drinking, Volvo-owning classes, so beloved of caricaturists of the SDP membership, were generally in limited supply north of the border. One of the constituencies which approximated most nearly to the Identikit

SDP seat, Glasgow Hillhead, was indeed won by the party in a by-election in 1982.

The Liberals remained confined to about three areas: the Highlands and Northern Islands, rural Aberdeenshire and the south-east. Occasionally, traditional strongholds could be won back: North-east Fife in 1987 exemplified this pattern. Elsewhere, if anything, the party could not always maintain its previous areas of strength: in Greenock, for example, its vote eroded badly, transforming this once winnable Liberal seat into a solid Labour seat, while in 1992 and 1997 the Liberals were placed fourth. The levels of support enjoyed in the 1980s had a high element of fortuitousness about them. The eclipse of the SNP robbed voters not thirled to Labour or Tory of a realistic alternative. When, as outlined below, the Nationalists set their house in order from the late 1980s, the Liberal vote tumbled. Between 1983 and 1992, the Liberal share of the poll virtually halved (from 24.5 per cent to 13.1 per cent) while the SNP nearly doubled (from 11.8 per cent to 21.5 per cent), but the combined share was almost static – 36.3 per cent in 1983, 33.3 per cent in 1987, 34.6 per cent in 1992 and 35.1 per cent in 1997.

IV

The SNP in a sense suffered in the 1980s rather as Labour in England did from internal feuding which diminished its electoral attractiveness. An influx of left-wingers took place from the mid-1970s into the early 1980s. Some had come via the Scottish Labour Party, including James Sillars and several of his henchmen, while others came direct from Labour in protest at that party's perceived dilution of socialism and abnegation of its Home Rule commitments. A few moved from more leftist groupuscules. It was contended by this faction, the 79 Group, that the only way to crack open the solid Labour territory of the west-central industrial belt was by offering socialist policies to the voters. This analysis derived from a belief that these voters were committed socialists and that Labour itself was drifting to the right, as its conduct in office between 1974 and 1979 demonstrated. The driving figure behind this group was Sillars, his rapport with the working class no doubt deepened by his experience with the SLP.

The strategy posited by this tendency was, however, problematic. First, of course, the British Labour Party did in fact become quite radical for the first half of the 1980s, so that allegations that Labour was diluting socialism out of existence looked rather odd in the high tide of Bennery. But, as Labour's left also discovered, it was unclear how far the working class were crying out for more committed socialism. Apathy and lethargy seemed to characterise the response by many in Scotland to the profound economic and social changes of the 1980s. The poll tax did not produce public disorder; it was the disturbances in London over its arrival in England, a good year after it had been introduced in Scotland, that precipitated its abandonment. In any event, the SNP failed to poll noticeably better in the industrial belt. Sillars's own remarkable victory at Govan in 1988 proved yet another temporary by-election gain, to be comfortably reclaimed by Labour at the following general election. Indeed, by 1987 the SNP had also lost its sole remaining urban-industrial constituency from the heady days of 1974–9: Dundee East was taken by Labour.

The problem for the Nationalists was very much akin to that faced by the Liberals. The areas of SNP support remained outside the central industrial areas. In all the elections, the Nationalists could rely on the Tayside and Grampian regions, with Galloway also supportive. In these parts their vote was above the SNP's national average. But in Strathclyde, Lothian and Fife, it was below par. Even though in 1997 the SNP was frequently second-placed in many seats in these three regions, the party was normally still some way from ousting the incumbents.

Within the SNP, the espousal of overtly socialist messages created unease among the traditional powerbases. It was difficult to believe the electors in Moray & Nairn or Banffshire were returning Nationalists because they believed this would realise John Maclean's vision of a Scottish republican soviet. Led by Mrs Ewing, Donald Stewart and Gordon Wilson, the last-named owing his return to an unspoken anti-Labour formation in Dundee East, there was a fight-back. After bloodletting, expulsions and resignations, mostly among the socialistic camp, the SNP regained a sort of equipoise in the later 1980s. Now it espoused what might be seen as rather social democratic polices. This made sense on a range of fronts: it struck a halfway point between the warring factions, and it projected the party as moderate but progressive, thus enabling it to appeal to the sorts of voters who in England could turn only to the Liberal–SDP alliance. Moreover it established a *modus vivendi* within the party, and some of those on the left who had been eclipsed earlier returned to positions of influence, notably Alex Salmond.

In the midst of these internal recriminations, the SNP lost the sure touch that had characterised its approach in the previous decade. Efforts to initiate civil unrest both to force the setting up of a Scottish parliament and to refuse to pay the poll tax were alike completely unsuccessful. These adventures only dented the image carefully cultivated in the preceding twenty years of the SNP as a wholly constitutional movement. Part of the problem for the party was that the 1980s were to a degree rather like the later 1950s and early 1960s. The Scottish people appeared to have persuaded themselves that salvation from the experiences of Conservative misrule lay with the return to power of Labour. In this climate, the constitutional question was rather subordinate, and in any event the débâcle over devolution in the 1970s left many in Scotland reluctant to reopen the question. It was not until the Constitutional Convention began to plan in detail for an assembly that this issue acquired public relevance. Here, too, the Nationalists may have miscalculated. Their decision to stay aloof from what was a remarkably broad coalition of civic society seemed a petty partisan stance, allowing the initiative to speak for the vast majority of Scots to pass into the hands of others.

V

Labour retained its support for a variety of reasons. On the one hand, it never succumbed to the manifestations of left-wing ultraism, thus avoiding alienating middle-of-the-road opinion, as noted earlier. The bulk of MPs were not identified with Tony Benn's group. Some factors may be adduced for this. On the one hand, some of the left-leaning Labour MPs were of an older tradition, and had little truck with the fashionable attitudes obtaining among the Bennites, some indeed still feeling loyalty to successive Tribuneite leaders, Michael Foot and Neil Kinnock, rather than to latterday radicals. Norman Buchan and Judith Hart would certainly fit this description. It is also possible that the social ingredients behind much of the left-wing surge in England did not operate in Scotland. For instance, there was less of a presence of ethnic minorities, whose social and political aspirations were skilfully welded by the likes of Ken Livingstone into a rainbow alliance. Feminism, too, was arguably less politically conscious in Scotland at this point. The much-ridiculed polytechnic lecturer in sociology, the intellectual momentum behind the left's surge in England, was a rarity in Scotland, where the higher education system was differently organised. At council level, the existing councillors in Scotland retained a firmer grip, perhaps because their patronage powers were greater, thanks to the larger role played by local government in the society and economy of the communities they served, via public sector housing, direct labour organisations and so forth.

Trade unions in Scotland were still very influential, and in general were not interested in extreme politics. The STUC was arguably better led in the 1980s – by first James Milne and then Campbell Christie – than was the TUC. The STUC and the whole union movement in Scotland avoided the fate of being marginalised and demonised. There was no equivalent of Wapping; the 1984–5 coal strike in Scotland was strongly supported by the broad union movement, but there were few incidents like the violent clashes between police and striking miners at Orgreave which a hostile media could exploit. The closure of factories, notably Caterpillar and Ravenscraig, elicited positive waves of sympathy and concern across a wide range of opinion in Scotland. The STUC carefully kept links with other elements in Scottish public life, so retaining esteem. Its recurring approach was to construct an alliance with other involved civic bodies, so making maximum impact in its campaigns. Perhaps the best instance of this approach came in 1986, when the Congress was instrumental with Strathclyde Regional Council in creating the Standing Commission on the Scottish Economy. Besides the unions and local government, this body included academics, church representatives, voluntary bodies, other political movements, businessmen and the Scottish Council Development and Industry. Christie's pivotal role in launching and influencing the Constitutional Convention emphasised this aspect very neatly.

Labour was able to present itself as the natural protector of 'traditional' Scottish values and institutions – in the sense that the party sought to defend the post-1945 Welfare State. Most Scots, as we have seen, were strongly attached to these institutions, and the social differences with England meant that there were fewer interstices in which the Conservatives could create support. Labour was able to cast Thatcherism as an extreme ideology which had been imposed on a hostile Scottish electorate.

The success of Labour in local government throughout the 1980s was a bonus: through its dominance of COSLA, it was able to create a united front of opposition to Conservative policy, as well of course as linking with the STUC. This broad stream of access to a coherent, uniform alternative to Conservative policy was not prevalent in England. There

Labour was internally preoccupied with the divide opened up by the strong Bennite and Militant Tendency presences. The voice of local authorities in England was less politically united, as the Tories and the Liberals both ran a sizeable number of town and county halls. Moreover, because local authorities in Scotland played a bigger providing role than in England, attempts to scale down public spending support were typified by councillors as a direct onslaught on Scottish interests and local democracy. Labour in Scotland thus portrayed itself as the defender of Scottish, not just working-class, interests in the teeth of the Tory onslaught. After all, the middle classes were also users of the excellent pubic sector provision of schooling, health and social care.

Labour became much keener on devolution than before. Under the Wilson–Callaghan administrations of 1974–9, there had been a strong sense that most Scottish Labour *prominenti* were at best lukewarm on self-government. But as John Smith and Donald Dewar in particular rose up the British party hierarchy, and as older MPs retired to be replaced by more pro-devolution figures, the party's stance became both more principled and more dedicated. Additionally, the rising eminence of Gordon Brown, a long-standing proponent of devolution, reinforced this decisive tilt. But lower political cunning was also at work. Labour's hand was forced by the defeats in 1987 and 1992, which gave enhanced credibility to the SNP's contention that voting Labour was not going to prevent the Conservatives, sustained by their large majority in England, from imposing their will on a hostile Scottish population. The surge in support for the SNP in 1992, accompanied by a decline in Labour's Scottish poll – when in England Labour was at last advancing – concentrated the attention of Labour on devolution.

The work of the Scottish Constitutional Convention was highly significant in ensuring that support for a devolved Scottish parliament would be both broader and deeper than in the 1970s, so that the unsatisfactory outcome of the 1979 referendum would not be repeated. First, it maintained the issue of devolution at the centre of Scottish politics. Secondly, it established the case for self-government as non-partisan. A wide spectrum of Scottish society engaged in its proceedings: not simply politicians, but also academics, trade unionists, local government representatives, the churches, plus a plethora of interest groups.

The instigators of the Convention sought to bestow enhanced status for its project by issuing a *Claim of Right* in 1988. This document, with its allusion to earlier assertions of Scottish Presbyterian pretensions, rehearsed the intellectual and moral assumptions behind self-government for Scotland. The Scottish Constitutional Convention itself was launched in January 1989, with Professor Sir Robert Grieve, the first chairman of the Highlands & Islands Development Board, a classic product of the consensual corporatist age, in the chair. The detailed proposals of the Convention were produced in 1995. The report outlined both the ambit of the institution's authority and the blueprint for electing members to it.

As to the latter, the mode of voting recommended was a form of proportional voting akin to the German 'list' method, the consequence of which was generally predicted to mean no single party would have an overall majority. This was a long-standing Liberal position, and so mollified a key element in the Convention. It had the added attraction of reassuring the outlying regions that domination by the political parties associated with the Central belt would be severely constrained. The disaffection shown by the Borders, Dumfries & Galloway, and the Highlands and Islands towards devolution in 1979 had been a very significant factor in delegitimising that poll. The cynical surmised that this was additionally a ruse to prevent the SNP from ever gaining outright power, so stymying any rapid path to independence. A major challenge to the male-dominated political culture of Scotland was posed in the assertion that there should be an equal number of men and women representatives in the new parliament.

Broadly speaking, the Convention argued for very wide powers being allotted to a Scottish Parliament – a term widely used in lieu of the 'Assembly' favoured in the 1970s. The most important changes from the 1970s legislation which were proposed related to reserved powers. Now the areas of government to be handled by Westminster were itemised – foreign policy, defence, central economic policy, social security and immigration – and all else was assumed to be the province of the Scottish parliament. This approach, reversing the 1977–8 measure, which had itemised those responsibilities devolved to Edinburgh, was politically adroit. Much of the opposition to that bill arose from disputes about the allocation of powers: this new formulation was simple and clear. Moreover, the vesting of additional powers made devolution more palatable to nationalist-inclined segments within Labour and the Liberals. Edinburgh would now, unlike 1978, deal with economic development, aid to industry, forestry, police and prisons, transport, training and universities.

While the Convention's plan was given widespread publicity and was, for the most, warmly endorsed by influential sections of the media, it is not clear that this report galvanised the wider nation into a greater appetite for devolution. A public opinion survey taken when the Convention's proceedings were at an important phase revealed that only 18 per cent of respondents professed awareness of its deliberations. The alleged excesses of the Conservative government in the 1980s, climaxing with the imposition of the community charge (poll tax), and the concomitant debate on the democratic deficit, seem not to have instantly pushed the Scots into a more pro-devolutionary approach. Opinion polls reported fairly stable endorsement for the three main constitutional options (full independence, full union, devolution) for most of the 1980s and 1990s.

It was nevertheless highly beneficial to Labour that it not only participated fully in the Scottish Convention with other parties and sectors of Scottish civil society, but also that it substantially accepted the Convention's's constitutional framework. The party was not now seen, as had been the case in the 1970s, to be endorsing Home Rule merely as a response – made under pressure and with marked reluctance – to political exigencies. Moreover, Labour achieved two extra bonuses. First, it had accepted the type of inclusive politics identified with Blairite Labour later in the decade: sharing the decision-making process with the Liberals, local government, church and union leaders and agreeing to proportional representation and enhanced women's representation in the proposed assembly. This was all evidence of a non-dogmatic approach which struck a chord with a large swathe of opinion which felt that splintered opposition since 1979 to the economic and social radicalism of Conservative governments had vitiated effective resistance. Secondly, Labour in Scotland seemed to embody the aspirations of the nation: it was a government-in-waiting long before the British party established its credentials in this respect.

A crucial factor in the arrival of the Scottish parliament was the conduct of the Blair government after its 1997 electoral triumph. The referendum on setting up a parliament in Edinburgh was held in September 1997. Many proponents of the Convention's report had been unhappy when Labour in 1996 announced that it would hold a plebiscite, and they contended that a manifesto commitment by Labour was sufficient grounds for legislative action. But the government feared a backlash, particularly in England, if a clear test of opinion in Scotland was not conducted. By holding the vote very soon after the sweeping general election victory, when afflatus was at peak levels, Labour guaranteed a decisive favourable verdict. This contrasts vividly with the 1979 referendum, which came at the fag-end of the 1974 parliament, when the government's popularity was very low, and factors other than the merits of devolution therefore affected voters' decisions.

Hence the vote was cast for or against the broad principle of devolution in 1997, as there were no detailed legislative proposals, but only a general White Paper, produced at high speed over the summer, available for scrutiny. This further tended to boost the vote in favour, as there were no details which might disconcert electors, as had happened in 1979. The decision by the new government to insert a separate question on support for additional tax-raising powers for the Scottish parliament was also vociferously opposed by keen devolutionists. But from the standpoint of the government, this removed a major weapon in the armoury of the antis, and also conferred stronger justification for any fiscal adjustments later effected by the Edinburgh administration.

With the Conservatives still reeling from the total demolition of their Westminster representation, the campaign for devolution was overwhelmingly superior, and the verdict at the polls was emphatic beyond earlier expectations. Whereas in 1979, 51.6 per cent supported and 48.4 per cent opposed the scheme, now the respective figures were 74.3 per cent and 25.7 per cent. These results were in stark contrast to Wales, whose referendum – held on the same day – produced the most narrow margin of backing for self-government: 50.3 per cent for, 49.7 per cent against. Turn-out in Scotland, at 60.4 per cent, was also much higher than in 1979. Although the 40 per cent threshold requirement of the 1979 referendum was dropped in 1997, it is instructive that 44.9 per cent of the total electorate sanctioned the new measure, while in 1979, a mere 32.5 per cent of the eligible electorate had done so. In striking contrast to the previous referendum, the proposals were supported by every geographical region: now areas hostile in 1979, notably in the Highlands and Islands and the south-west, came out in favour. Again, sampling polls revealed that there was general approval across the social spectrum, although in 1979 middle-class voters had been resistant. There was also strong endorsement of the right to raise taxes, albeit not at the levels of support for governmental devolution: 63.5 per cent for, 36.5 per cent against. Now there could be no mistaking the settled will of the Scots.

With a massive parliamentary majority and the rout of the 'No' camp in the referendum, the passage of the subsequent bill was rapid and subjected to few disruptive manoeuvres in parliament. The concomitant promise of regional devolution within England, especially in the matter of economic development, helped to appease the northern English Labour MPs who had been strong opponents of Scottish devolution in the 1970s. The Scotland Act was passed in 1998, with some modifications from the Convention's blueprint. Some cabinet ministers had insisted on retaining elements of their portfolio under their jurisdiction. Other proposals had to be jettisoned because legal advice pronounced them likely to be untenable in the courts – this was the reason for dropping the intention to have equal male and female representation in the parliament.

The general election for the Scottish parliament, held in May 1999, produced, as was anticipated, an assembly in which no single party had a majority. Labour was the biggest party, securing 56 seats. The SNP, significantly improving on its 1997 Westminster election support, but not polling as well as had seemed likely in the pre-election period, was the second largest, with 35 MSPs. The Tories, despite winning no seats in the constituency component, nonetheless had a reasonable tally of 18. The Liberals, with 17 members, joined with Labour to set up a coalition administration.

The new set-up has a number of features which, if maintained, represent a major new departure in British and Scottish politics. The balance of authority and the demarcation of responsibilities between the head of the Scottish administration and the Secretary of State for Scotland remains fluid. But subsequent events underlined the impact powerful proactive figures can have on a fuzzy structure. Again, the problems of co-ordinating policy between ministries in Wales, Scotland and Britain are being pointed to as a potentially destabilising feature. But the only change is that these policy clashes are being now conducted in public, rather than, as hitherto, within the corridors of Whitehall.

The formation of a coalition government is distinctly innovative, as these have been rare in peace-time Britain, and have left an ambiguous legacy. The 1918–22 coalition collapsed, speeding the disintegration of the Liberals. The coalition formed in 1931 was somewhat artificial, as it was overwhelmingly Conservative, with other parties holding seats by dint of a sort of pact with local Tories. Labour has traditionally been against peace-time coalitions: in 1924 and 1929, the party opted to form a minority administration, and even with precarious majorities in 1950, 1964 and 1974, it insisted on governing alone. The Lib–Lab pact formed in 1976 was never more than a highly fissile deal, with no power-sharing. Even at the level of local government in Scotland there was no tradition of Labour forming a coalition to run a local authority, rather again preferring to run affairs single-handedly as a minority administration.

The system of proportional representation has also yielded the prospect of an altered politics. As noted above, coalitions are virtually inevitable under the system. But it has permitted minorities to secure a presence in the parliament, underscoring the inclusive nature of the institution. The main beneficiary of PR has been the Conservatives, who won none of the constituency contests but nevertheless secured a respectable number of seats from the list section.

Additionally, much smaller parties – the Greens and the ultra-left Scottish Socialist Party – were also represented, and there was even a seat for an Independent, Dennis Canavan. Canavan, a Labour MP, had not been selected by his Party as a Scottish parliament candidate, but stood successfully against Labour's official choice in his Falkirk constituency. It is possible to see these as momentary phenomena, as much as signs of permanent sea-change. Support for the Green Party has flickered up and down for nearly twenty years, so this result could prove another transient blip. The Scottish Socialist Party, a hangover from the Militant Tendency, is a salutary reminder that many in the peripheral estates and run-down inner cities remain deeply alienated from mainstream politics.

Backing for Canavan is part of a long tradition, where a long-serving, highly regarded local MP can fight against his party machine, and triumph. The cases of S. O. Davies, Eddie Milne and Dick Taverne are all reminders from the recent past of this pattern. But, significantly, none of them contrived to sustain their challenge beyond a single contest. These examples occurred in England and Wales, but a parallel Scottish model is J. H. Mackie. Mackie had been the Tory MP for Galloway from 1931, but in 1945 his local party declined to reselect him. Instead they chose a military hero and scion of a prominent South Ayrshire lairdly family with historic links to the Conservative party – Col. Bernard Fergusson. Mackie ran as an Independent Unionist and effortlessly demolished the hapless colonel, who came third behind Labour. Mackie by 1950 was endorsed as the official Tory candidate, and sat until his death in 1958, after an utterly insignificant twenty-seven-year career in parliament.

But it is useful to be cautious about the extent to which the big parties' monopoly is at peril. First, it is possible that electors, using the scheme for the first time, made miscalculations about how to deploy their votes. In subsequent contests, greater voter sophistication could produce less unpredictability. It is striking how quickly the parties worked out how to manipulate the system of proportional representation under which Scottish Universities constituency returned three MPs between 1918 and 1950. School board elections between 1872 and 1918 also used a form of proportionality, a loophole which sectional interests rapidly exploited to maximise their representation on the authorities. Indeed, the first success in mobilising the Irish Catholic vote came here, as the Glasgow Catholic Union marshalled supporters to return church candidates. Again, PR was quite quickly abandoned in Northern Ireland in the 1920s, as it became apparent that all sides had worked out how to bypass the intended moderating impact of the system.

To some extent, the elections proved disappointing as an exercise in changing the political culture of Scotland. Not a single member of an ethnic minority was returned. Women made up just over one-third of the total (49 out of 129). The calibre of many MSPs was perceived to be somewhat lacklustre. Too many, particularly on the Labour side, seemed to be part of the old tradition of over-promoted councillors, while a number of SNP people were Westminster rejects being given a safe nest for their declining years. There was no obvious unleashing of swathes of hitherto untapped talent, unable or unwilling to find a berth in the existing set-up, but available to devote time and energy to revitalising Scotland – this was a long-standing argument of proponents of devolution and outright independence. The early activities, or lack thereof, of the MSPs seemed to reinforce this perception. Long deliberations on holiday entitlements, members' expenses and so forth preoccupied the new Edinburgh parliamentarians in their first summer of power. Many in Scotland were not over-impressed; it seemed as if in the new Eden there were too many old Adams and Eves.

APPENDIX I GENERAL ELECTION RESULTS IN SCOTLAND, 1900–97

	Con.		Lab.		Lib.		SNP	
	1	2	1	2	1	2	1	2
1900	49.0	36	–	–	50.2	34		
1906	38.2	10	2.3	2	56.4	59		
1910 (Jan.)	39.6	9	5.1	2	54.2	59		
1910 (Dec.)	42.6	9	3.6	3	53.6	58		
1918	52.3■	54■	24.7	6	I 15.0	8		
	2.0	2						
1922	25.1	13	32.2	29	I 21.5	15		
					N 17.7	12		
1923	31.6	14	35.9	34	28.4	22		
1924	40.7	36	41.1	26	16.6	8		
1929	35.9	20	42.3	36	18.1	13		
1931	55.3*	57*	32.6	7	8.6	7	1.0	0
1935	49.8*	43*	41.8♦	24♦	6.7	3	1.1	0
1945	41.1	27	49.4♦	40♦	5.0	0	1.2	0
1950	44.8	31	46.2	37	6.6	2	0.4	0
1951	48.6	35	47.9	35	2.7	1	0.3	0
1955	50.1	36	46.7	34	1.9	1	0.5	0
1959	47.2	31	46.7	38	4.1	1	0.8	0
1964	40.6	24	48.7	43	7.6	4	2.4	0
1966	37.7	20	49.9	46	6.8	5	5.0	0
1970	38.0	23	44.5	44	5.5	3	11.4	1
1974 (Feb.)	32.9	21	36.6	40	8.0	3	21.9	7
1974 (Oct.)	24.7	16	36.3	41	8.3	3	30.4	11
1979	31.4	22	41.6	44	9.0	3	17.3	2
1983	28.4	21	35.1	41	24.5+	8+	11.8	2
1987	24.0	10	42.4	50	19.3+	9+	14.0	3
1992	25.6	11	39.0	50	13.1	8	21.5	3
1997	17.5	0	45.6	56	13.0	10	22.1	6

Note: Column 1 is share of poll won; column 2 is number of MPs elected.

Key: ■ Includes all 'Coalition' labels.
    I Independent (Asquithian) Liberal.
    N National (Lloyd George) Liberal.
    * Includes all 'National' labels.
    ♦ ILP results are included with Labour.
    + Sum of SDP and Liberal.

Appendix II   Scottish Electoral Statistics in Relation to England, 1900–97

	Con.		Lab.		Lib.	
	1	2	1	2	1	2
1900	93.5	70.6	–	–	114.1	183.2
1906	86.2	53.4	43.4	50.1	115.1	123.5
1910 (Jan.)	80.3	25.2	73.9	39.5	126.0	201.0
1910 (Dec.)	87.3	25.2	56.3	57.5	120.7	202.0
1918	99.6■	94.8■	106.9	95.5	I 102.0	217.3
1922	60.5	28.9	111.8	208.6	I 109.7	232.9
					N 242.5	264.4
1923	79.4	43.3	120.9	168.3	94.9	122.2
1924	85.3	70.9	141.7	163.0	94.3	287.6
1929	92.5	61.8	114.6	108.8	76.7	253.7
1931	80.3◆	89.5◆	107.9	165.0	143.3	239.3
1935	85.0◆	88.4◆	108.3*	141.2*	106.3	186.3
1945	102.2	116.0	101.9*	86.8*	53.2	–**
1950	102.3	73.2	100.0	105.1	70.2	712.6
1951	99.6	92.0	98.2	107.1	117.4	356.2
1955	99.4	86.4	99.8	113.3	73.1	359.7
1959	94.4	70.8	107.1	141.7	65.1	239.8
1964	92.1	65.9	112.0	125.8	62.9	959.6
1966	88.3	65.7	104.0	115.8	75.6	599.8
1970	78.7	56.7	102.5	145.3	69.6	1072.3
1974 (Feb.)	81.8	57.0	97.3	122.7	37.6	244.0
1974 (Oct.)	63.5	45.2	90.5	115.7	41.1	272.3
1979	66.5	52.3	113.4	156.8	58.4	311.3
1983	61.7	42.7	130.5	204.1	92.8+	446.9+
1987	51.9	20.3	143.7	234.0	80.8+	653.8+
1992	56.3	25.0	115.0	187.1	68.2	652.9
1997	51.9	–++	104.6	124.9	72.6	231.1

Notes:

1   In all of the above, the figure for England is taken as 100, and the Scottish figures calculated in relation thereto.

2   Column 1 refers to share of the poll, and column 2 to share of seats won.

Key: ▪   Covers all 'Coalition' labels; the data for 'uncouponed' Conservatives is too small to calculate relative performance.

   I   Independent (Asquithian) Liberal.

   N   National (Lloyd George) Liberal.

   ♦   Includes all 'National' labels.

   *   Includes ILP.

   **   No Liberal was elected in Scotland.

   +   Sum of SDP and Liberal.

   ++   No Conservative was elected in Scotland.

NOTES

1 The Liberal Ascendancy, 1900–14

1. Unless otherwise indicated, throughout the text the Scottish Universities' seats are not included in data relating to Scottish election results. There were two such seats in 1900–18, three in 1918–50.
2. I. G. C. Hutchison, *A Political History of Scotland, 1832–1924* (Edinburgh, 1986), p. 241.
3. See C. G. Brown, *Religion and Society in Scotland since 1707* (Edinburgh, 1997), pp. 44–55; cf. Hutchison, *Political History of Scotland*, p. 335–7.
4. J. G. Kellas, 'The Liberal Party and the Scottish Church Disestablishment Crisis', *English Historical Review*, 79 (1964), pp. 31–46.
5. W. Knox, 'Religion and the Scottish Labour Movement, 1900–39', *Journal of Contemporary History*, 23 (1988), pp. 615–17.
6. S. J. Brown, '"Echoes of Midlothian": Scottish Liberalism and the South African War, 1899–1902', *SHR*, 81 (1992), pp. 156–83; Hutchison, *Political History of Scotland*, pp. 175–9.
7. See J. F. McCaffrey, 'The Origins of Liberal Unionism in the West of Scotland', *SHR*, 50 (1971), pp. 47–71; Hutchison, *Political History of Scotland*, pp. 162–7.
8. Brown, '"Echoes of Midlothian"', pp. 180–3; Hutchison, *Political History of Scotland*, pp. 237–40.
9. Quoted in Hutchison, *Political History of Scotland*, p. 243.
10. J. Cannon, *Parliamentary Reform, 1640–1832* (London, 1973), p. 279. English voters grew from 344,000 to 652,000.
11. J. Hunter, 'The Politics of Highland Land Reform, 1873–95', *SHR*, 53 (1974), pp. 45–68.
12. J. Brown, 'Scottish and English Land Legislation, 1905–11', *SHR*, 47 (1968), pp. 72–85.
13. N. Blewett, *The Peers, the Parties and the People* (London, 1972), pp. 402–3.
14. I. Packer, 'The Land Issue and the Future of Scottish Liberalism in 1914', *SHR*, 85 (1996), pp. 52–6; Hutchison, *Political History of Scotland*, pp. 242–5.
15. Packer, 'Land Issue', pp. 56–71.
16. Cited in Hutchison, *Political History of Scotland*, p. 245.
17. R. Finlay, *A Partnership for Good?* (Edinburgh, 1997), pp. 54–60; Hutchison, *Political History of Scotland*, pp. 241–2.

18. Cited in Hutchison, *Political History of Scotland*, p. 240; and see pp. 237–45 generally for this.

19. L. Leneman, *A Guid Cause. The Women's Suffrage Movement in Scotland* (Aberdeen, 1991), pp. 58–63, 101–8, 118–19; L. Moore, 'The Women's Suffrage Campaign in the 1907 Aberdeen By-election', *Northern Scotland*, 5 (1983), pp. 155–78.

20. Leneman, *A Guid Cause*, pp. 118–19.

21. Ibid., pp. 63–8, 86–90, 188–9.

22. Hutchison, *Political History of Scotland*, pp. 230–4 for this and the following three paragraphs.

23. Finlay, *A Partnership for Good?*, p. 52–60; Hutchison, *Political History of Scotland*, pp. 232–3.

24. Hutchison, *Political History of Scotland*, pp. 218–21 for this and the succeeding paragraph.

25. Cited in Hutchison, *Political History of Scotland*, p. 222.

26. R. H. Campbell, *Owners and Occupiers. Changes in Rural Society in South West Scotland before 1914* (Aberdeen, 1991), pp. 108–50.

27. T. M. Devine (ed.), *Farm Servants and Labour in Lowland Scotland 1770–1914* (Edinburgh, 1984), pp. 10–142.

28. I. G. C. Hutchison, 'The Nobility and Politics in Scotland, *c*.1880–1939', in T. M. Devine (ed.) *Scottish Elites* (Edinburgh, 1994), pp. 135–6.

29. McCaffrey, 'Origins of Liberal Unionism', pp. 47–71.

30. Hutchison, *Political History of Scotland*, pp. 207–12, 225–7.

31. E. McFarland, *Protestants First! Orangeism in 19th Century Scotland* (Edinburgh, 1990), esp. pp. 70–2, 160–211.

32. Hutchison, *Political History of Scotland*, pp. 222–5.

33. The Unionist share of the vote rose by over 3 per cent in only three of nine such contests, and it actually fell in four. In only one of the three gains did their poll share rise. The seats (with Unionist share of the poll in December 1910 and the subsequent by-election) are: Glasgow, St Rollox (44.2 per cent, 48.6 per cent); Glasgow, Tradeston (39.5 per cent, 41.8 per cent); Kilmarnock (39.1 per cent, 31.0 per cent): Lanarkshire, Govan (43.1 per cent, 46.5 per cent); Lanarkshire, North East, (42.0 per cent, 38.4 per cent); *Lanarkshire, South (43.9 per cent, 42.8 per cent); *Leith (42.8 per cent, 37.8 per cent); *Midlothian (39.1 per cent, 41.7 per cent); West Lothian (39.2 per cent, 47.6 per cent). * Denotes a Unionist gain.

34. Hutchison, *Political History of Scotland*, pp. 221–7 for the following four paragraphs.

35. Cited in Hutchison, *Political History of Scotland*, p. 227.

36. G. D. Phillips, *The Diehards. Aristocratic Society and Politics in Edwardian England* (Cambridge, Mass., 1979), tables 3.2, 3.3 (pp. 29, 30–1).

37. J. Smith, 'Labour Traditions in Glasgow and Liverpool', *History Workshop*, 17 (1984), p. 46.

38. Leneman, *A Guid Cause*, pp. 69–70, 94–8, 125–6; S. S. Hetherington, *Katharine Atholl, 1874–1960. Against the Tide* (Aberdeen, 1989).

39. See J. Melling, 'Scottish Industrialists and the Changing Nature of Class Relations in the Clyde Region, 1880–1914', in T. Dickson (ed.), *Capital and Class in Scotland* (Edinburgh, 1982), pp. 61–142; W. Knox, *Hanging by a Thread: the Scottish Cotton Industry, c.1850–1914* (Preston, 1995), pp. 115–40.

40. C. C. M. MacDonald, 'The Radical Thread: Political Change in Scotland. Paisley Politics, 1885–1924', Strathclyde Univ. Ph.D. thesis (1996), pp. 164–71.
41. W. Knox, 'Politics and Workplace Culture', in W. H. Fraser and R. J. Morris (eds), *People and Society in Scotland*, vol. II, *1830–1914* (Edinburgh, 1990), pp. 149–50.
42. M. Keating and D. Bleiman, *Labour and Scottish Nationalism* (London, 1979), pp. 40–3.
43. W. H. Fraser, 'The Labour Party in Scotland', in K. D. Brown (ed.), *The First Labour Party, 1900–14* (London, 1985), pp. 40–52; Hutchison, *Political History of Scotland*, pp. 250–4.
44. J. J. Smyth, 'Labour and Socialism in Glasgow, 1880–1914: the Electoral Challenge prior to Democracy', Edinburgh Univ. Ph.D. thesis (1987), pp. 94–101.
45. Hutchison, *Political History of Scotland*, p. 261.
46. G. Brown, *Maxton* (Edinburgh, 1986), chs 3, 5; G. Walker, *Thomas Johnston* (Manchester, 1988), pp. 3–23.
47. Smyth, 'Labour and Socialism', pp. 278–86; J. Smith, 'Class, Skill and Sectarianism in Glasgow and Liverpool, 1880–1914', in R. J. Morris (ed.), *Class, Power and Social Structure in British Nineteenth Century Towns* (Leicester, 1986), pp. 195–8.
48. Walker, *Johnston*, pp. 7–16, 179–82.
49. C. W. M. Phipps, 'Aberdeen Trades Council and Politics, 1900–39. The Development of a Local Labour Party in Aberdeen', Aberdeen Univ. M.Litt. thesis (1980), chs 2, 3.
50. W. Kenefick and A. McIvor (eds), *Roots of Red Clydeside, 1910–14? Labour Unrest and Industrial Relations in West Scotland* (Edinburgh, 1996).
51. MacDonald, 'Radical Thread', pp. 178–80; Phipps, 'Aberdeen Trades Council', pp. 78–83.
52. J. Smith, 'Taking the Leadership of the Labour Movement: the ILP in Glasgow, 1906–14', in A. McKinlay and R. J. Morris (eds), *The ILP on Clydeside, 1893–1932: from Foundation to Disintegration* (Manchester, 1991), pp. 73–9.
53. Hutchison, *Political History of Scotland*, pp. 261–5.
54. Percentage of Labour councillors in 1898: 14.7 per cent; in 1914, 15.4 per cent. Cf. Smyth, 'Labour and Socialism', pp. 109–48.
55. J. F. McCaffrey, 'The Irish Vote in Glasgow in the Later Nineteenth Century: a Preliminary Survey', *Innes Review*, 21 (1970), pp. 30–7; Blewett, *The Peers, the Parties and the People*, pp. 151–3.
56. I. Wood, *John Wheatley* (Manchester, 1990), chs 2, 3; D. Howell, *A Lost Left: Three Studies in Socialism and Nationalism* (Manchester, 1986), pp. 229–37.
57. Smyth, 'Labour and Socialism', ch. 5; cf. Leneman, *A Guid Cause*, pp. 118–19.
58. Smyth, 'Labour and Socialism', ch. 6.
59. Labour share of vote: 1901, 21.7 per cent; 1904, 27.9 per cent; 1906, 29.2 per cent; Jan. 1910, 11.8 per cent; 1911, 16.3 per cent. These were all three-cornered fights.
60. Fraser, 'Labour Party in Scotland', pp. 52–9.

2   The Rise of Unionism and of Labour, 1914–39

1. West central region as defined here is: Ayrshire (4 seats), Dunbartonshire (2), Lanarkshire & Glasgow (21), Renfrewshire (4).

2. M. Dyer, *Capable Citizens and Improvident Democrats: The Scottish Electoral System, 1884–1929* (Aberdeen, 1996), pp. 104–12.

3. Edinburgh was the exception, with the Unionist *Scotsman* the sole daily, although the Liberals had a staunch evening champion, the *Edinburgh Evening News*.

4. E[dinburgh] U[niversity] L[ibrary], S[cottish] L[iberal] P[arty] MSS, H 20/12, SLF Exec. Min. Bk, 16 Sep. 1936, 31 Mar., 19 May, 17 Nov. 1937, 2 Mar. 1938.

5. Hutchison, *Political History*, pp. 319–27.

6. S. J. Brown, '"A Solemn Purification by Fire": Responses to the Great War in the Scottish Presbyterian Churches, 1914–19', *Journal of Ecclesiastical History*, 45 (1994), pp. 82–104.

7. S. J. Brown, '"Outside the Covenant"; the Presbyterian Churches and Irish Immigration, 1922–38', *Innes Review*, 42 (1991), pp. 19–45; R. J. Finlay, 'Nationalism, Race, Religion and the Irish Question in Inter-war Scotland', Ibid., 42 (1991), pp. 46–67.

8. S. J. Brown, '"A Victory for God": Scottish Presbyterian Churches and the General Strike of 1926', *J. Eccl. Hist.*, 42 (1991), pp. 596–617.

9. R. Ferguson, *George MacLeod. The Founder of the Iona Community* (London, 1990), ch. 9, cf. pp. 236–7.

10. N[ational] L[ibrary of] S[cotland], S[cottish] C[onservative &] U[nionist] A[ssociation] MSS, Acc. 10424/26(vi), Glasgow UA, *Annual Report*, 1933.

11. Cf. I. G. C. Hutchison, 'The Impact of the First World War on Scottish Politics', in C. M. M. Macdonald and E. W. McFarland (eds), *Scotland and the Great War* (East Linton, 1999), pp. 41–3.

12. Hutchison, *Political History of Scotland*, p. 310.

13. *Stirling Journal*, 1 Nov. 1922; Aberdeen University Library, Aberdeen Liberal Association MSS, MS 2472, Exec. Comm. Min. Bk, 23 Mar. 1920, 4 Apr. 1922.

14. EUL, SLP MSS, H 20/11, SLA Exec. Min. Bk, 27 Feb., 10 May, 19 Jul. 1929, 21 Jan. 1930.

15. *Alloa Advertiser*, 17 October 1931.

16. EUL, SLP MSS, H20/12, SLF Exec. Comm. Min. Bk, 10 Oct. 1934.

17. Ibid., H20/12, SLF Exec. Comm. Min. Bk, 17 Oct. 1935.

18. Dundee C[ity] A[rchives], Dundee L[iberal] A[ssociation] MSS, GD/DLA 1/1, Exec. Comm. Min. Bk, Ann. Reps 1932–3, 1933–4, 1935–6.

19. EUL, SLP MSS, H20/12, SLF Exec. Comm. Min. Bk, 10, 29 June 1932; 23 Dec. 1932, 11 Jan. 1933; 5 Apr. 1935, 8 Jan. 1936; 9 Dec. 1936; 30 Nov. 1938.

20. Ibid., H20/11, SLF Exec. Comm. Min. Bk, 20 Jan. 1928.

21. Ibid., H20/12, SLF Exec. Comm. Min. Bk, 17 Oct. 1935.

22. EUL, SLP MSS, H 20/11, SLF Exec. Comm. Min Bk, 23 Sep., 29 June 1926.

23. EUL, SLP MSS, H20/11, SLF Exec. Comm. Min. Bk, 27 Feb. 1929.

24. Based on Dundee CA, Dundee LA MSS, GD/DLA/1/8,12, 5th and 9th Ward Committee Min. Bks.

25. EUL, SLP MSS, H 20/11, SLF Exec. Comm. Min. Bk, 27 Jul. 1928.

26. Ibid., H20/11, SLF Exec. Comm. Min. Bk, 27 Feb. 1929, cf. 3 Oct., 7 Dec. 1928, 23 Apr. 1929.
27. Ibid., H 20/12, 13, SLF Exec. Comm. Min. Bk, 5 May 1937, 11, 25 May, 9 Nov. 1938.
28. S. Ball, 'Asquith's Decline and the General Election of 1918', *SHR*, 61 (1982), pp. 58–61.
29. EUL, SLP MSS, H 20/11, SLF Exec. Comm. Min. Bk, 21 Feb. 1928; 12 Jul. 1927, cf. 6 Mar. 1928.
30. Dundee CA, Dundee LA MSS, GD/DLA/4/11, Press-cuttings, *Dundee Evening Telegraph*, 20 Dec. 1928; *Broughty Ferry Guide*, 8 Mar. 1929.
31. EUL, SLP MSS, H 20/12, SLF Exec. Comm. Min. Bk, 21 Oct. 1935.
32. Dundee CA, Dundee LA MSS, GD/DLA/4/14, Press-cuttings, *Dundee Courier & Advertiser*, 4 Nov. 1935; cf. GD/DLA/4/13, Press-cuttings, *Dundee Courier & Advertiser*, 28 Nov. 1933.
33. EUL, SLP MSS, H10/12,13, SLF Exec. Comm. Min. Bk, 15 Sep. 1937, 11 May 1938.
34. Hutchison, *Political History of Scotland*, pp. 326–7.
35. This excludes the unusual case of Sir Alec Douglas-Home, who became a Scottish MP after being appointed Prime Minister in 1963. George Younger, Defence Secretary from 1986, was the first Scottish Tory MP already in the House of Commons to gain a Cabinet post other than the Scottish Office in the post-1945 era.
36. See A. Seldon and S. Ball (eds), *Conservative Century. The Conservative Party since 1900* (Oxford, 1994), pp. 59, 326, for the most recent discussion. Skelton used the term in his *Constructive Conservatism* (Edinburgh, 1924), p. 17.
37. NLS, SCUA MSS, Acc. 10424/27(vii), SUA, *Ann. Rep.*, 1936–7.
38. Ibid., Acc. 10424/27(viii), SUA, *Ann. Rep.*, 1938–9.
39. Ibid., Acc. 10424/27(v), SUA East. Div. Council, *Ann. Rep.*, 1931–2. The pamphlet was: Scottish Unionist Whip's Office, *Scottish Nationalism* (n.p., 1932).
40. Ibid., Acc. 10424/27(iv), SUA, *Ann. Rep.*, 1923–4.
41. Ibid., Acc. 10424/; cf. Acc. 10424/27(vii), SUA West. Div. Council, *Ann. Rep.*, (1937–8).
42. Ibid., Acc. 10424/27(vii), SUA West. Div. Council, *Ann. Rep.*, 1935–6; Acc. 10424/31, West. Div. Council Min. Bk, 31 May 1933.
43. Ibid., Acc. 10424/26(vi), Glasgow Unionist Association, *Ann. Rep.*, 1936 (Kelvingrove Constituency Association).
44. On inspection, only about one-quarter of a claimed 2,400 members in Cathcart Association in 1933 were found to exist: ibid., Acc. 10424/26(vii), Glasgow UA, *Ann. Rep.* (1934) – Cathcart UA.
45. Hutchison, *Political History of Scotland*, p. 316.
46. Cf. Hutchison, 'The Impact of the First World War on Scottish Politics', pp. 45–7.
47. NLS, SCUA MSS, Acc. 10424/126, 1931 Election Manifesto of Major MacAndrew (Glasgow Partick).
48. Mining seats won by Unionists: 14 (South Ayrshire, Fife West, Kirkcaldy, Lanarkshire Bothwell, Lanarkshire Coatbridge, Lanarkshire Lanark, Lanarkshire Motherwell, North Lanarkshire, Lanarkshire Rutherglen, North Midlothian, South Midlothian, Stirling East, Stirling West, West

Lothian; Stirling & Falkirk); by National Liberals: 1 (Dunfermline); by Labour: 1 (Lanarkshire Hamilton).

49. NLS, SCUA MSS, Acc. 10424/30, SUA West. Div. Council Min. Bk, 5 June 1929.

50. Ibid., Acc. 10424/64, SUA Cent. Council Min. Bk, 17 Nov. 1938; cf. Acc. 10424/31, SUA West. Div. Council Min. Bk, 13 Jan. 1932, for the earliest complaint.

51. C. Thornton-Kemsley, *Through Winds and Tides* (Montrose, 1974), p. 107.

52. Hutchison, *Political History of Scotland*, p. 314.

53. G. Brown, 'The Labour Party and Political Change in Scotland, 1918–29', Edinburgh Univ. Ph.D. thesis (1982), pp. 219–20, 237–40, 252–65, 289–307, 329–52, 463–72.

54. H. J. Moss, *Windjammer to Westminster* (London, 1941), pp. 131–3.

55. NLS, SCUA MSS, Acc. 10424/9(ii), L. Shedden MSS, P. J. Blair (?) to Prof. G. Kerr and Sir F. Thomson (Copies), 24 Nov. 1933.

56. *Questions of the Day in Scotland* (Edinburgh, 1928), pp. 7–10, cf. p. 31.

57. G. Walker, 'The Orange Order in Scotland between the Wars', *International Review of Social History*, 38 (1992), pp. 177–206; cf. T. Gallagher and G. Walker, 'Protestantism and Political Culture, 1890–1990' in T. Gallagher and G. Walker (eds), *Sermons and Battle Hymns: Protestant Popular Culture in Modern Scotland* (Edinburgh, 1990), pp. 89–91.

58. NLS, SCUA MSS, Acc. 10424/26(vii), Glasgow Unionist Association, *Ann. Rep.*, 1937.

59. Interestingly neither was Conservative: they were Dr R. Forgan (Labour, Renfrewshire West), and C. R. Dudgeon (Liberal, Dumfriesshire).

60. J. Mitchell, *Conservatives and the Union. A Study of Conservative Party Attitudes to Scotland* (Edinburgh, 1990), pp. 21–6, 45–8.

61. The Liberal ministers were: Robert Munro, (1918–22), Viscount Novar (1922–3), Sir Archibald Sinclair (1931–2), Sir Godfrey Collins (1932–6); the Unionists were: John Gilmour (1924–9), Walter Elliot (1936–8), John Colville (1938–40).

62. R. R. James, *Bob Boothby: Portrait of a Rebel* (London,1991), p. 67, cf. pp. 72–4, 133–4, 155–7, 185–9, 234–5.

63. Hetherington, *Katharine Atholl*, chs 15–19; S. Ball, 'The Politics of Appeasement: the Fall of the Duchess of Atholl and the Kinross & West Perthshire By-election, December 1938', *SHR*, 69 (1990), pp. 49–83; Hutchison, *Political History of Scotland*, p. 322.

64. NLS, SCUA MSS, Acc. 10424/27(vi), SUA, *Ann. Rep.*, 1934–5.

65. *Stirling Journal*, 15 Mar. 1923.

66. NLS, SCUA MSS, Acc. 10424/27(v), SUA, *Ann. Rep.*, 1934–5. Cf. Acc. 10424/64, SUA Cent. Council Min. Bk, 23 Nov. 1934.

67. Ibid., Acc. 10424/63, SUA Cent. Council Min. Bk, 13 Nov. 1925; Acc. 10424/27(v), SUA, *Ann. Rep.*, 1934–5.

68. T. Begg, *Fifty Special Years. A Study in Scottish Housing* (London, 1987), pp. 57–9.

69. NLS, SCUA MSS, Acc. 10424/31, SUA West. Div. Council Min. Bk, 29 Apr., 10 May 1935; also 3 Jan., 1, 6, 26 Feb., 6 Mar, 1, 10 May 1935; Acc. 10424/64, SUA Cent. Council Min. Bk, 10 Jan., 15, 18 May 1935.

70. Ibid., Acc. 10424/29, SUA Cent. Council Min. Bk, 10 Nov. 1924; Acc. 10424/27(v, vi), SUA, *Ann. Reps.*, 1924–5, 1932–3.

71. *Glasgow Herald*, 13 Nov. 1935.

72. *The National Government. What Has It Done? What Is It Doing?* (Edinburgh, 1935), pp. 17–18. Note, too, the Tories' advocacy in the 1930s of public funding to construct a Forth–Clyde canal, which flew in the face of economic orthodoxy: NLS, SCUA MSS, Acc. 10424/31, SUA West. Div. Council Min. Bk, 3 May 1933.

73. Ibid., Acc. 10424/, SUA West. Div. Council Min. Bk, Acc. 10424/63, SUA Cent. Council Min. Bk, 13 Nov. 1925.

74. *Questions of the Day in Scotland* (Edinburgh, 1928), pp. 139–42; *The Unionist Scheme of Rating and Local Government Reform. Its Effects on Industry and Agriculture* (2nd edn, Edinburgh, 1928), esp. pp. 8–22.

75. E. M. M. Taylor, 'The Politics of Walter Elliot, 1929–36', Edinburgh Univ. Ph.D. thesis (1979), chaps 5, 8.

76. There are more index references for Weir than any other non-politician in K. Middlemas, *Politics in Industrial Society* (London, 1979), the classic study of the tendency to corporatism. See also D. Ritschel, *The Politics of Planning: Debates on Economic Planning in Britain in the 1930s* (Oxford, 1997), pp. 186–8 (Nimmo quote), 150, 189, 195, 215, 294–5.

77. NAS, Gilmour of Montrave MSS, GD 393/23/6, E. R. Mitchell to J. Gilmour, 15 Feb. 1926.

78. Three useful expressions of the varying standpoints are: I. MacLean, *The Legend of Red Clydeside* (Edinburgh, 1983); J. Foster, 'Strike Action and Working Class Politics on Clydeside, 1914–19', *International Review of Social History*, 35 (1990), pp. 33–70; T. Brotherstone, 'Does Red Clydeside Really Matter Any More?', in A. MacIvor and R. Duncan (eds), *Militant Workers* (Edinburgh, 1992), pp. 52–80.

79. J. Holford, *Reshaping Labour. Organisation, Work and Politics in Edinburgh in the Great War and After* (London, 1988), p. 102.

80. Ibid., ch. 3, for the Edinburgh experience.

81. J. M. Craigen, 'The STUC (1897–1973) – a Study of a Pressure Group', Heriot-Watt Univ., M. Litt. thesis (1974), pp. 117–23, 137–9.

82. Holford, *Reshaping Labour*, pp. 168–232.

83. Stirling C[ouncil] A[rchives], Stirling [& Falkirk Burghs] L[abour] P[arty] MSS, PD 38/1/1, Stirling Trades & Labour Council Min. Bk, 27 Oct. 1915; cf. 1 Sep. 1915, 28 Nov. 1917, 20 Mar. 1918.

84. Craigen, 'STUC', pp. 159–70; K. Aitken, *The Bairns O'Adam. The Story of the STUC* (Edinburgh, 1997), pp. 107–15.

85. Craigen, 'STUC', pp. 151–73.

86. W. Walker, 'Dundee's Disenchantment with Churchill', *SHR*, 49 (1970), pp. 85–109. Dundee had the highest proportion of Irish-born of any Scottish town.

87. I. Patterson, 'The Impact of the Irish Revolution on the Irish Community in Scotland, 1916–23', Strathclyde Univ. M.Litt. thesis, (1990), pp. 218–45.

88. McCaffrey, 'The Irish Vote in Glasgow', pp. 30–7.

89. J. F. McCaffrey, 'Irish Issues in Nineteenth and Twentieth Century Radicalism in a Scottish Context', in T. M. Devine (ed.) *Irish Immigration and Scottish Society* (Edinburgh, 1991), pp. 126–31.

90. J. McGovern, *Neither Fear nor Favour* (London, 1960), pp. 67–80.

91. Hutchison, *Political History of Scotland*, pp. 290–2; R. Duncan, '"Motherwell for Moscow": Walton Newbould, Revolutionary Politics and the Labour Movement in a Lanarkshire Constituency', *Scottish Labour History Society Journal*, 28 (1993), pp. 47–70.
92. Macdonald, 'Radical Thread', pp. 181–92.
93. Hutchison, *Political History of Scotland*, p. 288.
94. In England, 7 Co-operative and 291 Labour candidates ran, a ratio of 1:42; in Scotland, the respective figures are 3 and 39, a ratio of 1:13.
95. Macdonald, 'Radical Thread', pp. 217–28; Hutchison, *Political History of Scotland*, pp. 301–3.
96. A. B. Campbell, 'From Independent Collier to Militant Miner: Tradition and Change in the Trade Union Consciousness of Scottish Miners, 1874–1929', *Scottish Labour History Society Journal*, 25 (1989), pp. 8–23; S. MacIntyre, *Little Moscows. Communism and Working Class Militancy in Inter-war Britain* (London, 1980), esp. pp. 48–111.
97. Manchester, N[ational] M[useum of] L[abour] H[istory], L[abour] P[arty] MSS, NEC Min. Bk, 6,7 Feb. 1928 (Kelvingrove); 22, 24 Mar. 1926 (delegate); SAC Min. Bk, 12 Oct. 1925, 16 Aug. 1926 (Glasgow and Bannockburn); 12 Jan., 8 June, 13 Jul., 14 Sep. 1925, NEC Min. Bk, 24 Feb. 1926, 30 Sep., 1,3 Oct. 1927, 6–7 Feb. 1928 (Greenock and Glasgow Trades Councils); SAC Min. Bk, 12 Apr., 13 Sep. 1926 (St Rollox, etc).
98. Ibid., LP MSS, SAC Min. Bk, 17 Jan. 1927.
99. Ibid., LP MSS, SAC Min. Bk, 11 May 1925; 18 Jan. 1926, 21 May, 17 Dec. 1928, 18 Mar. 1929, 17 Feb. 1930.
100. Ibid., LP MSS, SAC Min. Bk, 14 Apr. 1926.
101. Ibid., LP MSS, NEC Min. Bk, 27 Feb. 1929.
102. Ibid., LP MSS, SAC Min. Bk, 24 Apr. 1939.
103. Ibid., LP MSS, 18 Nov. 1930.
104. Ibid., LP MSS, SAC Min. Bk, 18 Jan. 1932.
105. Ibid., LP MSS, SAC Min. Bk, 16 Nov. 1933; NEC Min. Bk, 27 Mar. 1935, cf. 6–7 Feb. 1928; 21 Jan. 1925.
106. NLS, Woodburn MSS, Acc. 7656/4/1, 'Some Recollections by A. W.', p. 59.
107. See W. W. Knox and A. MacKinlay, 'The Remaking of Scottish Labour in the 1930s', *Twentieth Century British History*, 6 (1994), pp. 174–93, for a general interpretation.
108. NMLH, LP MSS, SAC Min. Bk, 6, 16 Nov. 1931.
109. J. Wood, 'The Labour Left and Constituency Politics, 1931 to 1951', Warwick Univ. Ph.D. thesis, (1982), pp. 184–96.
110. NMLH, LP MSS, NEC Min. Bk, 5 May 1938.
111. Ibid., LP MSS, SAC Min. Bk, 19 Nov. 1934.
112. Ibid., LP MSS, NEC Min. Bk, 8 Dec. 1931, 23 Jan., 27 Apr., 1932, 15. Dec. 1933, 21–2 May 1935; SAC Min. Bk, 11 Dec. 1931, 18 Jan. 1932.
113. Ibid., LP MSS, NEC Min. Bk, 4 Sep. 1935; SAC Min. Bk, 15 Oct. 1934.
114. Ibid., NEC Min. Bk, 24 Jan. 1934; SAC Min. Bk, 17 Feb. 1939.
115. Ibid., LP MSS, SAC Min. Bk, 19 June 1933.
116. Ibid., LP MSS, SEC Min. Bk, 17 Oct. 1938.
117. Ibid., LP MSS, NEC Min. Bk, 27 Mar. 1927.
118. Ibid., LP MSS, NEC Min. Bk, 21–2 May, 19 June 1935.

119. Ibid., SAC Min. Bk, 17 Oct. 1938.
120. Ibid., LP MSS, SAC Min. Bk, 27 Sep., 15 Nov. 1937, cf. 3 Apr., 17 Oct. 1938.
121. Ibid., LP MSS, SEC Min. Bk, 17 Aug., 6 Nov. 1931, 13 Feb. 1933, 27–8
      Sep. 1935, 15 Nov. 1937.
122. Ibid., SAC Min. Bk, 15 Oct. 1934.
123. Ibid., SAC Min. Bk, 19 Oct. 1936.
124. Ibid., LP MSS, SAC Min. Bk, 17 Oct. 1938.
125. Ibid., LP MSS, NEC Min. Bk, 27 Feb. 1936; SAC Min. Bk, 20 Mar. 1933, 21
      Oct. 1935, 17 Oct. 1938.
126. Ibid., LP MSS, SAC Min Bk, 3 Jul., 28 Aug. 1939.
127. Ibid., LP MSS, NEC Min. Bk, 17 Jul. 1935; SAC Min. Bk, 20 Aug. 1934,
      17 Oct., 9 Dec. 1938.
128. Ibid., LP MSS, SAC Min. Bk, 16 June 1935, 27 Feb. 1938; see also 3 Jul., 28
      Aug. 1939.

3   Consensus and Convergence?, 1939–59

1.   NLS, SCUA MSS, Acc. 10424/33, SUA West. Div. Council Min. Bk, 2 Mar.
     1945; Acc. 10424/27(viii), SUA West. Div. Council *Ann. Rep.* (1945), p. 6.
2.   D. E. Butler, *The Electoral System in Britain since 1918* (2nd edn, Oxford,
     1963), pp. 146–7 for this; cf. R. B. McCallum and A. Readman, *The British
     General Election of 1945* (Oxford, 1947), App. II.
3.   The apparent exception, 1951, is in reality aberrant because one-third of
     the total Liberal vote was cast in one seat (Dundee West), where no Tory was
     standing.
4.   NLS, SCUA MSS, Acc. 10424/33, SUA West. Div. Council Min. Bk, 26 Apr.
     1944, 3 Sep. 1945.
5.   Ibid., Acc. 10424/64, SUA Cent. Council Min. Bk, 28. Jul. 1941; Acc. 10424/
     27(viii), SUA West. Div. Council, *Ann. Reps* (1940–1, 1942–3, 1943–4).
6.   Ibid., Acc. 10424/36, SUA West. Div. Council Min. Bk, 26 May 1953, where
     148,770 members are claimed.
7.   NLS, SCUA MSS, Acc. 10424/35, SUA, West. Div. Council Min. Bk, 31 May
     1950; Acc. 10424/94(i), SUA, East. Div. Council *Ann. Rep.* (1949–50); Acc.
     10424/27(ix), West. Div. Council, *Ann. Rep.* (1950).
8.   Ibid., Acc. 10424/27(ix), SUA West. Div. Council, *Ann. Rep.* (1953).
9.   Ibid., Acc. 10424/97 SUA West. Div. Council, Org. Sec. Jt Mtg Min. Bk, 26
     Feb. 1953; 27 Jan., 26 May 1949; 29 Sep. 1950, 25 Jan. 1951; 15 Dec. 1953.
10. Ibid., Acc. 10424/64, SUA Cent. Council Min. Bk, 31 Oct. 1946; Acc. 11368/
     4, SUA Cent. Council Min. Bk, 24 Feb. 1953.
11. I.e., Ayr Burghs, Ayrshire Central, Berwick & East Lothian, Invernessshire
     and Lanark.
12. NLS, Central Ayrshire UA MSS, Acc. 9079/30, 'General Election Campaign
     1955 – Report by Organising Secretary.'
13. S. Rose and J. H. Burns, 'A Scottish Constituency' in D. E. Butler (ed.), *The
     British General Election of 1951* (London, 1952), pp. 186–8.

14. NLS, SCUA MSS, Acc. 10424/33, SUA, West. Div. Council Min. Bk, 5 Nov. 1941.

15. C. Coote, *A Companion of Honour. The Story of Walter Elliot in Scotland and Westminster* (London, 1965), p. 215, for Elliot. The other two Scottish members of the Progress Trust were E. G. R. Lloyd (Renfrewshire East) and Sir Douglas Thomson (Aberdeen South).

16. NLS, SCUA MSS, Acc. 10424/33, SUA West. Div. Council Min. Bk, 6 Mar. 1940, 25 Feb. 1943; Acc. 10424/64, SUA, Cent. Council Min. Bk, 21 Mar. 1945.

17. Ibid., Acc. 10424/64, SUA Cent. Council Min. Bk, 21 Mar. 1945.

18. Ibid., Acc. 10424/64, SUA Cent. Council Min. Bk, 21 Mar. 1945.

19. Between 1947–50, a total of 85,018 houses were built, 80,042 by local authorities. Between 1952–5, 142,817 houses were completed in all, 131,303 by local authorities.

20. NLS, SCUA MSS, Acc. 10424/94(i), SUA Cent. Council Min. Bk, 18, 19 May 1950.

21. Ibid., Acc. 10424/27(ix), SUA Cent. Council, *Ann. Rep.* (1953).

22. I.e., Ayrshire, Dunbartonshire, Lanarkshire, and Renfrewshire.

23. Thornton-Kemsley, *Through Winds and Tides*, pp. 228–9.

24. Dundee CA, Dundee LA MSS, GD/DLA/5/1,3,44, J. Carson to L. B. Weatherhead, and reply, 20 Feb., 8 May 1948, G. Wilson to L. [Weatherhead], 7 Mar. 1949; GD/DLA/1/1, Dundee LA Exec. Comm. Min. Bk, 13 Feb., 6 Mar., 24 Apr. 1950; *Dundee Courier & Advertiser*, 6 Oct. 1951. Cf. J. Junor, *Memories. Listening for a Midnight Tram* (London, 1991), p. 48, for the 'enormous pressure' placed on him to withdraw as Liberal candidate in the West seat. A similar sort of pact operated at Greenock: in 1950, no Tory stood, while in 1951 and 1955 no Liberal ran.

25. Mitchell, *Conservatives and Union*, pp. 27–34, 43–4, 48–50; cf. *Scottish Control of Scottish Affairs. Unionist Policy* (n.p., 1949).

26. The seats were Dundee West, Edinburgh East and North, and Motherwell.

27. J. Fowler (ed.), *Bannerman. The Memoirs of Lord Bannerman of Kildonan* (Aberdeen, 1972), pp. 106–13.

28. EUL, SLP MSS, H20/13, SLA Min. Bk, 30 Jan. 1946.

29. Junor, *Memories*, pp. 7–10, 18–19, 48, 50.

30. Dundee CA, Dundee LA MSS, GD/DLA/5/23, Lady Glen-Coats to L. B. Weatherhead, 10 May 1947.

31. Ibid., GD/DLA/5/28, Mrs H. R. Mill to L. Weatherhead, n.d. [c. Feb. 1948].

32. EUL, SLP MSS, H20/13, SLA Min. Exec. Comm. Bk, 21 Mar., 21 Nov. 1945.

33. Dundee CA, Dundee LA MSS, GD/DLA/2/2, Dundee LA Accounts, 1947/8–1958/9.

34. EUL, SLP MSS, H20/13. SLA Exec. Comm. Min. Bk, 29 Apr. 1942, 10 Feb. 1943, 6 Dec. 1944, 7 Mar. 1945.

35. Ibid., H20/13, SLA Exec. Comm. Min. Bk, 28 Oct. 1942.

36. NLS, Scottish Secretariat MSS, Acc. 3721/41/11, Lady Glen-Coats to R. E. Muirhead, 8 Jan. 1952, cf. 28 Nov. 1951.

37. EUL, SLP MSS, HO 20/13, SLF Exec. Comm. Min. Bk, 15 Feb., 30 Jan. 1946.

38. Ibid., H20/13, SLA Exec. Comm. Min. Bk, 28 June, 29 Sep. 1944, 21 Nov. 1945.

39. M. C. Dyer, 'The Politics of Kincardineshire', Aberdeen Univ. Ph.D. thesis (1973), vol.I, pp. 366–75.

40. R. J. Finlay, *Independent and Free* (Edinburgh, 1994), pp. 1–205, is the authoritative treatment of Scottish Nationalist politics in this period.

41. Ibid., pp. 206–50.

42. The Nuffield study of the 1945 election included the SNP vote under the general heading of 'Labour'.

43. Finlay, *Independent and Free*, pp. 238–43.

44. W. Wood, *Yours Sincerely for Scotland* (London, 1970) conveys the glorious dottiness of fringe nationalism. The chapter on her visit to London in 1951 during a Wembley football international is particularly entertaining: pp. 83–95.

45. McCallum and Readman, *The General Election of 1945*, pp. 120–1.

46. The study of the 1951 election in North Aberdeen concluded that there was 'little interest' in Scottish Home Rule among voters: Rose and Burns, 'A Scottish Constituency', p. 191.

47. ILP share of poll: Glasgow Pollok (1940), 11.9 per cent; East Renfrewshire (1940), 19.3 per cent; Edinburgh Central (1941), 29.0 per cent; Glasgow Cathcart (1942), 13.8 per cent; Hamilton (1943), 18.9 per cent.

48. C. Harvie, 'Labour in Scotland during the Second World War', *Historical Journal*, 26 (1983), pp. 934–6.

49. Stirling CA, Stirling LP MSS, PD 38/2/3, Exec. Comm. Min. Bk, 23 Sep. 1950.

50. NMLH, LP MSS, NEC Min. Bk, 20 Feb. 1948 – Appendix, Election Sub-Committee Mins.

51. NLS, SCUA MSS, Acc. 10424/34, SUA West. Div. Council Min. Bk, 3 Feb. 1948.

52. S. B. Chrimes (ed.), *The General Election in Glasgow, February 1950* (Glasgow, 1950), pp. 90–2.

53. NMLH, LP MSS, NEC Min. Bk, 21 Mar., 15 Sep. 1948.

54. Ibid., LP MSS, NEC Mins., 21 Mar. 1948 (Organisation Sub-Committee); 20 Feb. 1948 (Elections Sub-Committee). Glasgow City Labour Party, *Ann. Reps*, 1951, 1952.

55. Stirling CA, Stirling LP MSS, PD 38/2/3, CLP Min. Bk, 5 Nov. 1949; 6 Aug. 1950; PD 38/2/4, CLP Min. Bk, 10 Aug. 1952; PD 38/2/3, 23 Sep. 1950; 5 Nov. 1950; 25 Nov. 1951; PD 38/2/4, 13 Sep. 1953; PD 38/2/3, 14 May [1950].

56. NMLH, LP MSS, NEC Min. Bk, 9 Feb., 6 Dec. 1951. There were 10 Scottish seats (14.1 per cent of all seats) with no women's section; 15 (3.0 per cent) in England and 1 (2.8 per cent) in Wales. Scotland in fact had fewer women's branches than Wales – 178 to 258 – despite Scotland having double the population. There were 1,777 branches in England.

57. Exec. Comm. of the Scottish Council of the Labour Party, *Ann. Rep.*, 1950 [i.e., 1949], p. 11.

58. Ibid., 1956 [i.e., 1955], p. 42.

59. Stirling CA, Stirling LP MSS, PD 38/2/3, CLP Min. Bk, 4 June [1950].

60. Exec. Comm. SCLabP, *Ann. Rep.*, 1956.
61. I.e., Caithness & Sutherland, Invernessshire, Moray & Nairn and Ross & Cromarty. Labour already held the Western Isles, and had come third in Orkney & Shetland, but very close to the second-placed Liberal.
62. NMLH, LP MSS, NEC Min. Bk, 17 Sep. 1947.
63. Stirling CA, Stirling LP MSS, PD 38/2/3, CLP Min. Bk, 5 Nov. 1950.
64. R. H. Campbell, 'The Committee of Ex-Secretaries of Scotland and Industrial Policy, 1941–5', *Scottish Industrial History*, 2 (1979), pp. 3–11, is a penetrating critique of this talking-shop.
65. MacCallum and Readman, *General Election of 1945*, pp. 96–105.
66. Stirling CA, Stirling LP MSS, PD 38/2/3, CLP Min. Bk, 4 Mar., 15 Apr. 1944, 14 Aug. 1943, 7 Oct. 1944, 4 Feb. 1945 (quote).
67. SAC LP, *Ann. Reps*, (1956), p. 10; (1960), pp. 14–15.
68. W. C. Watson, 'Clydebank and the Inter-War Years: a Study in Economic and Social Change', Glasgow Univ. Ph.D. Thesis, (1984), pp. 312–39.
69. Cf. J. Schneer, *Labour's Conscience: the Labour Left, 1945–51* (London, 1988), App. I; M. Jenkins, *Bevanism. Labour's High Tide* (Nottingham, 1979), pp. 307–12.
70. F. Bealey and J. Sewel, *The Politics of Independence: a Study of a Scottish Town* (Aberdeen, 1981), pp. 51–4, 100–5; Dyer, 'Politics of Kincardineshire', pp. 349–52, 396–406.
71. W. Hamilton, *Blood on the Walls* (London, 1992), pp. 61–3.
72. NMLH, LP MSS, NEC Min. Bk, 4 June 1945; for McGovern's move to Labour: 6 Feb., 19 Mar. 1947; for Stephen's, 16 Jul., 17 Sep. 1947.

4   The Dominance of Labour and the Challenge of Nationalism, 1959–79

1. L. Chester and J. Fenby, *The Fall of the House of Beaverbrook* (London, 1979), pp. 54–7.
2. Although this somewhat overstates the increase; as the *Daily Mirror* effectively withdrew from Scotland, selling only about 25,000 copies against 100,000 before the takeover: C. King, *Strictly Personal* (London, 1969), pp. 120–2.
3. The circulation of the *Record* rose by 120,000 between 1956 and 1961.
4. See Ferguson, *George MacLeod*, pp. 234–6.
5. R. Ferguson, *Geoff. The Life of Geoffrey M. Shaw* (Gartocharn, 1979).
6. Ferguson, *George MacLeod*, p. 393.
7. NLS, SCUA MSS, Acc. 11368/4, SUA Cent. Council Exec. Min. Bks, 14 Apr. 1958; Exec. Comm., Scottish Council of the Labour Party, *Ann. Rep.*, 1955, p. 34.
8. For two lively overviews, see D. Seawright and J. Curtice, 'The Decline of the Scottish Conservative and Unionist Party, 1950–92: Religion, Ideology and Economics', *Contemporary Record*, 9 (1995), pp. 319–42; D. McCrone, 'Politics in a Cold Country', in *Understanding Scotland. The Sociology of a Stateless Nation* (London, 1992), pp. 146–73.

9. R. Saville (ed.), *The Economic Development of Modern Scotland, 1950–80* (Edinburgh, 1985), pp. 1–113; C. H. Lee, *Scotland and the United Kingdom. The Economy and the Union in the Twentieth Century*, (Manchester, 1996), chs 3 and 4 provide two clear outlines of the economic disparities.
10. NLS, SCUA MSS, Acc. 11368/4, SUA Cent. Council Min. Bk, 30 Nov. 1959. Cf. Acc. 10424/27(ix), SUA West. Div. Council, *Ann. Rep.*, 1959.
11. These were: Ayrshire Central, Glasgow Craigton, Glasgow Kelvingrove, Glasgow Scotstoun, Glasgow Woodside, Lanark, Renfrewshire West, Rutherglen.
12. These were: Aberdeenshire East & West, Angus South, Argyll, Banff, Caithness & Sutherland, Galloway, Invernessshire, Moray & Nairn, Perthshire East, Ross & Cromarty.
13. Cf. Bealey and Sewel, *Politics of Independence*, pp. 54–62; Dyer, 'Kincardineshire Politics', pp. 322–7.
14. NLS, SCUA MSS, Acc. 11368/4, SUA Cent. Council Min. Bk, 13 Nov. 1964.
15. By contrast, controls on cheaper housing stock – those with an annual rental of less than £40 – ended only upon a change of tenant.
16. NLS, SCUA MSS, Acc. 11368/5, SUA Cent. Council Min. Bk, 13 Nov. 1964.
17. Scottish Council (Development and Industry), *Inquiry into the Scottish Economy, 1960–1* (Edinburgh, n.d.) [the Toothill Report], pp. 134–7.
18. Begg, *Fifty Special Years*, pp. 180–8; *Glasgow Herald*, 11 Sep. 1959 (this article was written by R. D. Kernohan, a leading Glasgow Conservative, who stood as a candidate in 1959, as well as in several other elections, always unsuccessfully); J. MacInnes, MP, *Rent and Rates. The Inside Story* (Glasgow, n.d., but c. 1957).
19. NLS, Central Ayrshire CUA MSS, Acc. 9079/7, SUA New Towns Committee Min. Bk, 11 Apr. 1972.
20. Mitchell, *Conservatives and the Union*, chs 4, 5 spares no detail.
21. NLS, SCUA MSS, Acc. 10424/98, SUA West. Div. Council, Org. Secs Jt Mtg Min. Bk, 29 Oct. 1964.
22. Ibid., Acc. 11368/5, SUA Cent. Council Min. Bk, 13 Nov. 1964.
23. Ibid., Acc. 10424/97, SUA, West. Div. Council Org. Secs Jt Mtg Min. Bk, 29 Jan. 1959; NLS, Central Ayrshire CUA MSS, Acc. 7029/4, Exec. Comm. Min. Bk, 9 Sep. 1975.
24. NLS, SCUA MSS, Acc. 10424/97, 98, SUA West. Div. Council, Org. Secs Jt Mtg Min. Bk, 26 May 1959, 28 Feb. 1963.
25. Ibid., Acc. 11368/4, SUA Cent. Council Min. Bk, 22 June 1951; Acc. 10424/98, SUA West. Div. Council Org. Secs Jt Mtg Min. Bk, 28 May 1964, 25 Mar. 1965.
26. Ibid., Acc. 10424/97, SUA West. Div. Council Org. Secs Jt Mtg Min. Bk, 28 May 1959; Central Ayrshire CUA MSS, Acc. 9079/4, Exec. Comm. Min. Bk, 7 Dec. 1965, 13 Sep. 1966.
27. NLS, SCUA MSS, Acc. 10424/97, SUA West. Div. Council, Org. Secs Jt Mtg Min. Bk, 31 May, 29 Nov. 1956.
28. I.e., Lady Tweedsmuir (Aberdeen South, 1946–66), B. Harvie Anderson (Renfrewshire East, 1959–79).
29. NLS, SCUA MSS, Acc. 10424/98, SUA West. Div. Council, Org. Secs Jt Mtg Min. Bk, 31 Jan. 1963, 26 Mar., 29 Oct. 1964.
30. Ibid., Acc. 10424/98, SUA West. Div. Council, Org. Secs Jt Mtg Min. Bk, 2 Nov., 29 Oct. 1964.

31. Ibid., Central Ayrshire CUA MSS, Acc. 9079/3,4, Exec. Comm. Min. Bk, 4 Oct. 1956, 24 Feb. 1965, 16 Feb. 1967, 4 Nov. 1968, 19 Jan. 1971, 26 Feb. 1976, 11 Dec. 1979; *Ann. Rep.*, 1975–6.

32. Ibid., Central Ayrshire CUA MSS, Acc. 9079/4, Exec. Comm. Min. Bk, 9 Sep. 1975.

33. For example, in Glasgow, Conservative candidates first ran in 1967.

34. NLS, Central Ayrshire CUA MSS, Acc. 9079/4, Exec. Comm. Min. Bk, 5 Feb., 15 May, 11 Nov. 1981, 26 Nov. 1981.

35. NLS, SCUA MSS, Acc. 11368/4, SUA Central Council Min. Bk, 17 Nov. 1962.

36. NLS. SCUA MSS, Acc. 11368/4, SUA Cent. Council Min. Bk, 13 Dec. 1963.

37. Ibid., Central Ayrshire CUA MSS, Acc. 9079/3, Exec. Comm. Min. Bk, 26 May 1960.

38. Ibid., Central Ayrshire CUA MSS, Acc. 9079/4, Exec. Comm. Min. Bk, 10 Jan. 1978; SCUA MSS, Acc. 11368/4,5, SUA Central Council Min. Bk, 13 Dec. 1963, 13 Nov. 1964. In England, paid missioners had been used in the late 1940s, but thereafter constituency association members undertook this work.

39. J. H. Young, *A History of Cathcart Conservative & Unionist Association, 1918 to 1993* (n.p., n.d.), pp. 48, 4–5, 69–70.

40. NLS, SCUA MSS, Acc. 10424/35, 37, SUA West. Div. Council Min. Bk, 1 Dec. 1950; [2 Jan.], 6, 28 Mar. (quoted), 1 June 1951; 30 Nov. 1954.

41. NLS, Central Ayrshire CUA MSS, Acc. 9079/4, Exec. Comm. Min. Bk, 5 Feb., 11 Dec. 1979.

42. I. Levitt, 'New Towns, New Scotland, New Ideology, 1937–57', *SHR*, 76 (1997), pp. 222–38.

43. NLS, Central Ayrshire CUA MSS, Acc. 9079/7, SUA New Towns Comm. Min. Bk, esp. 29 Mar. [1967], 10 Apr., 26 June 1968, 26 June, 16 Oct. 1969, 3 Dec. 1970, 1 Jul. 1971, 11 Apr. 1972.

44. Ibid., SCUA MSS, Acc. 10424/97, SUA West. Div. Council Org. Secs Jt Mtg Min. Bk, 26 Jan., 28 Sep. 1961.

45. Ibid., Central Ayrshire CUA MSS, Acc. 9079/4, Exec. Comm. Min. Bk, 26 May, 8 Sep. 1960, 8 Feb., 26 June 1961, 19 Apr. 1962, 5 May 1963, 30 Jan. 1964.

46. Young, *Cathcart Unionist Association*, p. 54.

47. Ibid., pp. 69–70.

48. Ibid., pp. 55–60.

49. *Stirling Journal*, 12 Apr. 1962; NLS, Central Ayrshire CUA MSS, Acc. 9079/ 4, Exec. Comm. Min. Bk, 25 Sep., 11 Oct. 1967.

50. C. Lythe and M. Majmudar, *The Renaissance of the Scottish Economy?* (London, 1982), pp. 107–9.

51. While about 15 per cent of pupils in England attended grant-maintained or independent schools, only about 4 per cent in Scotland did so.

52. T. H. Hollingsworth, *Migration. A Study based on the Scottish Experience, 1939– 64* (Edinburgh, 1970), pp. 54–5.

53. B. Ashcroft and J. Love, 'New Firm Formation in the British Counties and the Regions of Scotland', *Scottish Economic Bulletin*, 49 (1994), pp. 13–21. This study relates to the period 1980–90.

54. In 1965–6, managers, professionals and clerical workers constituted 40.1 per cent of the total adult males, and in 1975–6, 47.9 per cent. See H. Jones,

'Modern Emigration from Scotland to Canada', *Scottish Geographical Magazine*, 95 (1979), pp. 4–12, esp. table 1.

55. D. G. Mercer and D. J. C. Forsyth, 'A Scottish Brain Drain. The University Experience', *Scottish Geographical Magazine*, 90 (1974), pp. 134–5; cf. *Toothill Report*, App. 34.

56. Thus in 1973, 45.8 per cent of households in England, but 39.2 per cent in Scotland, owned one car; the respective figures for refrigerators were 81.3 per cent and 73.2 per cent; for central heating, 42.1 per cent and 35.7 per cent.

57. R. H. S. Crossman, *Diaries of a Cabinet Minister*, Vol. 1, *Minister of Housing, 1964–66* (London, 1975), p. 159 (14 Feb. 1965).

58. Ashcroft and Love, 'New Firm Formation', pp. 13–21.

59. Greenock is an exception only because the Tories had effectively ceased to work the constituency in a serious manner.

60. NLS, SCUA MSS, Acc. 11368/5, SUA Cent. Council Min. Bk, 13 Nov. 1964.

61. Dyer, 'Politics of Kincardineshire', pp. 319–22, 366–75.

62. D. Butler and D. Kavanagh, *The British General Election of February 1974* (London, 1974), pp. 318–23.

63. *Labour Party Campaign Handbook. Scotland* (n.p., 1979), pp. 43–6.

64. Forty-five per cent of Scottish Tory manifestos alluded to the Empire, 55 per cent in England. For foreign affairs, the respective figures are 57 per cent and 71 per cent, and for defence, 50 per cent and 59 per cent. With Labour, the respective Scottish and English statistics are: Empire, 11 per cent, 24 per cent; foreign affairs, 77 per cent, 84 per cent; defence, 2 per cent, 12 per cent. See MacCallum and Readman, *General Election of 1945*, pp. 104–5. Cf. K. Robbins, 'This Grubby Wreck of Old Glories: the United Kingdom and the End of the British Empire', in *History, Religion and Identity in Modern Britain* (London, 1993), pp. 281–92.

65. C. Harvie, *Fool's Gold*, (London, 1995), chap. 8 is an excellent distillation of the welter of material on the impact of North Sea oil.

66. J. Brand, *The National Movement in Scotland* (London, 1978), p. 150, reports a survey finding that 49 per cent of those under 24 would support the SNP, but only 24 per cent of those over 65 would do so.

67. None of the eleven MPs in October 1974 had a working-class occupation, and none were upper-middle-class. There were four teachers (Andrew Welsh, Iain MacCormick, George Thompson, Margaret Bain), two lawyers (Winifred Ewing, Gordon Wilson), two business consultants (Douglas Crawford and Douglas Henderson), and one each of broadcaster (George Reid), farmer (Hamish Watt), and small businessman (Donald Stewart).

68. Butler and Kavanagh, *The February 1974 General Election*, p. 246–7.

69. R. Levy, *Scottish Nationalism at the Crossroads* (Edinburgh, 1990), pp. 10–17, 77–85.

70. Levy, *Scottish Nationalism at the Crossroads*, p. 13; cf. Dyer, 'Politics of Kincardineshire', pp. 406–11.

71. Bealey and Sewel, *Politics of Independence*, pp. 53–4; Dyer, 'Politics of Kincardineshire', pp. 322–7.

72. W. L. Miller, *The End of British Politics?* (Oxford, 1981), chs 4, 5; cf. D. McCrone, *Understanding Scotland. The Sociology of a Stateless Nation* (London, 1992), pp. 164–7.

73. Glasgow City Labour Party, *Ann. Rep.*, (1968).
74. *Scottish Co-operator*, 9 Apr., 21 May 1955; 13 June 1975.
75. Glasgow City Labour Party, *Ann. Reps*, 1968, 1967. The problem of membership is referred to every year in the 1960s.
76. See: *Labour Party Campaign Handbook. Scotland*, (n.p., 1979), for much on this, esp. pp. 7–21, 24–35.
77. W. Miller, 'The Scottish Dimension', in D. Butler and D. Kavanagh (eds), *The British General Election of 1979* (London, 1980), pp. 98–9.
78. Lythe and Majdumar, *Renaissance of Scottish Economy?*, pp. 107–9.
79. J. Brand and W. L. Miller, *The Labour Party in Scotland in 1979: Advance or Retreat?* (Glasgow, 1983), pp. 6–18.
80. M. Keating *et al.*, *Labour's Elites in Glasgow* (Glasgow, 1989), pp. 8–16.
81. Scottish Council of the Labour Party, *Ann. Rep.*, 1980 (i.e., for 1979).
82. T. Gallagher, *Glasgow. The Uneasy Peace* (Manchester, 1987), pp. 323–7.
83. Brown, *Religion and Society in Scotland*, fig. 5, pp. 62–3, cf. pp. 158–61.
84. Keating *et al.*, *Labour's Elites in Glasgow*, pp. 20–2.
85. Ferguson, *Geoff, passim*.
86. Ferguson, *Geoff*, pp. 187–98, 229–30, 266–9.
87. This and the following paragraph is taken from the Labour Party Scottish Council, *Ann. Reps*, 1974–9.
88. H. Drucker, *Breakaway: the Scottish Labour Party* (Edinburgh, n.d.) gives a clear account.

Epilogue: Since 1979

1. Young, *Cathcart Conservative Association*, p. 79–83.
2. I. Crewe and A. King, *SDP: the Birth, Life and Death of the Social Democratic Party* (Oxford, 1995), table 13.2.
3. Ibid., pp. 292–8.

BIBLIOGRAPHY

This survey is confined to items with a strong Scottish content: works dealing primarily with Britain as a whole are not included. Only secondary works are listed.

For the **general background**, T. M. Devine, *The Scottish Nation, 1700 to 2000* (London, 1999) is up to date and scholarly. T. M. Devine and R. J. Finlay (eds), *Scotland in the Twentieth Century* (Edinburgh, 1996) is authoritative; C. Harvie, *No Gods and Precious Few Heroes: Scotland since 1914* (new edn, Edinburgh, 1987) is lively; W. Ferguson, *Scotland since 1689* (Edinburgh, 1968) is solid but a little elderly; J. G. Kellas, *Modern Scotland. The Nation since 1870* (2nd edn, London, 1980) is helpful. General treatments of politics can begin with: C. Harvie, 'Scottish Politics', in A. Dickson and J. Treble (eds), *People and Society in Scotland. Vol. III, 1914–90* (Edinburgh, 1992), which is brief but rewarding; M. Fry, *Patronage and Principle. A Political History of Modern Scotland* (Aberdeen, 1987), a stimulating treatment from the later eighteenth century to the present; I. G. C. Hutchison, *A Political History of Scotland, 1832–1924. Parties, Elections, Issues* (Edinburgh, 1986), which covers the early years of this century. A broad account of the Scottish electoral system is afforded by M. Dyer, *Capable Citizens and Improvident Democrats. The Scottish Electoral System, 1884–1929* (Aberdeen, 1996).

The **central government of Scotland** can be approached through: two works by I. Levitt, *Government and Social Conditions in Scotland, 1845–1919* (Edinburgh, 1988), and *The Scottish Office: Depression and Reconstruction, 1919–59* (Edinburgh, 1996); J. S. Gibson, *The Thistle and The Crown: A History of the Scottish Office* (Edinburgh, 1988); L. Paterson, *The Autonomy of Modern Scotland* (Edinburgh, 1994) is a highly stimulating panoptic view; H. J. Hanham, 'The Development of the Scottish Office', in J. N. Wolfe (ed.), *Government and Nationalism in Scotland. An Enquiry by Members of the University of Edinburgh* (Edinburgh, 1969); two essays by R. H. Campbell: 'The Scottish Office and the Special Areas in the 1930s', *Historical Journal*, 22 (1979), and 'The Committee of Ex-Secretaries of State for Scotland and Industrial Policy, 1941–45', *Scottish Industrial History*, 2 (1979) ; J. Mitchell, 'The Gilmour Report on Scottish Central Administration', *Juridical Review* (1989); G. S. Pottinger, *The Secretaries of State for Scotland 1926–76* (Edinburgh, 1979) has brief biographies, often with insider knowledge. J. Brand, *British Parliamentary Parties: Policies and Power* (Oxford, 1992), chap. 7, is astute. W. L. Miller, 'Politics in the Scottish City, 1832–1982', in G. Gordon (ed.), *Perspectives of the Scottish City* (Aberdeen, 1985) is about the only consideration of municipal politics.

175

For the **Conservatives** there is very little. G. Warner, *The Scottish Tory Party* (London, 1988) is, to be charitable, disappointing. There are interesting papers in C. C. M. MacDonald (ed.), *Unionist Scotland*, (Edinburgh, 1998); J. G. Kellas, 'The Party in Scotland', in S. Ball and A. Seldon (eds), *Conservative Century: The Conservative Party since 1900* (Oxford, 1994) is a brisk tour of the topic; as is R. Finlay, 'Scottish Conservatism and Unionism since 1918', in M. Francis and I. Zweiniger-Bargielowska (eds), *The Conservatives and British Society, 1880–1990*, (Cardiff, 1996). J. Mitchell, *Conservatives and the Union. A Study of Conservative Party Attitudes to Scotland* (Edinburgh, 1990) is wide-ranging; narrower themes are covered in D. W. Urwin, 'The Development of Conservative Party Organisation in Scotland until 1912', *Scottish Historical Review*, 44 (1965); S. Ball, 'The Politics of Appeasement: the Fall of the Duchess of Atholl and the Kinross and West Perth By-election, December, 1938', *Scottish Historical Review*, 69 (1990). J. H. Young, *A History of the Cathcart Conservative and Unionist Association, 1918–93* (Glasgow, 1994) has interesting nuggets. D. Seawright and J. Curtice, 'The Decline of the Scottish Conservative and Unionist Party, 1950–92: Religion, Ideology or Economics?', *Contemporary Record*, 9 (1995), uses opinion polls ingeniously. Biographies of relevance are: R. Blake, *The Unknown Prime Minister* (London, 1955) for Bonar Law; S. Hetherington, *Katharine Atholl, 1874–1960: Against the Tide.* (Aberdeen, 1989); R. R. James, *Bob Boothby : A Portrait* (London, 1991); C. Coote, *A Companion of Honour. The Story of Walter Elliot in Scotland and Westminster* (London, 1965).

For **Labour**, there is, relatively speaking, a superabundance. I. Donnachie, C. Harvie and I. Wood (eds), *Forward! Labour Politics in Scotland, 1888–1988* (Edinburgh, 1989) is series of essays on the history of the party from its origins; M. Keating and D. Bleimann, *Labour and Scottish Nationalism* (London, 1979) ranges more widely than the title suggests. W. H. Fraser, 'The Labour Party in Scotland', in K. Brown (ed.), *The First Labour Party, 1900–14* (London, 1983) is particularly sensible and thoughtful; two papers by J. Smith, 'Class, Skill and Sectarianism in Glasgow and Liverpool, 1880–1914', in R. J. Morris (ed.), *Class, Structure and Power in Nineteenth Century British Towns* (Leicester, 1986), and 'Labour Traditions in Glasgow and Liverpool', *History Workshop*, 17 (1984), take a long perspective.

For the debate on **Red Clydeside**, there are two older books still of some value: B. Pribicevic, *The Shop Stewards Movement and Workers' Control, 1910–22* (Oxford, 1959) and K. Middlemas, *The Clydesiders* (London, 1965). The more recent phase of the controversy starts with J. Hinton, *The First Shop Stewards Movement*, (London, 1973) and I. McLean, *The Legend of Red Clydeside* (Edinburgh, 1983); see also the latter's 'Red Clydeside, 1915–19', in R. Quinault and J. Stevenson (eds), *Popular Protest and Public Order. Six Studies in British History, 1790–1920* (London, 1974). G. Rubin, 'Explanations for Law Reform: The Case of War-Time Labour Legislation in Britain, 1915–16', *International Review of Social History*, 38 (1987); A. Reid, 'Dilution, Trade Unionism and the State in Britain during the First World War', in S. Tolliday and J. Zeitlin (eds), *Shop Floor Bargaining and the State*, (Cambridge, 1985) both argue against the more radical interpretation. J. Melling, 'Whatever happened to Red Clydeside?', *International Review of Social History*, 35 (1990) attempts to strike a balance between the two schools. J. Foster, 'Strike Action and Working Class Politics in Clydeside, 1914–19', *International Review of Social History*, 35 (1990) seeks to resurrect the revolutionary interpretation; see also his 'Red Clyde, Red Scotland', in I. Donnachie and C. A. Whatley (eds), *The Manufacture of Scottish History*, (Edinburgh, 1992); T. Brotherstone, 'Does Red Clydeside Really Matter any More?', in R. Duncan and A. J. McIvor (eds), *Militant Workers. Labour and Class Conflict on the Clyde, 1900–50* (Edinburgh, 1992) makes an interesting summary of the present state of the argument. On the rent strikes, J. Melling, *Rent Strikes: The People's Struggles for Housing in the West of Scotland, 1890–1916* (Edinburgh, 1983) is authoritative, but see also: S. Damer, 'State, Class and Housing in Glasgow, 1885–1919', in J. Melling (ed.), *Housing, Social Policy and the State* (London, 1980); J. J. Smyth, 'Rents, Peace, Votes: Working Class Women and Political Activity in the First World War', in E. Breitenbach and E. Gordon (eds), *Out of Bounds. Women in Scottish Society, 1800–1945*, (Edinburgh, 1992). R. J. Morris and A. MacKinlay (eds), *The ILP on Clydeside* (Manchester, 1991) contains careful reassessments.

J. D. Young, *The Rousing of the Scottish Working Classes* (London, 1979) ends in the inter-war period. The **inter-war years** are treated spasmodically: J. Holford, *Reshaping Labour: Organisation, Work and Politics in Edinburgh during the Great War and After* (London, 1988) is a study of Labour in Edinburgh; R. Gallagher, 'The Vale of Leven, 1918–75: Changes in Working Class Organisation and Action', in T. Dickson (ed.), *Capital and Class in Scotland* (Edinburgh, 1982); J. Skelly (ed.), *The General Strike* (London, 1976) and M. Morris (ed.), *The General Strike* (Harmondsworth, 1976) both have sections on Scotland, with widely differing interpretations; W. W. Knox and A. MacKinlay, 'The Re-making of Scottish Labour in the 1930s', *Twentieth Century British History*, 6 (1994) is invaluable. C. Harvie, 'Labour in Scotland during the Second World War', *Historical Journal*, 26 (1983) takes the chronology a little further. A. Tuckett, *The Scottish Trades Union Congress. The First Eighty Years, 1897–1977* (Edinburgh, 1986) is rather uncritical; K. Aitken, *The Bairns O' Adam. The Story of the STUC* (Edinburgh, 1997) covers the first hundred years of the STUC; R. P. Arnot, *A History of the Scottish Miners* (London, 1955) and A. Tuckett, *The Scottish Carter. The History of the Scottish Horse and Motormen's Association*, (London, 1967) are both also highly sympathetic to their subjects.

Biographical studies of **Labour party leaders** include: W. W. Knox, *Scottish Labour Leaders 1918–39* (Edinburgh, 1984), with an exceptionally strong introductory essay; D. Howell, *A Lost Left: Three Studies in Socialism and Nationalism* (Manchester, 1986) deals with John Wheatley and John Maclean; G. Walker, *Thomas Johnston* (Manchester, 1988); G. Brown, *Maxton* (Edinburgh, 1986); W. W. Knox, *James Maxton* (Manchester, 1987); A. J. B. Marwick, 'James Maxton: His Place in Scottish Labour History', *Scottish Historical Review*, 43 (1964); P. Slowe, *Manny Shinwell* (1993); A. McKinlay and M. Black, '"Never at rest": The Diary of John S. Taylor, 1885–1916', *Journal of the Scottish Labour History Society*, 29 (1994); I. Wood, *John Wheatley* (Manchester, 1990). R. Ferguson, *Geoff: The Life of Geoffrey M. Shaw* (Gartocharn, 1979) covers the first leader of the Strathclyde Regional Council.

The **Liberals** are extremely thinly covered. S. J. Brown, '"Echoes of Midlothian": Scottish Liberalism and the Boer War, 1899–1902', *Scottish Historical Review*, 71 (1992) deals with the Liberal Imperialist feud; J. Brown, 'Scottish and English Land Legislation, 1905–11', *Scottish Historical Review*, 47 (1968) is helpful; I. Packer, 'The Land Issue and the Future of Scottish Liberalism in 1914', *Scottish Historical Review*, 75 (1996) illuminates a wide range. See also E. A. Cameron,

'Politics, Ideology and the Highland Land Issue, 1886 to the 1920s', *Scottish Historical Review*, 72 (1993). On the post-1918 era, see S. Ball, 'Asquith's Decline and the General Election of 1918', *Scottish Historical Review*, 61 (1982); W. Walker, 'Dundee's Disenchantment with Churchill', *Scottish Historical Review*, 49 (1970). R. Jenkins, *Asquith* (London, 1964) and S. Koss, *Asquith* (London, 1976) both have discussions of the Scottish context; G. De Groot, *Liberal Crusader. The Life of Sir Archibald Sinclair* (London, 1993) has remarkably little on the general crisis of Scottish Liberalism in the period of Sinclair's career.

Scottish Nationalism is well served. A. C. Turner, *Scottish Home Rule* (Oxford, 1952) is a pioneering study; H. J. Hanham, *Scottish Nationalism* (London, 1969) is entertaining; C. Harvie, *Scotland and Nationalism: Scottish Society and Politics, 1707–1994* (2nd edn, London, 1994) is sweeping and invigorating; J. Mitchell, *Strategies for Self-Government. The Campaign for a Scottish Parliament* (Edinburgh, 1996) has a historical portion; J. Brand, *The Nationalism Movement in Scotland*, (London, 1978) is a blend of historical material and contemporary political science; K. Webb, *The Growth of Scottish Nationalism* (Glasgow, 1978) is also valuable; T. Nairn, *The Break-up of Britain* (London, 1981) mixes history and polemics. R. J. Finlay has established himself as the authority on the early phase of the Nationalist parties: *Independent and Free: Scottish Politics and the Origins of the Scottish National Party, 1918–45* (Edinburgh, 1994); *A Partnership for Good? Scottish Politics and the Union since 1880*, (Edinburgh, 1997); '"For or Against?": Scottish Nationalists and the British Empire, 1918–39', *Scottish Historical Review*, 71 (1992); 'Pressure Group or Political Party? The Nationalist Impact on Scottish Politics, 1928–45', *Twentieth Century British History*, 3 (1992); 'National Identity in Crisis: Politicians, Intellectuals and the "End of Scotland"', *History*, 79 (1994). R. Levy, *Scottish Nationalism at the Crossroads* (Edinburgh, 1990), does have a brief historical section.

Minority parties and movements are unevenly treated: J. McKay, 'Communist Unity and Division, 1920: Gallacher, Maclean and "Unholy Scotch Currents"', *Journal of the Scottish Labour History Society*, 29 (1994) considers the formation of the Communist Party; S. MacIntyre, *Little Moscows* (London, 1980), analyses two Scottish communities where the Communist Party was influential. Three papers by A. Campbell – 'From Independent Collier to Militant Miner: Tradition and Change in the Trade Union Consciousness of Scottish Miners, 1874–1929', *Scottish Labour History Society Journal*, 25 (1989), 'The Communist Party in the Scots Coalfields in the Inter-war Period', in N. Fishman and K. Morgan (eds), *Opening the Books: the Social and Cultural History of British Communism* (London, 1995), and 'The Social History of Political Conflict in the Scots Coalfields, 1910–39', in A. Campbell, N. Fishman and D. Howell (eds), *Miners, Unions and Politics, 1910–47* (London, 1996) – look at inter-war Communism and militancy in the mining areas; R. Duncan, 'Motherwell for Moscow: Walton Newbould, Revolutionary Politics and the Labour Movement in a Lanarkshire Constituency, 1918–22', *Journal of the Scottish Society of Labour History*, 28 (1993) gives an account of the election of the first Communist MP in Scotland. For the late 1950s and after there is W. Thomson, 'The New Left in Scotland', in I. MacDougall (ed.), *Essays in Scottish Labour History* (Edinburgh, n.d.). B. J. Ripley and J. McHugh, *John MacLean* (Manchester, 1989) is the best biography, along with D. Howell's consideration in *A Lost Left: Three Studies in Socialism and Nationalism* (Manchester,

1986). H. M. Drucker, *Breakaway: the Scottish Labour Party* (Edinburgh, n.d.) deals with the ill-fated secession of the devolution age.

Fascist tendencies are discussed in: H. Maitles, 'Fascism in the 1930s in the West of Scotland – the British Context', *Journal of the Scottish Labour History Society*, 27 (1992); L. Kibblewhite and A. Rigby, *Fascism in Aberdeen. Street Politics in the 1930s*, (Aberdeen, 1978); C. Holmes. 'Alexander Ratcliffe, Militant Protestant and Anti-Semite', in T. Kushner and K. Lunn (eds), *Traditions of Intolerance* (Manchester, 1989).

Female suffrage is fully explored in L. Leneman, *A Guid Cause: The Women's Suffrage Movement in Scotland* (Aberdeen, 1991); L. Moore, 'The Women's Suffrage Campaign in the 1907 Aberdeen By-election', *Northern History*, 5 (1983) looks at a specific episode; E. King, 'The Scottish Women's Suffrage Movement', in E. Breitenbach and E. Gordon (eds), *Out of Bounds. Women in Scottish Society, 1800–1945* (Edinburgh, 1992).

The **political dimensions of religion** are well covered. C. G. Brown, *Religion and Society in Scotland since 1707* (Edinburgh, 1997) is the best overall survey. W. W. Knox, 'Religion and the Scottish Labour Movement, 1900–39', *Journal of Contemporary History*, 23 (1988) has valid points to make. Two papers by S. J. Brown: '"A Solemn Purification by Fire": Responses to the Great War in the Presbyterian Churches, 1914–19', *Journal of Ecclesiastical History*, 45 (1994), and '"A Victory for God": the Scottish Presbyterian Churches and the General Strike of 1926', *Journal of Ecclesiastical History*, 42 (1991) reveal the Church of Scotland's stance on public issues. On Orangeism and popular Protestantism, E. McFarland, *Protestants First! Orangeism in Nineteenth Century Scotland* (Edinburgh, 1990) is sound on the role of the Orange Order in the pre-1914 period; and G. Walker, 'The Orange Order in Scotland between the Wars', *International Review of Social History*, 37 (1992) expands the chronological analysis. G. Walker, *Intimate Strangers: Political and Cultural Interaction between Scotland and Ulster in Modern Times* (Edinburgh, 1994) studies the links between Ulster Protestantism and Scotland. G. Walker and T. Gallagher (eds), *Sermons and Battle Hymns. Popular Protestant Culture in Modern Scotland* (Edinburgh, 1990) is a compilation of papers on modern popular Protestantism. T. Gallagher also discusses ultra-Protestant politics in the 1930s in 'Protestant Extremism in Urban Scotland, 1930–39: Its Growth and Contraction', *Scottish Historical Review*, 64 (1988).

Roman Catholics and Irish Nationalists are dealt with in two works by T. Gallagher: *Glasgow. The Uneasy Peace* (Manchester, 1987) and *Edinburgh Divided* (Edinburgh, 1987); J. McCaffrey, 'Politics and the Roman Catholic Community', in D. McRoberts (ed.), *Modern Scottish Catholicism, 1878–1978* (Glasgow, 1979), and 'Roman Catholics in Scotland in the Nineteenth and Twentieth Centuries', *Records of the Scottish Church History Society*, 21 (1983); I. Patterson, 'The Activities of Irish Republican Physical Force Organisations in Scotland, 1919–21', *Scottish Historical Review*, 72 (1993); R. Finlay, 'Nationality, Race, Religion and the Irish Question in Inter War Scotland', *Innes Review*, 42 (1991); S. Brown, '"Outside the Covenant": the Scottish Presbyterian Churches and Irish Immigration, 1922–38', *Innes Review*, 42 (1991).

For the very **recent past**, it is of course difficult for a scholarly secondary literature to have established itself, but the following constitute at least a beginning towards such an approach. A. Marr, *The Battle for Scotland* (Harmondsworth,

1992); A. Kemp, *The Hollow Drum. Scotland since the War* (Edinburgh, 1993) are both by journalists with a sense of perspective; C. Harvie, *Fool's Gold* (London, 1994) examines the impact of North Sea oil. W. L. Miller, *The End of British Politics? Scottish and English Political Behaviour in the 1970s* (Oxford, 1981) has a useful historical section. The **current political set-up** is accessible through: J. Kellas, *The Scottish Political System* (4th edn, Cambridge, 1989); A. Brown, D. McCrone and L. Paterson, *Politics and Society in Scotland* (London, 1996) – by three Edinburgh-based academics, while a view from the west is A. Midwinter, M. Keating and J. Mitchell, *Politics and Public Policy in Scotland* (London, 1991). The **1992 and 1997 general elections in Scotland** are surveyed in, respectively, L. Bennie, J. Brand and J. Mitchell, *How Scotland Votes* (Manchester, 1997) and A. Brown, D. McCrone, L. Paterson and P. Surridge, *The Scottish Electorate* (London,1999). There is much of value in D. McCrone, *Understanding Scotland: The Sociology of a Stateless Nation* (London, 1992); see also A. Dickson, 'Scotland is Different – OK?', in D. McCrone *et al.* (eds), *The Making of Scotland: Nation, Culture and Social Change* (Edinburgh, 1989).

INDEX